Music, Health, and Power

Music, Health, and Power offers an original, on-the-ground analysis of the role that music plays in promoting healthy communities. The book brings the reader inside the world of kanyeleng fertility societies and HIV/AIDS support groups, where women use music to leverage stigma and marginality into new forms of power.

Drawing on ethnographic research conducted over a period of 13 years (2006–2019), the author articulates a strengths-based framework for research on music and health that pushes beyond deficit narratives to emphasize the creativity and resilience of Gambian performers in responding to health disparities. Examples from Ebola prevention programs, the former President's AIDS "cure," and a legendary underwear theft demonstrate the high stakes of women's performances as they are caught up in broader contestations over political and medical authority.

This book will be of interest to scholars and students of ethnomusicology, medical anthropology, and African studies. The accompanying audio examples provide access to the women's performances discussed in the text.

Bonnie B. McConnell is a lecturer in the School of Music at the Australian National University.

SOAS Studies in Music Series

Series Editors:
Rachel Harris, SOAS, University of London, UK
Rowan Pease, SOAS, University of London, UK

Board members:
Angela Impey, SOAS, University of London, UK
Noriko Manabe, Temple University, US
Suzel Reily, Universidade Estadual de Campinas, Brazil
Martin Stokes, Kings College London, UK
Richard Widdess, SOAS, University of London, UK

SOAS Studies in Music Series is today one of the world's leading series in the discipline of ethnomusicology. Our core mission is to produce high-quality, ethnographically rich studies of music-making in the world's diverse musical cultures. We publish monographs and edited volumes that explore musical repertories and performance practice, critical issues in ethnomusicology, sound studies, and historical and analytical approaches to music across the globe. We recognize the value of applied, interdisciplinary, and collaborative research, and our authors draw on current approaches in musicology and anthropology, psychology, media and gender studies. We welcome monographs that investigate global contemporary, classical, and popular musics, the effects of digital mediation, and transnational flows.

Becoming a Garamut Player in Baluan, Papua New Guinea: Musical Analysis as a Pathway to Learning
Tony Lewis

Music Theory in the Safavid Era
Owen Wright

Arnold Bake: A Life with South Asian Music
Bob van der Linden

Music, Health, and Power: Singing the Unsayable in The Gambia
Bonnie B. McConnell

For more information about this series, please visit:
https://www.routledge.com/music/series/SOASMS

Music, Health, and Power

Singing the Unsayable in The Gambia

Bonnie B. McConnell

LONDON AND NEW YORK

First published 2020
by Routledge
2 Park Square, Milton Park, Abingdon, Oxon OX14 4RN

and by Routledge
605 Third Avenue, New York, NY 10017

First issued in paperback 2021

Routledge is an imprint of the Taylor & Francis Group, an informa business

Publisher's Note
The publisher has gone to great lengths to ensure the quality of this reprint but points out that some imperfections in the original copies may be apparent.

British Library Cataloguing-in-Publication Data
A catalogue record for this book is available from the British Library

Library of Congress Cataloging-in-Publication Data
A catalog record has been requested for this book

ISBN 13: 978-1-03-223996-5 (pbk)
ISBN 13: 978-0-367-31272-5 (hbk)

Typeset in Times
by Deanta Global Publishing Services, Chennai, India

For Fatou and Mama Wini

Contents

Figures

Recorded selections on the accompanying website

Track 1 *"Kolonba"* ("Big Well")
APGWA Kanyeleng Group, 2013

Track 2 *"Teriyaa"* ("Friendship")
From the Allatentu Support Band *Teriyaa* remix album, 2010

Track 3 *"Girim"* ("Orphan")
From the Allatentu Support Band *Teriyaa* remix album, 2010

Track 4 "HIV *Be Keering*" ("HIV Is Real")
From the Allatentu Support Band *Teriyaa* remix album, 2010

Track 5 *"Cati Oo, Kana Kumboo"* ("Youngest Child, Don't Cry")
Jainaba Saho and the Brikama Nyambai College Kanyeleng Group, 2013

Track 6 "HIV/AIDS"
Jainaba Saho and the Brikama Nyambai College Kanyeleng Group, 2013

Track 7 "Malaria"
Jainaba Saho and the Brikama Nyambai College Kanyeleng Group, 2013

Track 8 *"Ngaanyaa Baadinyaa"* ("Pride in *Baadinyaa*")
Jainaba Saho and the Brikama Nyambai College Kanyeleng Group, 2013

 Tracks are available for download from the "eResources" tab on the website: https://www.routledge.com/9780367312725

Tracks 2, 3, and 4 used with permission from the Allatentu Support Group. All remaining tracks recorded by and copyright the author, used with permission of performers.

Orthography and pronunciation

The transcriptions of Mandinka language materials in this book follow the conventions established in *A Practical Orthography of Gambian Mandinka* (WEC 1988), with the omission of tone markings for readability. For Mandinka terms used frequently in the text, I have adapted the spelling to aid pronunciation for English language readers. For example, I write *tulungo* rather than *tuluŋo* to refer to women's percussion and dance performances. For readability and consistency with other scholarship, I use the noun stem form for terms such as jali and kanyeleng, rather than the definite forms, *jalo* (*jaloolu*, pl.), or *kanyelengo* (*kanyelengoolu*, pl.). Translations of frequently used Mandinka terms are provided in the Glossary.

For translations of Mandinka words, I draw primarily on the *Mandinka-English Dictionary* published by WEC International (1995 Revised Edition). I also draw on knowledge of the use of terms in musical contexts gained from interviews, lessons, observation, and participation in performances. Unless otherwise indicated, all translations are my own.

Vowels

a is pronounced as in "father"
e is pronounced as in "let"
i is pronounced as in "it"
o is pronounced as in "on"
u is pronounced as in "soup"

The length of vowel sounds is indicated through the use of a single letter (a, e, i, o, u) for short vowels and double letters (aa, ee, ii, oo, uu) for long vowels.

Consonants

c is pronounced "ch" as in "check"
ñ (or *ny*) is pronounced as in "onion"
ŋ (or *ng*) is pronounced as in "sing"
r is rolled

List of abbreviations

APGWA	Association for Promoting Girls' and Women's Advancement in The Gambia
APRC	Alliance for Patriotic Reorientation and Construction (political party)
ART	Antiretroviral Therapy
GAMCOTRAP	Gambian Committee on Traditional Practices Affecting the Health of Women and Children
GFPA	Gambia Family Planning Association
GRTS	The Gambia Radio and Television Services
NGO	nongovernmental organization
TC	traditional communicator
UNAIDS	Joint United Nations Program on HIV/AIDS
UNICEF	United Nations Children's Fund
WHO	World Health Organization
WID	women in development

Acknowledgments

This project was supported by funding from the Fulbright-Hays Program (the US Department of Education) and the American Association of University Women. I am grateful to the series editors and editorial staff at Routledge who helped bring this project to fruition.

I offer my wholehearted thanks to all the performers and health workers in The Gambia who contributed to this project. In particular, I would like to recognize Binta Jammeh Sidibeh and the members of the APGWA kanyeleng: you taught me so much about performance, friendship, and the meaning of kanyelengyaa. Big thanks are also due to the women's performance groups from Brikama Nyambai College, Kembujeh, Lamin, Farato, Missirah, Dobong Kunda, Samba Tako, Farafenni, Wassu, Genieri, Bati Njol, Soma, Bwiam, Sintet, Gunjur, and Manduar. Thank you for teaching me your songs and sharing your knowledge of music and health with me. I am also grateful to Neneh Jali Suso, Sambou Suso, Tatadinding Jobarteh, Pabobo Jobarteh, Bai Jobarteh, Dawda Camara, Alasan Trawally, Alhagie Minteh, Omar Traore, Jaliba Kuyateh, ST Brikama Boyo, Jainaba Saho, Nyima Cham, Kejawo Juwara, Haruna Baldeh, and Ebrima Camara.

This research would not have been possible without the support of the many dedicated health workers from the Gambia Ministry of Health and Social Welfare who took the time to contribute their knowledge and expertise to this project. I am grateful to Momat Jallow, Lamin Barrow, Saharu Kante, Basiru Bojang, Dembo Fatty, Kura Joof, Bubacarr Sillah, Ndey Gibba, Baba Samateh, Omar Ceesay, Hajara Huma, and Malick Gaye. Extra thanks are due to Buba Darboe for supporting this project right from the beginning up until the end. Thank you for helping with last minute questions and permissions, and for being toma to Bubadinding.

To the current and former staff of GAMCOTRAP (Dr. Isatou Touray, Amie Bojang, Baai Jaabang, and many more), your input was invaluable during the first stage of research for this book. Thank you for sharing your wisdom and supporting this project; you are an inspiration.

I am grateful to The Gambia's National Centre for Arts and Culture for supporting this research. Hassoum Ceesay, thank you for sharing your expertise and guidance. Sheikh Omar Jallow, your insight on kanyelengyaa has been invaluable.

I am indebted to the members of the University of Washington community who contributed so much to the development of these ideas. Philip Schuyler, I am always grateful for your support and sense of humor. Rachel Chapman, thank you for reminding me to believe in this project (and to keep my priorities straight). Special thanks are also due to Christina Sunardi, Shannon Dudley, and Lynn Thomas for insightful, constructive feedback on this manuscript. My graduate student colleagues, thank you for sharing ideas and feedback, and for making the first stage of this project so enjoyable.

I am grateful to Fraser McNeill for constructive feedback that helped improve the manuscript. Thank you for your thoughtful reading and insightful comments. Many thanks also to Julia Day for the unique combination of ethnomusicologist-editor feedback that made this book better in innumerable ways. Thanks to James Morford, for the informative discussions of rhythm and meter.

I am grateful for the research community at the Australian National University who supported this project after I moved to Canberra. In particular, I would like to thank my wonderful colleagues in the School of Music, as well as the members of the anthropology "gender node" writing groups who gave valuable feedback on chapter drafts and the motivation to keep writing. A special thanks is due to Matt Barnes for assistance with preparing audio files.

I am grateful to my family for their patience, support, and encouragement. Special thanks to my mother, Joanne Clark, for your enthusiasm and feedback, and to Erin, for your map-making skills. To Micah and Xander, this book would not have been written without your support (and your willingness to travel the world with me).

I am indebted to Awa Jatta and my host families in Kembujeh and Brikama whose compounds became homes away from home. Lastly, but most importantly, I would like to thank Fatou as well as the members and staff of the Allatentu Support Kafoo. Our conversations, music, and friendship are the inspiration behind this project.

1 Introduction

Music, health, and power

Introduction

Shortly after evening prayers, Fatou[1] stepped onto the stage amid cheers from the audience at the Paradise Suites seaside concert venue. The cool breeze off the Atlantic was refreshing after the long, hot day and there was an atmosphere of festivity and celebration among audience members. Fatou moved close to the microphone and her rich, emotive voice filled the night air. She sang in Mandinka, "Friendship, oh friendship is not an easy thing." To Fatou's left, Bai played a brisk reggae beat on the drum set, while Alhagie's syncopated patterns on the *kutiro* drums inspired audience members to get up and dance. Occasional breaks in Fatou's voice inserted a sense of emotional sincerity and poignancy into the band's celebratory sound, which incorporated influences from the Senegambian dance music styles of *mbalax* and Afro-Manding. Fatou sang, "You know I am HIV positive and taking my treatment. Don't worry, let's join hands and fight the virus."

A group of women in the audience stood up and approached the stage to elegantly hand Fatou bank notes one by one. Waving money in their hands, the women danced carefully in high-heeled shoes that matched their glittering, colorful dresses. During the cascading solos on the guitar, reminiscent of the improvisatory melodic lines of the kora,[2] Fatou also danced, stylish in her long yellow gown. But to Fatou's right, as I played the keyboard, I felt a sense of unease. In the front row of the audience sat the Vice President of The Gambia, Dr. Isatou Njie Saidy, and the Minister of Health and Social Welfare, Dr. Tamsir Mbowe.

The 2007 release of Fatou's album *Teriyaa*, featuring the Allatentu Support Band, was a momentous occasion for the HIV/AIDS service community and members of HIV support groups in The Gambia. Fatou's songs challenged the stigma associated with HIV and encouraged testing and treatment. Disclosing her own status through song, Fatou put a human face on the disease and urged listeners to take care of friends and family members with HIV. Just as the *Teriyaa* album was nearing completion, however, The Gambia's eccentric and authoritarian President Yahya Jammeh had made a momentous announcement that would fundamentally change the way the album was received. On January 17, 2007, Jammeh announced that he had discovered a cure for AIDS, along with several other diseases, including diabetes and hypertension. As one of few public figures who were open about their HIV status, Fatou faced strong political pressure to join Jammeh's treatment program. She died in July 2007 after ceasing antiretroviral medication in order to participate in the President's controversial treatment.

For years, in the shadow of Jammeh's authoritarian regime, discussions of Fatou's death were hidden and muted. In earlier versions of this ethnography, I tried to tell Fatou's story without discussing her death. It was a story full of painful silences and missing pieces. *Music, Health, and Power* is in part an attempt to understand Fatou's story, and the stories of other musicians like her, who work in the context of authoritarian national politics and extreme health inequality to make a positive difference in the lives of their communities. In the climate of openness following Jammeh's electoral defeat and subsequent removal from office in early 2017, it is time to fill in some of the missing pieces.

In 2007, Fatou was one of just a few hundred people on antiretroviral treatment in The Gambia as part of the Global Fund[3] initiative. In the United States and other wealthy countries, highly active antiretroviral therapy (ART) became available in 1996, greatly extending the life expectancy for people living with HIV/AIDS. Largely because pharmaceutical companies refused to allow generic drugs on the market, ART only became available in The Gambia in 2004, thanks to an international movement protesting the valuing of company profits over African lives (see Flint 2011). The delay in treatment provision caused a tragedy of epic proportions across the African continent, as millions of people died needlessly, causing enormous trauma for families, communities, and society at large. In The Gambia, a small country of 2.1 million people with a relatively low adult HIV prevalence rate of 1.9 percent (UNAIDS 2018), the tragedy was no less devastating for those affected. By the time Fatou started treatment, she had been in and out of hospital for years. Just when her health had finally stabilized, thanks to hard won access to medication, she was compelled to abandon ART to undergo President Jammeh's treatment. Fatou's story demonstrates the way music, medicine, and the bodies of people with chronic disease are caught up in contestations over power at the intersection between global inequalities and national politics.

The World Health Organization revised guidelines recommend universal treatment for people with HIV. Yet still today, as a result of high levels of HIV-related stigma and funding shortfalls, only 29 percent of Gambians with HIV are accessing lifesaving treatment (UNAIDS 2018). This book is in part inspired by the frustration I have felt watching friends die of AIDS and other treatable diseases without access to the medicine that would save their lives. Their lives are the casualties of "structural violence" rooted in unequal global political and economic relationships (Farmer 2004, 2001).

In the aftermath of Fatou's death, I have been forced to think more deeply about the complex politics of health funding and knowledge production. I committed to research that interrogates global power structures that perpetuate health disparities, while highlighting the creativity of local actors who use music to address complex social and health problems. In this endeavor, I have been inspired by the work of Gregory Barz (2006), who demonstrates an emotionally engaged ethnomusicology of HIV/AIDS in Uganda, and Paul Farmer who argues that an anthropology of structural violence must go beyond the "ethnographically visible" to examine "the dead and those left for dead" (2004: 305–307). But what does it mean to listen to the music of the dead and those left for dead? And what can music tell us about health, inequality, gender, and power? These questions are the focus of this book.

To illuminate questions of music, health, and power, I examine the popular songs of Fatou and the Allatentu Support Band as well as the health-related performances of Gambian *kanyeleng* women who have experienced infertility or child deaths. Just as Fatou encountered stigma and discrimination because of her HIV positive status, kanyeleng women similarly face stigma because of their failure to achieve societal ideals of motherhood. Rather than being defined by their marginalized social positions, however, these female performers use music to influence public opinion, promote health, and redefine their position in society.

Working both independently and in collaboration with health service organizations, female performers use songs to communicate information about health topics ranging from malaria, tuberculosis, and HIV/AIDS, to breastfeeding practices, childhood immunizations, and Ebola. Performances bring women's concerns to the public sphere, address sensitive and difficult topics, and promote community engagement with health issues. At the same time, through their performances, women critique dominant biomedical models of health promotion and emphasize local understandings of health grounded in caring relationships (*baadinyaa*[4]) and joking relationships (*sanuwuyaa*). I demonstrate that in the face of global health inequality and authoritarian national politics, female performers have adapted indigenous musical healing practices in order to assert new forms of women's power in twenty-first-century Gambia.

This project explores the ways in which female performers have taken on additional labor as communicators in the development sector even as they continue to perform for a variety of community events such as naming ceremonies, weddings, and circumcision-related occasions. Collaborations with health and development organizations have enabled female performers to earn additional income and to bring women's perspectives to the public sphere in a patriarchal society. At the same time, female performers' labor intensification is an indication of the challenges of the neoliberal economy, and the gendered politics of international development (Kea 2013). In the twenty-first century, many Gambians have to struggle to pay for basic items such as food, health care, and school fees. Contemporary political and economic conditions have placed added strain on female performers as they seek to earn more income while maintaining longstanding practices of health performance grounded in relations of reciprocity.

Female performers' involvement in health promotion in contemporary Gambia draws on deeply rooted practices of "public healing" that go beyond physical illness to address social relations (Berger 2014; Feierman 1999). In her article on women's movements and healing practices in Africa, Iris Berger (2014) explains that during the nineteenth century indigenous concepts of public healing were challenged by European medical practitioners who "insisted that therapy be directed only at the physical body, isolated from the interpersonal relationships that can determine health and wellness" (Berger 2014: 9). Despite the challenges they faced during the colonial and postcolonial periods, however, African women have sustained and transformed practices of public healing in order to address issues such as gender inequality as well as political and economic injustices that produce ill health.

In the Gambian context, music performance represents an important form of public healing through which women negotiate the politics of health promotion and foreground aspects of health that are neglected in global health discourse and programming. Women use musical performance to heal broader social conditions even as they simultaneously address particular physical ailments. This is consistent with ethnomusicological perspectives on healing as a process that integrates "a multiplicity of life's intertwined strands" (Roseman 2008: 18). That is, female performers' contribution to health promotion in The Gambia emerges through a process of integrating different "strands," or different ways of knowing and being.

A strengths-based approach

Music, Health, and Power outlines what I call a strengths-based approach for research on music and health, which responds to two major problems of representation that plague efforts to improve the lives of people in Africa. The first is the tendency to represent Africa and Africans primarily in terms of what they *lack*, emphasizing "absences, failing and problems, plagues and catastrophes" (Ferguson 2006: 2). The second is the emphasis on symptoms, rather than root causes of social and health problems. The response to HIV/AIDS in the 1990s and 2000s, and still to some extent today, demonstrates these problems of representation. From the period 2003–2007, when I was working in health education in The Gambia and Tanzania, the overwhelming emphasis was still the ABCs of HIV prevention (abstinence, being faithful, or using condoms), rather than the provision of equitable access to antiretroviral medication which, it turns out, also prevents HIV transmission (Jon Cohen 2011). The ABC behavior change approach faults African sexual practices for the spread of HIV, neglecting the role of political and economic inequalities; the result is that Africans are still far more likely to die from AIDS and other treatable diseases than are people in the United States and other wealthy countries.

Ethnomusicological scholarship already demonstrates powerful alternatives to these problems of representation by exploring music and health in cultural context, and attending to issues of power and inequality (e.g. Barz 2006; Barz and Cohen 2011; Van Buren 2010; R. Stone 2017; Koen et al. 2008; Allison, Reed, and Cohen 2017). I suggest that more must be done, however, to understand and communicate across disciplines the roles that music plays in "times of trouble" (Rice 2014: 191). The strengths-based approach that informs this volume brings close examination of musical performance together with analysis of the political economy of global health in order to illuminate both the strength and creativity of Gambian musicians, as well as the broader global contexts that enable and constrain their work. I build on existing work in the overlapping fields of medical ethnomusicology, which investigates intersections between music, health, and culture (Barz 2006; Barz and Cohen 2011; Koen et al. 2008), and applied ethnomusicology, which emphasizes social responsibility in research addressing real world problems (Pettan and Titon 2015; Harrison 2014; Dirksen 2012). The strengths-based approach foregrounds questions of power and value in relation to diverse epistemological and ontological frameworks of music and health.

The strengths-based approach draws on Aaron Antonovsky's (1996) salutogenic theory of health promotion, which pushes beyond a focus on risk factors to emphasize salutary factors that support health. This model challenges the dichotomy between health and ill health evident in pathology-focused models of health promotion, and in the World Health Organization definition of health as "a state of complete physical, mental, and social well-being" (WHO 2006: 1). Women's performances in The Gambia do not just convey information; they serve as "generalized resistance resources" that build a "sense of coherence" and enable people to cope with adversity (Antonovsky 1996: 15). In other words, music performance can serve as a positive social determinant of health by promoting meaning, motivation, and belonging (Sunderland et al. 2018).

The strengths-based approach is aligned with integrative perspectives on health and wellness in ethnomusicology (e.g. Roseman 2008; de Quadros 2017; Hoesing 2013) and music therapy (e.g. Batt-Rawden 2010). These perspectives highlight the complexity of human experiences of health and illness that cut across the intersecting domains of culture, physiology, psychology, and sociality. Through music, the women discussed in these pages integrate disparate epistemologies and ontologies, drawing on biomedical knowledge as well as indigenous approaches to music and medicine. In the context of severe health disparities and gender inequality, performers inspire collective action, promote understanding, and create meaning with music.

Women and music in The Gambia

I met the members of the Talinding kanyeleng group for the first time at a naming ceremony in 2006. The kanyeleng were wearing matching outfits, long beaded necklaces draped over each shoulder, and calabash hats covered in colorful beads. The leader of the group sang loudly into a megaphone, while another group member played a yellow *bidong* (20-liter plastic jerry can) with two sticks. She was joined by another percussionist playing a calabash gourd overturned in a tub of water. It had an unusual timbre, similar to the sound of clapping hands. In a circle (*luwo*) consisting almost entirely of women, the rest of us clapped and sang in call-and-response style. After some time, the percussionists increased the tempo and began playing more complex, syncopated patterns. One by one, women entered the circle to dance vigorously, stamping their feet in the dirt while raising their hands to the front and then to the side. Propelled by nervous excitement, I kicked off my sandals and entered the circle to dance, emerging breathless and laughing as the next dancer jumped in.

After this initial encounter with the Talinding kanyeleng, I met kanyeleng groups at community gatherings everywhere. With kanyeleng in my neighborhood in Kembujeh, I learned the songs and moves of the *musuba* ("big woman") dance.[5] I also learned to appreciate kanyeleng musical skill, sense of humor, and outspoken mockery of authority figures. Kanyeleng are noisy. I wondered why, in my reading on Gambian music, I had seldom heard of them.

To learn more, I joined the Talinding kanyeleng group and performed with them throughout the region. The Talinding group are commonly referred to as the APGWA kanyeleng, because of their connection with the Association for Promoting Girls and Women's Advancement in The Gambia, an organization run by prominent gender activist Binta Jammeh Sidibeh. Among the most active in public health work, the APGWA kanyeleng were the ideal collaborators for this project. While I interviewed and observed performances of kanyeleng groups throughout the country, performing alongside members of the APGWA kanyeleng group generated particularly valuable insights and friendships.

Kanyeleng use music, prayer, and trickery to outwit evil spirits and beseech God to have pity on them and grant them a child who survives (Hough 2006). Other terms for kanyeleng include *dimba kafoo* (mother's group) or *tole kafoo* (fool's group).[6] Kanyeleng describe their rituals first and foremost as prayer, challenging those who see them as a form of idolatry incompatible with Islam in this predominately Muslim society. Kanyeleng come together as a group to implore God to have pity on them. They also demonstrate to God their desperation for a child by dressing in ragged or ill-fitting clothing and eating disgusting food. These humiliating practices can also take away the envy and malevolent attention which may inspire witchcraft or sorcery. In contemporary Gambia, women

Figure 1.1 The APGWA kanyeleng group performing, October 2013, photograph by the author.

from any ethnic group may become kanyeleng, but the practice is particularly associated with Mandinka and Jola ethnic groups.[7] In Mandinka communities in eastern Gambia, full kanyeleng membership is restricted to women who belong to particular families, including *garanke* (leatherworker) or *jongo* (descendant of slaves). If other women have fertility challenges, they may go to the kanyeleng for assistance without taking on a kanyeleng identity. Kanyeleng groups in western Gambia do not have these restrictions on membership.

Kanyeleng practices have changed considerably as groups have taken on roles in health and development communication. While in the past kanyeleng faced high levels of stigma for their childlessness and shameful behavior, in contemporary Gambia, kanyeleng groups have begun to attract women who have not experienced reproductive challenges. Some women choose to join kanyeleng groups because they want to have opportunities to perform and, in the case of more financially successful groups, they want to earn income. The weakening of the association with infertility has also changed the meaning of the word "kanyeleng" in The Gambia. While most people with whom I spoke associated kanyeleng membership with problems of infertility and child mortality, others defined kanyeleng simply as "traditional communicators" and had little knowledge of other aspects of kanyeleng practice. While kanyeleng are among the most prominent and prolific performers in contemporary Gambia, this book represents the first extended study of kanyeleng performance practice.[8] In the chapters that follow, I investigate complex dynamics of gender and power as kanyeleng adapt their unique skills and knowledge in the context of social and economic change.

The Gambia Ministry of Health and Social Welfare works with a variety of performers, including popular musicians such as Fatou and the Allatentu Support Band, and groups that were originally neighborhood associations, or age-group societies. The most conspicuous performers in health programs, however, are kanyeleng. Even groups that are formed specifically for health promotion purposes such as theater groups, or groups dedicated to a particular health issue such as exclusive breastfeeding[9] (*Suusundi Timmaring*), often consist primarily of kanyeleng. Kanyeleng's skill as entertainers, as well as their special ability to address sensitive topics, make them valuable assets in public health programs. Focusing on kanyeleng in addition to Fatou and the Allatentu Support Band enables me to tease out differences and commonalities in the way particular performers approach issues of health. Health-related events often combine music, dance, drama, and costuming. I use the term "music" to describe sound practices that are but one component of a "constellation of the arts" (R. Stone 2008: 7–12) that comes together in women's performances in The Gambia.

The strength and diversity of women's musical practices in The Gambia today are the product of a long history of exchange between people with different languages and musics. The Gambia is part of the Mande cultural area, which encompasses those parts of West Africa influenced by the Mali Empire of the thirteenth–fifteenth centuries (Mali, Guinea, Senegal, The Gambia, Guinea-Bissau, Ivory Coast, and Burkina Faso) (Diawara, Mamadou 1997). Like much of the Mande area, The Gambia has long been an economic and cultural meeting point for diverse peoples and cultures. The largest ethnic groups in The Gambia include the Mandinka, Fulbe (Tukulor, Fula, Peul), Wolof, Jola (Diola, Karoninka) and Serahule (Soninke). Concepts of ethnicity in the Senegambia region are fluid, and intermarriage between individuals of different ethnic backgrounds is common.

Women's performance practices are also shaped by religious discourse in The Gambia where over ninety percent of the population is Muslim. The majority of Gambians practice a Sufi-oriented[10] form of Islam that incorporates local practices such as sainthood and guidance from marabouts (Sufi religious specialists) (Janson 2006). Reformist branches of Islam are also playing an increasingly important role in The Gambia. I use "reformist" to refer to Muslims who wish to reform Islam as it is practiced locally to align it with Islam as it is practiced in the Arab Middle East (see Janson 2006). Competing religious discourses shape the context in which female musicians perform. In general, however, The Gambia is characterized by a high degree of religious tolerance. Many families have both Muslim and Christian members, and people with different religious beliefs frequently come together to celebrate each other's holidays. Although less than one percent of the population identifies as practicing traditional religions, both Islam and Christianity have absorbed elements of indigenous religious beliefs and practices. A syncretic approach to religion is evident in therapeutic practices, as well as in kanyeleng performances, as I will discuss further in Chapter 2.

Music, Health, and Power focuses primarily, though not exclusively, on Mandinka-language concepts and songs. Many of the groups I work with are multiethnic, and because of the long history of close interaction among ethnic groups in The Gambia, there are many cultural and linguistic commonalities (Wright 2010). Even groups that identify as Mandinka often perform songs in multiple languages, including Wolof, Pulaar, and Jola, as well as Mandinka. This is particularly common in the Western Region where ethnic integration is more extensive. In this multilingual nation, singing songs in multiple languages is a strategy for musicians to increase their impact and popularity. For example, the *Teriyaa* album produced by Fatou and the Allatentu Support Band incorporated English, Mandinka, Wolof, Jola, Pulaar, Serahule, and Swahili[11] lyrics.

The Mandinka are the largest ethnic group in The Gambia and, like other Mande groups, they have a tripartite system of social organization, which includes the categories of *foro* or *sulaa*[12] (freeborn or noble), *jongo* (descendant of slaves), and *nyamaaloo* (artisan). The *nyamaaloo* group is further broken down into the categories of *jali* (griot), *numu* (blacksmith), *garanke* (leatherworker), and *fino* (religious praise specialist).[13] These historically endogamous groups pass down specialized knowledge from generation to generation and depend upon patronage from freeborn people as well as other *nyamaaloo* groups with specialized skills (see Charry 2000: 48). Jali are often referred to as "griots" in English, which is a general term adapted from French that describes West African hereditary specialists with expertise in praise singing, genealogy, conflict mediation, instrumental performance, and other skills that vary by region, ethnic group, and family.

Much research on music in the Mande cultural area has focused on griots, providing important insight into the position of musicians in social life as well as rich and dynamic traditions of instrumental and vocal performance (e.g. Charry 2000; Conrad and Frank 1995; Durán 2013, 2007; Hale 1998; Knight 1973, 1982; Tang 2008; Janson 2002; Ebron 2002). The scholarly preoccupation with griots, however, has also contributed to misconceptions regarding the range of musical practices in the Mande area as well as the role of women in performance (Appert 2018). Griot performance, though important, represents just one slice of the diverse musical practices in the region, many of which are performed primarily by people – particularly women – who do not belong to griot families.[14] The lack of scholarly attention to kanyeleng performers in The Gambia is especially surprising considering the prominent role they play in many community events.

Though Wolof drum ensembles are typically comprised of griot performers (*géwël*) (Tang 2008), most percussion traditions in The Gambia, including the drum ensembles of the Mandinka and Jola, are not specifically associated with griots. In contrast to the "aura of exclusivity" attached to the music of griots (Knight 1974: 26), percussion and dance events are highly participatory and inclusive of people from different social groups. The difference between griot performance and percussion and dance events for Mandinka is illustrated by the difference in terminology used to refer to the events. Percussion and dance events are typically described as *tulungo* or "play," while jali performances are referred to as *jaliyaa* or "the art of the jali" (Knight 1973; Charry 2000; McConnell 2017). Popular music such as that performed by the Allatentu Support Band is often described as *musiko* in Mandinka, an adaptation from the English *music* or French *musique*. These somewhat distinct spheres of musical activity are accompanied by different norms and expectations shaping *who* participates as well as *how* they participate, as I will explore further in Chapter 6.

Scholarship on music in the Senegambia region (The Gambia and Senegal) has sometimes erroneously suggested (or implied by omission) that women do not play instruments. In fact, in addition to women's prominence as singers and dancers, there are a number of instruments specifically associated with women. There are also regional differences in performance practices; while drums are strongly associated with men in western Gambia, in the east, female drummers are common. Many women's instruments are adapted from the household items that women use in their daily domestic chores.[15] The most widespread of these is the 20-liter plastic jerry can, or bidong (from the French *bidon* for "container") (see Figure 1.2). Younger performers with whom I spoke referred to the bidong as a "traditional" (*coosaanoo*) instrument and could not remember a time when bidongs were not played. My interlocutors used the word coosaanoo to refer to performances that draw on a repertoire of songs and rhythms that have been handed down for generations; change and innovation within this repertoire is expected. From this perspective, female performers' flexibility in accommodating different instruments and playing techniques is a sign of the strength of their tradition.

Older performers remembered that the bidong had replaced the calabash water drum (*jiikijo),* which used to be the most important instrument for Mandinka

Figure 1.2 Khadijatou Mass playing the bidong in Talinding, February 2019, photograph
by the author.

women in dance events. They recollected that severe Sahelian droughts beginning in the 1970s reduced the supply of large calabash gourds, making the plastic
bidong an attractive alternative instrument. Women developed new playing techniques, utilizing every side of the bidong to produce resonant, strong sounds to
encourage dancing. The calabash water drum has not been abandoned, however,
although it is played less often than it was in the past. Mandinka instrumentalists
typically overturn the calabash in a tub of water and play it using two sticks (see
Figure 1.3).[16] Kanyeleng groups frequently perform with both bidong and calabash, as well as a wooden mortar (*kulungo*), which is played by striking a metal
lid against its lip to create a sharp, percussive sound.

Women's performance practices are often flexible, utilizing different combina-
tions of instruments based on the availability of materials and skilled performers.
Bamboo clapping sticks associated with the Jola ethnic group have become popular among some Mandinka women's groups in the western part of the country
such as the APGWA kanyeleng. Many kanyeleng groups also include one or more

Figure 1.3 Calabash *jiikijo* played by a performer in Wassu, Central River Region, April 2013, photograph by the author.

police whistles. Wolof women play metal bowls and plastic wash tubs, as well as dry calabash gourds laid on top of a cushion. The enormous diversity of women's performance practices in this part of West Africa deserves further research attending to variations based on region and ethnic group.

In addition to longstanding musical practices associated with non-griot women, performers such as Fatou of the Allatentu Support Band have found new opportunities in popular music genres such as mbalax, Afro-Manding, and reggae. One of the most popular genres of music in The Gambia today, mbalax emerged in the 1970s in Senegal when musicians incorporated *sabar* drum rhythms and West African vocal styles into Afro-Cuban style dance bands (Tang 2008). In The Gambia, the term Afro-Manding is used broadly to describe popular music with Mandinka roots. It typically features Mandinka-language songs and influences from Mande instruments such as the kora. The two categories of mbalax and Afro-Manding are not mutually exclusive. Musicians sometimes use the term *yey-engo* to refer to Gambian kora-based mbalax, which is also typically described as Afro-Manding because of its clear Mandinka influences. While griots often play central roles in mbalax and Afro-Manding bands, these styles are not restricted to griot performers. The popularization of these styles in contemporary Gambia has opened up diverse professional opportunities for non-griot performers such as Fatou of the Allatentu Support Band.

The neglect of these diverse performance practices associated with women in scholarship on music in the Senegambia region has reinforced what Catherine Appert refers to as the "invention of the griot" as a symbol of "an unchanging (masculine) repository of tradition" (2012: 35). The lack of attention to women's instruments such as the bidong is striking considering the prominent role that the instrument plays in many performance contexts in The Gambia and neighboring countries. In my view, the absence of scholarly discussion of the bidong and other practices associated with women reflects underlying ideas about authenticity and value. That is, scholarly preconceptions about what kinds of performances are worth studying[17] have contributed to the gender bias in research as well as the neglect of many of the most locally significant performance practices (Janson 2002; Hale 1998). *Music, Health, and Power* attempts to fill this gap by exploring the musical performances of kanyeleng groups, as well as Fatou and the Allatentu Support Band.

Transformative labor: promoting health in The Gambia

Female performers' involvement in health promotion in The Gambia must be understood in relation to the challenging political and economic realities of health funding in the country, which contribute to extremely limited access to basic health services and information. Building on the work of Leith Mullings, I approach Gambian women's music as a site of "transformative work" to configure female networks of social support and empowerment in the face of deprivation (1995: 123). That is, women engage in health-related performances to create continuity for themselves, their families, and their communities. This work is grounded in woman-centered support networks that cut across public and private spheres (Mullings 1995: 133).

Music, Health, and Power employs a constellation of terms related to health and development that require differentiation here. First, following common practice in The Gambia, I use the term "health communication" to describe the targeted dissemination of health information through songs. In contrast, I use the term "health promotion" to emphasize the broader impact of women's performances in "enabling people to increase control over, and to improve their health" (Nutbeam 1998: 1). That is, performances do not only disseminate information, they also contribute to social mobilization, women's empowerment, and community participation. The related terms *global health* and *public health* also require clarification. While public health generally refers to population-wide interventions in a national context, global health is concerned with addressing health disparities worldwide by focusing on issues that cut across national boundaries (Beaglehole and Bonita 2010). I use the term global health to situate the activities of female performers in The Gambia within the broader context of global health programming that both enables and restricts their work.

Global health promotion is also linked to the wider field of international development. In the decades after the Second World War, discourse and practices of international aid were built upon the modernization theory of development, which asserted that development problems were rooted in traditional cultural practices that were incompatible with modernity. According to modernization theory, poor countries needed aid to evolve from a "backward" state of poverty and ignorance to achieve modernity in the image of the West. Thoroughly critiqued in development studies, the traces of modernization theory nonetheless continue to inform global health practice (Obregon and Waisbord 2012). Health development programs tend to represent problems as primarily local, rendering invisible their roots in global political and economic inequalities (Ferguson 2006). Without ignoring problems that exist in Africa and other parts of the developing world, positive change must be grounded in strengths rather than weaknesses, as well as an understanding of the global political economic and historical bases of health disparities. As Chérie Rivers Ndaliko argues, international aid programs fail when they study only "human catastrophe … divorced from studies of human creativity" (2016: 3). Concentrating on the creativity and agency of performers brings into focus complex sociomusical practices, as well as their significance for promoting health and a sense of coherence in the face of change.

The Gambia is a medically pluralistic society in which people employ a variety of different types of therapies, including biomedicine,[18] indigenous herbal medicines, and spiritual or "metaphysical" treatments. In this predominately Muslim society, local therapeutic traditions are often intertwined with Islamic beliefs. Many of the most sought-after practitioners are marabouts (*moroolu*), who are Islamic scholars and teachers. Marabouts vary in their areas of expertise, but they are frequently called upon to prepare protective amulets with Qur'anic verse to be worn on the body (*safoolu*), or healing water for bathing (*nasoo*) which is instilled with ink from Qur'anic verse. Kanyeleng practices, including *kuuroo* ("washing" or "baptism," see Chapter 2) are widely recognized as one of the treatment options available to women who face reproductive challenges.

People in The Gambia make health care choices based on the options that are available to them, as well as ideas about the causes of different illnesses and the effectiveness of different treatment options. For illnesses that are attributed to spiritual causes such as *jinoolu* (spirits, *jinoo,* sing.) or *buwaalu* (witches, *buwaa,* sing.), people are more likely to consult a marabout than a village health worker.[19] For example, a drummer friend whose performing career was interrupted by a chronic hand injury attributed his problem to witchcraft and sought help from a number of marabouts. He believed that jealous rivals had resorted to witchcraft to destroy his career (see McNaughton 1988a: 155 for related discussion). In contrast, for illnesses such as malaria, which is widely recognized as being caused by a parasite spread by mosquitoes, people are more likely to seek biomedical treatment. People with HIV/AIDS, such as Fatou, typically employ multiple different treatment options, including consultations with marabouts as well as antiretroviral treatment. While President Jammeh required patients to cease ART in order to participate in his treatment program, these different treatment approaches are not usually seen as mutually exclusive.

In addition to the ongoing burden of infectious diseases such as malaria and diarrheal disease, The Gambia has a growing noncommunicable disease burden. Cancers, hypertension, and diabetes are now among the top ten causes of mortality in the country (WHO 2018). The Gambia has an average of just 1.1 physicians and 16.2 nurses and midwives per 10,000 people, well below the World Health Organization's health workforce targets (WHO 2018). The scarcity of skilled health professionals results in long wait-times and short consultations at government health facilities, and makes it extremely difficult for patients to meet their basic health care needs.

Following the 1978 Alma-Ata declaration cosponsored by the World Health Organization, the early 1980s saw increased attention to establishing affordable, community-based health care in The Gambia and other sub-Saharan African countries. By emphasizing the provision of primary health care services throughout the country, the Gambia Ministry of Health and Social Welfare (MoH) sought to overcome the British colonial legacy, which provided quality health care only to a select few located in the urban areas of western Gambia (Sundby 2014). As part of the primary health care initiative, the MoH established and trained Village Health Workers, Community Health Nurses, Public Health Officers, and Traditional Birth Attendants (now called Community Birth Companions) in rural areas in The Gambia. A longitudinal study conducted by the UK Medical Research Council based in The Gambia showed that the primary health care initiative significantly reduced infant and child mortality (Hill et al. 2000). Support for primary health care has waned since the 1990s, however, as a result of shifts in donor priorities, an increasing emphasis on disease-specific ("vertical") programs, and funding cuts associated with economic austerity programs. As a consequence, in The Gambia today, many rural health posts lack access to even the most basic equipment and medicine. Low pay and poor conditions have also resulted in extremely high turnover rates among government health workers (Sundby 2014).

Public health discourse and practices in The Gambia are shaped by global neoliberal ideologies, according to which, "rather than investing in structural interventions to protect the health of its citizens, the state frames health as the individual's moral responsibility to choose a lifestyle that avoids risk" (Bourgois and Schonberg 2009: 109). This approach does not adequately consider the ways in which individual choices are constrained by broader social, political, and economic conditions. In The Gambia, as is the case in sub-Saharan Africa more generally, chronic immiseration of the public health sector has contributed to a redefinition of the role of government in the provision of health care (Sama and Nguyen 2008; Pfeiffer et al. 2010). Approximately one-quarter of health and social welfare spending in The Gambia comes from the national budget, with the remainder coming from donors, nongovernmental organizations (NGOs), and the private sector (WHO 2016; MoH 2012). As a result, international aid and NGOs have increasingly taken on responsibilities for the provision of basic health services in the country. This has produced uneven and uncoordinated service provision, with some diseases, and some regions (particularly western Gambia) better served than others.

It is in this challenging healthcare landscape that female performers collaborate with health workers to communicate information and encourage community mobilization to address health problems. The underfunding and lack of sustainability that characterizes health programs in The Gambia also affects the work of the female performers who are the focus of this book. As I will discuss in Chapter 2, many rural women's groups became involved in health promotion work in the early 1990s as part of the World Bank-funded Women in Development project.

As is the case with many such programs, funding for performance groups since this initial project has been sporadic and uneven. While some groups have received frequent training and continue to work in close collaboration with health organizations, others have become less active. Health workers recognize that effective health promotion programs require ongoing funding and support. Although short-term, disease-specific programs can have some impact, there is a need for long-term collaborations between health workers and performers that make it possible to build on prior knowledge and address emerging public health crises.

Female performers' transformative labor responds to deteriorating political and economic conditions in contemporary Gambia. Gambian women typically engage in what Leith Mullings has called a "triple day" (1995: 62), combining responsibilities at home, work, and in the community. Economic austerity programs have contributed to the intensification of women's labor, particularly agrarian and domestic forms of labor (Kea 2013; Schroeder 1999; Carney and Watts 1991). As income from male cash crops and waged labor dropped in the 1980s and later, Gambian women were forced to compensate by taking on additional income generating activities, such as vegetable gardening (Schroeder 1999; Kea 2013).[20] In urban areas, women's musical labor has similarly been increased in response to decreases in men's income and the stripping of public services in the country. Examining gendered *musical* labor is complicated by the fact that music is not considered to be work (*dookuwo*), but rather play (tulungo), or jaliyaa, and yet similar forms of labor intensification may be observed in women's music performance practices. While international development programs emphasize women's empowerment and capacity building, they can paradoxically make women's lives harder by multiplying their responsibilities, including their musical labor. And yet, women welcome the opportunity to earn more income, as the revenue from men's groundnut farming no longer provides for household livelihoods in the context of increasingly erratic climate conditions, poor agricultural productivity, and fluctuations in the international market for groundnuts.

As medical anthropologist Rachel Chapman writes, "People do not often stand still in the face of hardship" (2010: 45). Rather, in the context of political and economic marginalization, as well as deteriorating access to medical care, Gambian women engage in transformative labor to sustain themselves and their communities. This transformative labor is multi-layered, linking together through musical sound and movement individual, family, and community-level concerns. While health development programs emphasize Muslim women's subordination, and attempt to exploit women's collective associations to further development goals, women themselves use music to produce a sense of coherence as they negotiate conflicting understandings of health, development, knowledge, and power.

Toward an ethnography of health performance

Music, Health, and Power is based on my engagement with performers and health workers in The Gambia over a period of thirteen years (2006–2019). In a sense, I was thrown into this research when I began collaborating with Fatou and the

Allatentu Support Band in 2006–2007. During subsequent ethnographic research (2009; 2012–2013; 2018–2019), I gained a deeper understanding of music, health, and power by performing with women's groups including the APGWA kanyeleng and the Bolonkono Kafoo ("upcountry group"), while continuing my involvement with the Allatentu Support Group. I also took lessons on *kutiro* drums from Haruna Baldeh in Lamin, and lessons on bidong (20-liter plastic jerry can) from Kejawo Juwara in Talinding in order to gain hands-on experience and greater insight into Mandinka rhythms and songs.

In addition to musical participation, I attended and participated in the activities of the Directorate of Health Promotion and Education in the Ministry of Health and Social Welfare, and the Gambia Committee on Traditional Practices Affecting the Health of Women and Children (GAMCOTRAP). The staff of the Directorate of Health Promotion located in the coastal town of Kotu facilitated this research by providing insight and expertise and including me in Communication Task Force meetings and activities. They connected me with Regional Health Education and Promotion Officers, Community Health Nurses, and kanyeleng groups in every region of the country. I also worked with GAMCOTRAP on community outreach activities, planning meetings, and research. Contrasting with the government-run Ministry of Health and Social Welfare, GAMCOTRAP provided a valuable model of an effective nongovernmental organization that involved female performers as an integral component of their education and awareness activities.

Through ethnographic interviews that often moved seamlessly between speaking, singing, and dancing, I gained an in-depth understanding of performers' experiences and perspectives on music, health, and illness. I used an approach that I describe as performance interviewing, inspired by kanyeleng communication practices, as well as Norman Denzin's (2003) method of reflexive interviewing, which emphasizes the emergent and performative quality of the interview as social interaction. In interviews with kanyeleng women in particular, they often moved back and forth between singing and speaking, sitting and dancing, performing their knowledge of music and health for me as well as for each other. Performance interviewing is relational and emergent, blurring the lines separating performance, conversation, and research. In total, I conducted individual or group interviews with 130 performers and health workers from throughout the country. I was based primarily in The Gambia's Western Region, but also observed performances and conducted interviews with performers in every region of the country (see Figures 1.4 and 1.5).

As part of the research for this book, I provided three women's groups with portable camcorders, along with basic training on their operation, to facilitate their participation in the research process through video documentation, or "field notes." The groups included the APGWA kanyeleng, the Bolonkono Kafoo, and the Farato kanyeleng. The goal of the video "field note" project was to produce a collection of miniature autoethnographies that, when brought together, illustrate "the push and pull between and among analysis and evocation, personal experience and larger social, cultural, and political concerns" (Adams and Holman Jones 2008: 374). Rather than serving as a textual authority on experience, I see

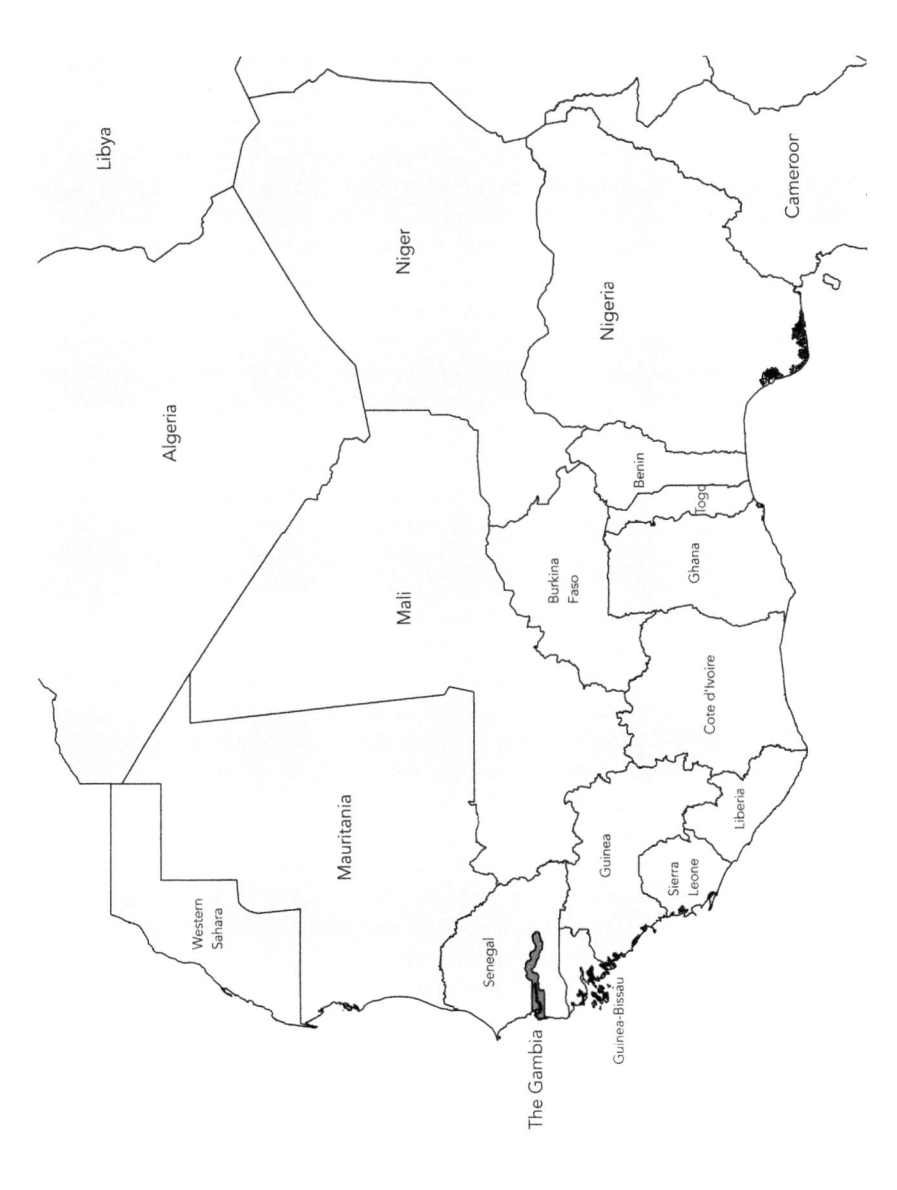

Figure 1.4 The Gambia and West Africa. Map by Erin McConnell.

these video "field notes" as part of an interactive process of reflection and mediation between embodied experience and its representation (Barz 2008). Instead of taking my single account of events as the authority, incorporating documentation from multiple perspectives highlights the convergences and divergences in our positions, experiences, and interpretations of events.

This project was fundamentally shaped by my position as a white American/ Australian woman and the relationships that I developed with people in The Gambia over a period of thirteen years. Assumptions about my identity and place of origin shaped the performances that I attended, as well as the information that was shared or withheld. In many cases, interactions were as much about my relationship with particular people, based on past actions and future responsibilities, as they were about the information shared. Gambian interlocutors often associated me with international development resources and biomedicine, sometimes assuming (despite my lack of medical training) that I was a doctor. This means that in some cases people may have withheld information, as they felt pressure to conform to the biomedical model of disease and prevention in their interactions with me. At the same time, as a result of my outsider status, some people with HIV and other chronic diseases felt more comfortable discussing sensitive topics with me. For example, many HIV positive friends disclosed their status to me even though they had not disclosed it to close family members. They saw me as a sympathetic listener who was somewhat apart from the local social networks that made secrets very hard to keep.

My relationships with people in The Gambia are also influenced by my connection with a particular host family. When I first moved to The Gambia with the US Peace Corps in 2006, I became a member of the Kah family in Kembujeh and received the name Anna Kah after the family's second eldest daughter. My interactions with people in The Gambia continue to be shaped by this family connection. My host family's identity as Fulas (Fulbe) who spoke primarily Mandinka was also passed on to me, further illustrating the high level of integration between ethnic groups in The Gambia and the fluidity of ideas about kinship and ethnicity. This is a contemporary example of longstanding "landlord-stranger" relationships in The Gambia that serve to integrate newcomers into local systems of relationality and responsibility (Wright 2010). Because relationships are framed in kinship terms, they carry with them more long-term obligations than would be the case in a purely economic landlord-tenant relationship.

Drawing on my experiences and observations over thirteen years, together the chapters of this book highlight multi-layered negotiations of gender, power, and health knowledge in women's performances. Chapter 2 investigates gendered understandings of music participation that have given women a strong platform to address health issues in the public sphere. Despite conservative ideals regarding Muslim womanhood and domesticity, female performers have engaged with Islamic discourse, and international movements for gender equality, to access new forms of public influence in contemporary Gambia. I argue that a strengths-based approach must be grounded in recognition of Muslim women's capabilities and knowledge, rather than assumptions of marginality and silence.

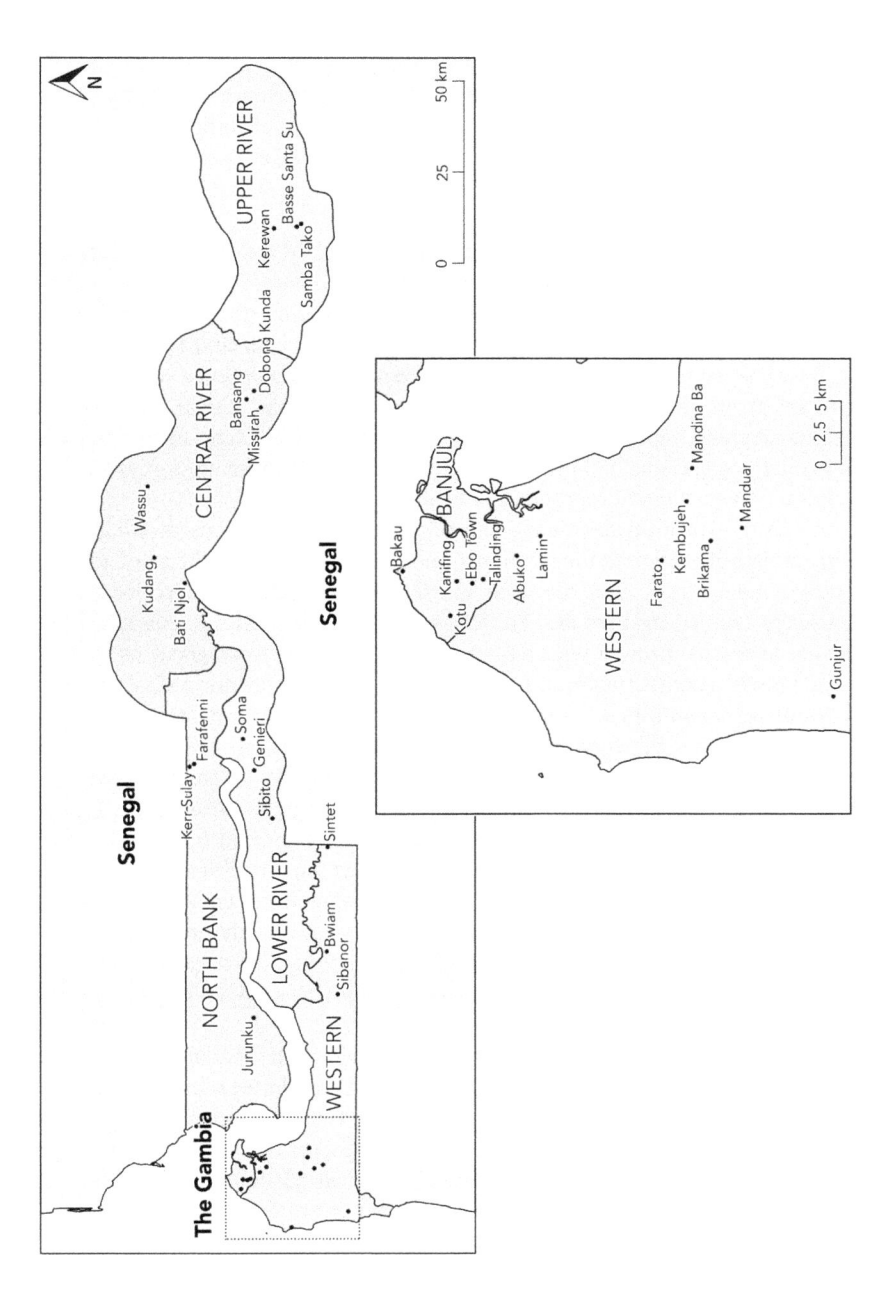

Figure 1.5 The Gambia and the primary research area in western Gambia. Named locations include sites where the author attended performances and/or conducted interviews for this book. Map by Erin McConnell.

Chapter 3 examines shifting interpretations of HIV treatment and shifting positions of power through the lens of Fatou's album *Teriyaa*. I suggest that Fatou's music is a form of transformative work to construct meaning and continuity in a world with HIV/AIDS. I attribute the power of *Teriyaa* primarily to Fatou's voice, a public expression of her private, embodied experience of disease. Even as Fatou's voice gave her the ability to influence public attitudes toward HIV, however, in the end her voice and body were caught up in competing political interests and agendas. This chapter illuminates the human stakes of contests over music, health, and power.

Chapter 4 investigates performative license. Why is it that musicians such as Fatou and the APGWA kanyeleng sing what they cannot say? Drawing on varied perspectives from musicians and health workers, I define performative license not as freedom of expression, but rather as freedom to hear and be heard. The social positions of performers, as well as the embodied experience of sound and movement, shape the form and content of communication. Using examples of kanyeleng women, and people with HIV, I show that music can enable participants to challenge stigma and promote dialogue on sensitive health topics such as those related to sexual and reproductive health.

The theme of baadinyaa (matrilineal relatedness) is the focus of Chapter 5. Baadinyaa literally refers to the relationship between children of the same mother in a polygynous family, but the term is used more broadly to describe caring relationships defined by love and collective responsibility. In this chapter, I use baadinyaa as a lens through which to explore women's performances as sites of collision between competing moral economies, which involve normative assumptions about responsibilities, ethics, and power. I show that performances challenge the dichotomy between capitalist commodity exchange and local spheres of exchange grounded in notions of reciprocity. Participants in performances use money, as both a material object and reference in songs, to affirm the value of human beings and human relationships. I demonstrate that performance norms of social interaction and exchange also carry over into health-related events. Through song and dance, women engage with, and sometimes critique, neoliberal public health discourse on individual responsibility and behavior change. They reframe performances as expressions of baadinyaa, collective responsibility, and care, even as they convey specific information about HIV prevention, hygiene, or vaccines.

Kanyeleng are notorious for their thievery. In 1970, the leader of the Banjul kanyeleng group boasted that she stole the president's underwear and she proudly wore them in performances throughout the region. Chapter 6 uses the legendary underwear theft as a starting point for an investigation of kanyeleng practices of embodying – or stealing – power through musical participation. I show that kanyeleng perspectives on sound and the body in performance events sometimes conflict with dominant paradigms of communication in global health discourse. I suggest that participatory norms of interaction and engagement in kanyeleng events facilitate social mobilization and transformation for health.

Finally, Chapter 7 examines female performers' work in health communication as a tradition defined by adaptability and innovation. It demonstrates that performers make new information accessible by integrating it within existing social relations and modes of communication. Drawing together central themes from the book, I argue that female performers are particularly skilled at involving local communities and promoting memory as well as emotional engagement. I suggest that in order to benefit from the special skills and capabilities that performers contribute, public health programs must build equitable, sustainable partnerships, going beyond the short-term funding models prevalent among international donors.

Notes

1 Because of the sensitive nature of the subject matter, I refer to many performers with their first names only. With the exception of Fatou, pseudonyms are used to refer to people with HIV/AIDS to protect their privacy.
2 The kora is a 21-string bridge harp associated with hereditary professional musicians (*jaloolu*, pl.; *jali/jalo* sing.).
3 Established in 2002, the Global Fund to Fight AIDS, Malaria and Tuberculosis is the main source of funding for HIV/AIDS treatment in The Gambia. The largest contributors to the Global Fund are the United States, France, the United Kingdom, Italy, and Japan, as well as private sector donors such as the Bill & Melinda Gates Foundation (Schocken 2004).
4 Unless otherwise indicated, all non-English terms are Mandinka.
5 According to Charry (2000: 240), musuba is also known as *nyaka*. However, like Knight (1974), I found that nyaka was used to refer to a different rhythm and dance connected with girls' initiation, whereas musuba is associated with kanyeleng, and has (together with lenjengo) become one of the most popular Mandinka dance rhythms among performers of all kinds in western Gambia. The musuba rhythm can be heard on Track 6 on the website: www.routledge.com/9780367731272.
6 While some people identified differences between kanyeleng, dimba, and tole groups, I found these terms were used fairly interchangeably (see Hough 2006 for discussion).
7 Weil (1976) asserts that Mandinka women along The Gambia's southern border adopted kanyeleng (spelled *kanyalang*) practices from Jola women in the Casamance region of Senegal in the 1950s. In contrast, Niang (1994) suggests that *dimba* fertility rituals among Mandinka communities in southern Senegal can be traced back to the Mali empire.
8 With the exception of Kirsten Langeveld's (2014) chapter on Jola kanyeleng songs in Senegal, existing research on kanyeleng has not focused primarily on musical performance practices, instead exploring questions of fertility, gender, ritual, and development (Hough 2006, 2010, 2008; Weil 1976; Fassin 1987; Fassin and Badji 1986; Skramstad 2008; Saho 2012; Niang 1994). Kanyeleng are briefly mentioned in Eric Charry's (2000) volume on Mande music and Roderick Knight's (1974) article on Mandinka drumming.
9 Exclusive breastfeeding refers to the practice of feeding infants only breast milk without supplementary water or food. The World Health Organization (WHO) recommends exclusive breastfeeding for the first six months of life.
10 While most Gambians do not identify as "Sufi," I use Janson's term "Sufi-oriented" as a way to describe an approach to Islam that incorporates local practices such as sainthood (Janson 2006).

11 Swahili is not spoken in this part of Africa. Swahili lyrics were included in an attempt to appeal to an East African audience.

12 The usage of these terms varies by region and appears to have changed over time as the freeborn/slave distinction has become less important. Knight (1973) treats *foro* as a broader freeborn category which includes *nyamaaloo* as well as *sulaa*. In eastern Gambia, the categories *foro* and *jongo* are still widely used, while in western Gambia they have become obsolete.

13 Though occupational specializations exist throughout West Africa, specific artisan categories and specializations vary by region and ethnic group.

14 Despite some representation of non-griot women performers in scholarship (e.g. Appert 2018; Durán 1995, 2003; Linford 2016; Modic 1996; N'Daou 2005; Sidikou and Hale 2012; Sidikou 2001), they continue to be seen as the exception to the (male griot) norm. I contend that the prominence of non-griot women documented by scholars such as Lucy Durán (1995; 2003), is more widespread than scholarship on the Mande area would suggest.

15 The practice of women converting household items into musical instruments is not specific to The Gambia. See Rasmussen (2014) and Penna-Diaw (2014) for related discussion.

16 The "water drum" has also been documented elsewhere in West Africa, including Mali and Nigeria, as well as in Haiti (Modic 1996).

17 Hale (1998) and Janson (2002), for example, have discussed the scholarly preference for epics and instruments associated with men, as well as more longstanding biases toward male informants in social science research.

18 Biomedicine is a form of clinical medical practice informed by biological science that locates the causes of disease in the physical body. Medical anthropological scholarship has demonstrated the way biomedicine, like other medical systems throughout the world, emerges from particular cultural, social, and historical contexts, with particular norms and biases (see Lock and Gordon 2012).

19 For a related discussion of the causes of illnesses and the role of marabouts in healing in Senegal, see Perrino (2002).

20 For discussion of the longer history of gendered labor practices in The Gambia, see Carney and Watts (1991).

2 Women's power

Gender, Islam, and health performance in The Gambia

Introduction

Niuminding Fatty was a prominent kanyeleng musician and community leader. She never went to school, but she was a successful businesswoman who traveled throughout the region for work, and also to serve as an advisor on kanyeleng practices. I learned about Niuminding from her son, Sheikh Omar Jallow, who goes by the name of Suntukung, as well as kanyeleng throughout the Western and North Bank Regions who remembered her fondly. Niuminding passed away in 2009. When we spoke in 2012, Suntukung told me one of the songs his mother used to sing still haunted him: *Yawulu Bande, nte ning Fulo le mu bang*? ("Yawulu Bande,[1] am I with a Fula?"). This is the chorus of the song that was composed for Suntukung, recognizing his Fula ancestry on his father's side. Today, the song is still widely sung for anyone of Fula ethnic background in community events. When Suntukung hears this song, it brings back happy memories of his childhood when he used to dance at kanyeleng events with his mother and eat different kinds of delicious food mixed together. Kanyeleng are notorious for their voracious and non-discriminating appetites. At the end of a ceremony, kanyeleng will often fill bags or pockets with leftovers, mixing together *benachin* (spiced rice), *supa kanja* (ochre stew), or *domoda* (peanut sauce), dishes with distinct flavors that are normally eaten separately. Niuminding would often bring bags of food home to her children.

Niuminding had decided to seek help from the kanyeleng group in Banjul after giving birth to twelve children who died in infancy. Following her initiation or *kuuroo*, Niuminding gave birth to a baby boy who the kanyeleng named Suntukung ("garbage dump" in Mandinka) to disguise him from evil spirits who wished to take the baby away. In accordance with kanyeleng ritual practice, the newborn baby was left on a pile of garbage in Banjul until a woman who lived nearby picked him up and brought him back to Niuminding. The kanyeleng ritual worked, and Suntukung survived.

Niuminding Fatty eventually became a prominent leader among the kanyeleng, and her influence went well beyond fertility-related issues. She worked as a political mobilizer who campaigned for the opposition party during the administration of The Gambia's first president, Dawda Jawara.[2] Niuminding sang a song about Jawara:

> This year it will not fail, the removal of the president will not fail, the catfish is coming, let's all boo him
>
> *Ñinang a te bayila, presidaŋ bondoo te bayi la, ngunja ka naa ali ye a wuure wuure*

(Sheikh Omar Jallow, personal communication, November 28, 2012)

In The Gambia in the 1970s and 1980s, catfish were disliked and seldom eaten. Comparing Jawara to an ugly, stinky catfish, Niuminding was suggesting, in comical kanyeleng style, that there were better candidates for president. Jawara was aware of Niuminding's influence, and according to Suntukung, he offered her land as a bribe to try to make her stop singing critical songs about him. Niuminding refused the offer.

During this period, kanyeleng performances became a privileged site of political discourse, and this has continued up to the present day. Kanyeleng songs often articulate political differences and insult specific politicians. Political rhetoric in kanyeleng songs can be heated. At the same time, expressing political differences through kanyeleng songs can serve to prevent violent conflict between political parties. This is because messages expressed in songs are placed within the framework of kanyeleng joking relations (see Chapter 4 for further discussion). During the 1970s and 1980s, kanyeleng groups were at the forefront of political campaigns for the incumbent People's Progressive Party (PPP) as well as the opposition National Convention Party (NCP). When political campaigns met along the road, the kanyeleng groups would insult one another and sing their songs, preventing violent conflict from developing (Sheikh Omar Jallow, personal communication, April 25, 2018).

Niuminding spearheaded kanyeleng involvement in health and development programs through partnership with Binta Jammeh Sidibeh and the Association for Promoting Girls and Women's Advancement in The Gambia (APGWA). Partly as a result of this partnership, kanyeleng have become increasingly professionalized as they have taken on roles in health and development communication. This has given kanyeleng greater prestige and decreased the stigma associated with kanyeleng membership.

Niuminding was also a pious Muslim. When she got older, her sons encouraged her to retire from kanyeleng performance, asserting that some aspects of kanyeleng practices were inappropriate for a devout Muslim woman of her age. The sons decided to give their mother a monthly retirement allowance (a "pension") so that she would not feel pressure to earn money through kanyeleng activities. Niuminding agreed to retire, but she continued to occasionally attend performances in secret, without telling her sons. She also played an important advisory role for younger women, both in relation to kanyeleng practices and

Muslim devotion (Sheikh Omar Jallow, personal communication, November 28, 2012).

Niuminding was an exceptional woman in many ways, but her story provides a starting point for a broader investigation of women's music and women's power in contemporary Gambia. Niuminding demonstrates both the enormous influence of female performers in politics and health, as well as contested ideas about music and appropriate behavior for Muslim women. In this chapter, I explore the cultural, historical, and political conditions that have combined to place women's associations, and Muslim women performers such as Niuminding, at the center of public life in The Gambia, challenging dominant portrayals of Muslim women as marginal and confined to the private sphere (Lachenmann and Dannecker 2008; Sidikou and Hale 2012). I investigate the contested terrain of Muslim women's musical practices in a context where ideas about gender and piety restrict performance opportunities, but also enable women to access new forms of power and influence in contemporary Gambia.

Shameless: music and femininity

An investigation of women's performances roles in The Gambia demands a broad view of musical participation. I use the word "participants" as an inclusive term to describe everyone involved with a music event, including singers, dancers, instrumentalists, listeners, organizers, and cooks (see Small 2011), recognizing that these categories overlap and many Gambian performances are highly participatory, without a clear division between audiences and performers (Turino 2008). Although men often comprise the majority of instrumentalists, when we consider other forms of musical participation such as singing, dancing, handclapping, *sooroo* (monetary donation in performance), and event organizing, women's musical prominence becomes clear. There are, of course, exceptions: reggae and hip hop shows, for example, as well as events associated with male circumcision, tend to feature a large proportion of male participants. At most of the performance events I attended, however, ranging from small-scale community celebrations to major celebrity shows at the Independence Stadium, participants were predominately female.

A central concept in explaining gendered musical participation for Mandinka and other Mande groups is *maloo* (shame). Maloo is associated with discretion, emotional restraint, and honesty. Groups that are expected to display high levels of maloo are less likely to engage in music performance (Grosz-Ngate 1989; Arnoldi 1995; Irvine 1990). Kanyeleng are notorious for their shamelessness (*malubaliyaa*) and their consequent ability to address taboo topics and make fun of authority figures, evident in Niuminding Fatty's comical songs about former president Dawda Jawara. According to the Mandinka system of hereditary professional groups or castes, *sulaa* (freeborn or noble) people are believed to have a more highly developed sense of maloo than their *nyamaaloo* (artisan) and *jongo* (slave) counterparts. These differences are also evident among non-Mande groups in the region, such as the Wolof (Irvine 1990). Even with changes in these social categories, including the decline of the freeborn/slave distinction in much of The Gambia, ideas about maloo continue to shape participation in musical performance in powerful ways. In eastern Gambia, where caste identities are stronger, most kanyeleng belong to *nyamaaloo* (particularly *garanke*) or *jongo* families. Women from other families who experience infertility or child deaths may seek help from kanyeleng without long-term engagement in ritual and performance activities. More generally, performers who are not from *nyamaaloo* families, such as Fatou of the Allatentu Support Band, often encounter opposition when they decide to pursue a career in music.

Older age and male gender are associated with a more highly developed sense of shame. Children are notorious for their shamelessness, as well as their love of music and dance. As people get older, they sometimes choose to cease participating actively in performances, explaining that it would be shameful for their children and grandchildren to see them dancing and singing. This attitude is evident in the experience of Niuminding Fatty, who faced pressure from her family to retire from kanyeleng performance as she grew older. This also relates to the broader expectation that people should become more pious as they age, turning more toward prayer and away from entertainment and material concerns.

Women of all ages are expected to experience less shame, and to be more emotionally and musically expressive than their male counterparts. In her discussion of related gender concepts in Mali, Maria Grosz-Ngate uses a Bamana proverb to demonstrate perceived differences between male and female experiences of shame:

> If you find a woman in trouble, help her. But if you find her in a shameful situation, leave her because she will get over it. If you find a man in trouble, leave him because he can get out of it on his own. But if you find him in a shameful situation, get him out of it because otherwise he might die.
>
> (1989: 171; see also Saho 2012: 118–119)

These starkly different expectations regarding men's and women's experiences of shame in Mande culture are linked to gendered constructions of expressivity and emotionality (McConnell 2015). That is, women and girls are believed to be naturally more emotionally expressive, which enables them to more easily overcome shame by releasing it, rather than holding it inside. I discussed these gender differences with my host father, a senior male community leader, who suggested that because men don't express their feelings through song, their hearts overflow; this can produce health problems, and may be the reason why men have a lower life expectancy. He gave the analogy of two plastic bags to explain gender differences. The empty plastic bag that is packed away (i.e. a woman's heart) will last much longer than the bag that is full to the brim (i.e. a man's heart overflowing with unexpressed emotion).

Although ideas about gender and music in West Africa connect to deeply rooted notions of masculinity, femininity, and shame, such ideas are neither static nor uncontested. In his research in Guinea, Manthia Diawara (1998) found that women had taken on roles in Mandinka performance that were formerly played by men. Diawara suggests that the dominance of women and the absence of men in performances such as male circumcision celebrations reflect a "weakening of tradition" (1998: 35). Diawara's perspective provides an important counter to the idea that women's prominent roles in performance in the region are "traditional" and highlights the way social and economic changes can transform musical performance contexts and participation. In The Gambia, as elsewhere in West Africa, male labor migration has left many rural areas with a higher proportion of women and a growing number of female-headed households (see Buggenhagen 2012). The extent to which this has affected music performance requires further research, but female performers in The Gambia do not view their prominent roles as a sign of the "weakening of tradition," nor do they inherit their musical roles passively. Rather, they are active in articulating performative responses to contemporary realities in The Gambia that are shaped but not defined by local ideas about gender and shame.

Sinful? Women, music, and Islam

Religious discourse also influences attitudes toward music participation in The Gambia, where the population is over ninety percent Muslim. For women such as Niuminding Fatty, a tension exists between idealized notions of Muslim womanhood and the demands of being a performer (see Janson 2002). A strong emphasis on women's domestic responsibilities and their roles as wives and mothers shapes their musical lives. Female performers work within an environment with particular gendered expectations and Islamic discourse that, to varying degrees, restricts their mobility and access to performance opportunities. At the same time, music is associated with femininity, and women have access to performance opportunities in The Gambia that men do not have. These opportunities emerge from local notions of gender, music, and Islamic practice.

While some pious Muslims choose not to participate actively in music events, for the majority of Gambian Muslims, music and dance are considered to be acceptable as long as they do not cause people to consume alcohol, commit adultery, or forget to pray. As a prominent Gambian Islamic scholar explained,

> Islam does not forbid all culture, but it does not accept all of it. … During the Prophet's time, songs were sung and it did not destroy anything. Songs were sung that made people happy … dancers also danced, because in the Prophet's own house, Isatou's father entered, he said, "Heh, stop, you stop that, in the prophet's house!" The prophet said, "No, leave them." The Prophet himself did not watch them, he directed his eyes away. He said, "leave them there." If it were forbidden, the prophet would not have agreed to that. … Some dance exists that is not bad. Some dance exists that is bad. … to throw the skirt, women's bodies all coming out, … all those dances, women and men hold each other, … Islam does not like that. … If it is your husband, you can do it, but another's husband [no].

Islamo, a maŋ culture bee bayi de. Bari a maŋ a bee accept. ... Kabiriŋ prophet la taimo, denkiloo ka laa le aniŋ a maŋ feŋ o feŋ tiñaa. Denkiloo ka laa le, meŋ i ye a loŋ ko, a ka moolu sewondi, ... prophet jamano ... doŋna fanaŋ ka doŋo ke, katuŋ prophet faŋo la buŋo kono, luŋ doo, ala musoo i ka fo a ye, Isatou, a ye moolu samba, i be doŋo la buŋo kono. Isatou faamaa dunta. A ko, "heh, stop, ali ye a bula, kiilaa la buŋo kono!" Kiilaa ko, "no, leave them." Kiilaa faŋo maŋ i juubee, a ye a ñaa tiliŋ teŋ mafaŋo. A ko a ye a bula jee. Niŋ a ye a tara a haramta, kiilaa te soŋ na wo la. Iyoo. Meŋ i ye a loŋ ko a maŋ kuu samba, a manke haram kuwo, wo ka ke le. Moo la culture ... doŋo doo be jee, wo maŋ jawuyaa. Doŋo doo be jee, wo jawuyaata le. ... ka faano fayi, musoolu baloo bee ye funti banta ... wo doŋo bee, musoolu niŋ kee ka ñoo muta. ... Islamo maŋ lafi wo la. ... Niŋ i kee le mu, i si a ke, bari wandi kee.

(Personal communication, September 25, 2013)

According to this perspective, musical sounds and movements are not problematic in themselves, but only for the danger represented by the exposure of women's bodies in dance, and the potential for adulterous sexual liaisons. Most of my interlocutors agreed with this view that music and dance are, within limits, acceptable.

Some kanyeleng rituals, however, are specifically condemned by Islamic leaders because they are seen as a form of idolatry with origins in pre-Islamic religious practices. Kanyeleng themselves emphatically refute this, asserting that their rituals are a form of prayer, and their primary goal is to inspire God to take pity on them and give them children who survive. I participated in an initiation ritual in October 2013 that exemplified kanyeleng's syncretic approach to fertility promotion and self-conscious framing of their practices as prayer. The initiation event, referred to as *kuuroo* (washing or baptism) was conducted by members of the APGWA kanyeleng, the group formerly led by Niuminding Fatty.

Before the initiation event, which took place in a large, shady compound in Fajikunda, the kanyeleng women filled a bucket with water and leaves from orange and mango trees. They also prepared a large bowl of millet porridge (*monoo*), and a cup of uncooked rice. One of the group members, Nyali Damba, explained that oranges, mangoes, millet, and rice were all very fertile. One millet seed, when you plant it in the ground, grows to produce hundreds of new seeds. Similarly, one mango tree bears hundreds of mangoes that passersby can eat. The kanyeleng used these grains and fruits in the initiation ceremony in the hope that their fecundity would rub off on the woman seeking a baby.

The initiate sat in the center of the circle and removed her clothing except for her underskirt. Her clothing was now the property of the kanyeleng group. The group sang songs that I later learned were part of a specific kanyeleng repertoire, even though they were performed with the more widely popular *lenjengo* and *musuba* rhythms. Musuba (lit. "big woman") is a popular dance that can be performed by anyone but is often preferred by older women and kanyeleng specifically. Lenjengo has a faster tempo than musuba, and it is preferred by young women who like to dance fast (see Chapter 6 for further discussion).

Dressed in a brilliant blue dress with a matching headscarf, Sunkari played the bidong to accompany the dancing and singing. The kanyeleng sang:[3]

> Big Well, that which you have done for [other] people, do it for me also
> *Koloŋbaa, i ye meŋ ke moolu le ye, koloŋbaa, a ke n fanaŋ ye*

The "big well" referenced in this song has multiple layers of meaning. Some kanyeleng suggested that the song refers to an allegorical story about a well that used to be full of water and has now dried up. Just as the well should have water, a woman should have a child. The well is therefore a symbol for a woman's fertility. Others described the "big well" as a reference to the ultimate power of God to grant fertility and healthy children, and some even used the term *Mansaba* ("Great King") instead of "big well." Nyali Damba and Khadijatou Mass from the APGWA kanyeleng said that the "big well" referred to in the song is a sacred site near the village of Gunjur where women go to pray for a child. In the past, many women went to pray at the big well and had healthy children who survived into adulthood. Khadijatou herself was taken there before she was initiated as a kanyeleng. Other similar sacred sites include the Kachikaly crocodile pond in Bakau (now a popular tourist destination) and the Folonko pond near Kartong. While some Gambians consider visits to sacred sites such as these to be a form of idolatry, kanyeleng describe them instead as sites for Muslim prayer.

The kanyeleng also performed a song that highlighted the importance of faith in God:

> Holding on to God, there is nothing like it, may you hold on, let it be strong
> *Alla mutoo, ñon te, i s'a muta a ye bambaŋ*

Nyali and Khadijatou explained that some women who are unable to conceive a child might be tempted to take outside lovers in order to try to conceive. In other cases, marriages end because the wife has not produced a child, in an environment where women face strong pressure to bear children and infertility is typically attributed to wives rather than husbands. This song cautions women to hold on to their faith in God so that their marriages will last. While struggles with infertility may cause a woman to lose her faith, kanyeleng emphasize patience, humility, and prayer to God as the ultimate source of fertility. When God sees a woman's faith and devotion, he may grant her a child.

These two songs are typical of kanyeleng repertoire in that they have relatively few words, yet they convey a great deal of meaning. The songs demonstrate the syncretic nature of kanyeleng rituals, which draw on pre-Islamic practices but reframe them in accordance with notions of Muslim prayer and faith in God. These songs also evoke the tension at the heart of kanyeleng practices. Their ultimate aim is to enable women to fulfill normative gender ideals of motherhood, but at the same time kanyeleng subvert those gender ideals, and provide solace for women who are unable to achieve them (Hough 2008; Saho 2012).

During the initiation event, the group members wore the funny clothing that is characteristic of kanyeleng. Some group members took off their dresses and put on large, ill-fitting trousers or oversized underwear over short pants. Their behavior was similarly outrageous. They joked, laughed, made sexually suggestive moves, and ridiculed the new initiate. Nyali was chosen as the primary "washer" of the new initiate because she had had many children. She, along with Binta and Fatou, washed the initiate with the water steeped in leaves from fertile mango and orange trees. They washed her hair and placed tiny grains of white rice in it. Finally, they wiped the sweet millet porridge all over the initiate's body. The rest of us danced and sang around her, stopping to scoop up some sloppy millet porridge as we passed by. It was a messy affair, with delicious but sticky millet porridge dripping over our faces and bodies.

Finally, the group stopped singing and began to pray, kanyeleng-style. Everybody prayed at once with emphatic speech and exaggerated gestures that marked this prayer as a kanyeleng activity. After the prayer was complete, the kanyeleng women chased the new initiate away, hitting her with small sticks and instructing her not to look back. She ran away down the street to her compound. Although she was covered in dried porridge, to maximize the effect of the intervention, the initiate would not bathe until the following day. She could wipe herself off with a dry cloth, but she was instructed not to wash with water. The kanyeleng explained that by subjecting herself to this treatment, the initiate could evade her spirit husband and demonstrate to God her desperation for a child.

In addition to initiation events such as this one, kanyeleng organize a variety of other events as part of their fertility-related practices. One of these is the kanyeleng "naming ceremony" where a new baby is given a kanyeleng name and a papaya is "slaughtered" in a comedic imitation of the killing of the ram at a Muslim naming ceremony seven days after birth (see Figure 2.1). Another common kanyeleng practice, also intended to evade the *kuntofengo* or spirit husband, is the custom of leaving a young baby at a crossroads or a garbage dump. The person who picks the child up will then usually take on the role of their namesake or guardian.

For individuals like Niuminding and Suntukung, it is sometimes difficult to reconcile a deep knowledge and appreciation of kanyeleng ritual practices with the perspectives of Islamic scholars who consider those practices to be *haram* (forbidden). Suntukung expressed concern and a sense of sorrow about the loss of kanyeleng wisdom as older kanyeleng die and the younger generation concerns itself with parties and development work rather than ritual knowledge. And yet, Suntukung and his brother encouraged their own mother to retire because they did not think kanyeleng practices were appropriate for an aging Muslim woman. Suntukung's ideas are informative because they demonstrate the complexity of debates about Islam, music, and traditional culture (*coosaanoo*), and the way conflicting perspectives may be held by a single individual. People such as Suntukung and Niuminding have also been at the forefront of efforts to adapt kanyeleng practices to meet the needs of contemporary Gambian communities, responding to the changing political, economic, and religious landscape.

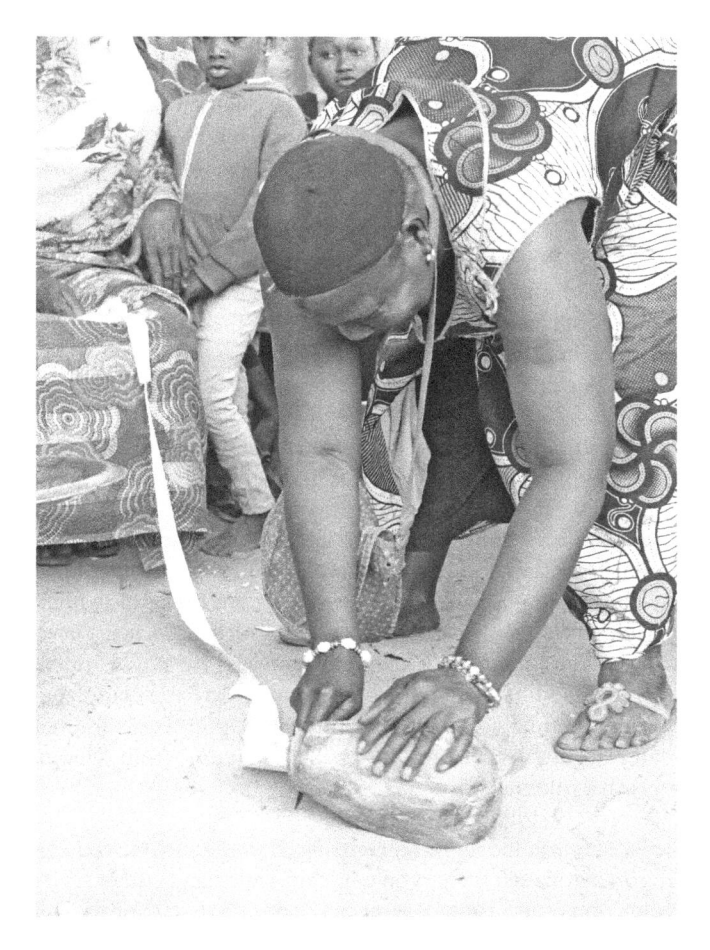

Figure 2.1 The papaya ram is "slaughtered" at a kanyeleng naming ceremony in Talinding in 2019, photograph by the author.

As evident in the initiation event, kanyeleng challenge the notion that their music is incompatible with Islam, interweaving their performances with Islamic references. Likewise, Mandinka *jalimusoolu* (female jali, sing. *jalimusoo*) proclaim that their profession originated with the Prophet Muhammad and connect Mande oral histories to historical Islamic figures (Janson 2002; Ebron 2002; see also Conrad 1985).

> Jaliyaa, we inherited it from the Prophet's time in the hands of our ancestors. Jaliyaa came from Surakata. That is the Prophet's jali.
>
> *Jaliyaa, ntolu ye a inherit kabiriŋ kiilaa rasuulu tumoo nna ancestor le bulu. Jaliyaa bota Surakata le bulu. Wo le mu kiilaa rasuulu la jaloo ti.*
>
> (Sambou Suso, personal communication, July 25, 2013)

The figure of Surakata, frequently referenced as the jali's ancestor, is inspired by Suraqa ibn Malik ibn Ju'shum who is a figure from Arabic literature (Conrad 1985). By claiming Surakata as their ancestor, female performers in The Gambia assert their legitimacy with regard to their religion. Though Sambou Suso, quoted above, is a jalimusoo, kanyeleng women similarly align themselves with Surakata and other Muslim figures in order to challenge those who question the compatibility of kanyeleng practice with Islam. In addition, female performers attribute their musical skill and inspiration to God. For example, Kejawo Juwara asserted that her ability to make the bidong "speak" (in a musical sense) was something that came from God and could not be taught. (While she agreed to give me lessons, she did not have great faith in my ability to learn to play the bidong). Female performers also demonstrate their legitimacy within Islam through song texts and speeches that incorporate Qur'anic verse and references (Charry 2000; Janson 2002; Knight 1973).

The hajj (the Muslim pilgrimage to Mecca) further demonstrates the way women actively negotiate their performance practices in relation to religious commitments. Because completing the hajj is believed to cleanse pilgrims of their sins, upon their return to The Gambia, women sometimes choose to cease performance practices that could potentially be sinful. Returned pilgrims must negotiate the profoundly socially and psychologically transformative experience of the hajj in relation to their everyday lives (see Hammoudi and Ghazaleh 2006 for related discussion). Even for those who do not associate performance with sin, an active performance role is seen as potentially dangerous for people who have completed the hajj. Gambian pilgrims often take special precautions in order to ensure that they will be able to safely continue performing when they return from Mecca. Kanyeleng performer Nyali explained,

> You know a place is there [on the hajj], a place that, if you go there, you can sing a song there, you can dance there, you can clap your hands there. … If you went there, when you return [home], you can continue [to perform]. But if you did not go there, you will not be able to.
>
> *I ye a loŋ dulaa be jee, dulaa meŋ i ye a long ko, niŋ i taata jee, i si denkiloo laa jee, i si i idoŋ jee, i si i buloolu kosi jee. Niŋ i ye a tara i taata wo to, niŋ i naata, i si kontinee noo, bari niŋ i maŋ taa wo to, i te a ke noo la.*
>
> (Personal communication, July 17, 2013)

Other kanyeleng and jali interlocutors likewise emphasized the need to sing and dance while on the pilgrimage in order to continue a performance career in The Gambia. Nyima, a jalimusoo from western Gambia, explained that some jali cease performing for a period of one year after their pilgrimage after which the restriction is lifted. She also stressed the importance of stating an intention to continue performing while in Mecca in order to ensure that one is able to perform safely upon returning to The Gambia. Nyima noted that while most jali continue vocal and instrumental performance after returning from Mecca, many choose not to dance again after completing the hajj (personal communication, September 30, 2013). Such accounts challenge a monolithic view of Islam in West Africa and foreground the agency of individual performers who seek to reconcile the demands of their faith and their music.

Scholarly and media accounts tend to portray Islam as a uniformly oppressive and silencing force in African women's lives, eliding the diversity and complexity of Muslim women's experience (Callaway and Creevey 1994; Masquelier 2009). Yet in The Gambia, Islamic discourse often serves to reinforce the association of music with femininity, thereby making space for women's voices to be heard in the public sphere. For example, many villages, neighborhoods, and family compounds have restrictions on music. These restrictions are usually based on directions from local Islamic leaders or marabouts, and they often apply specifically to instruments played by men and/or popular music recordings. Villages that performers and health workers identified as having such restrictions included Badibu Gunjur (North Bank Region), Bati Njol (Central River Region), Ballanghar (Central River Region), and Kiang Keneba (Lower River Region), among others.

A resident of the Central River Region attributed the instrument restrictions in Balangharr to the community's commitment to the "Islamic path." He explained, "They also don't accept these drums in their village. It's on the top of the hill. They call it Arafat. ... They will entertain those things [calabash and bidong], but the drums, no" (personal communication, July 7, 2013). The name Arafat here is a reference to the holy site in Saudi Arabia where the Prophet Muhammad delivered his last sermon. Referring to their village as Arafat and restricting music activity are means by which Islamic leaders in Balangharr assert their piety and devotion. While drums are considered incompatible with the community's religious commitments, women's percussion instruments are tolerated.

In other cases, instrument restrictions are attributed to the presence of Muslim jinn,[4] or spirits. Khadijatou explained that her compound in Kiang was home to a jinn who did not like drums[5] or *kankurang* masquerades associated with circumcision activities and recreational events:

> They have a jinn who does not like kankurang entering there, or playing drums there. They play the calabash there! They don't refuse that, but [if you bring] these Mandinka drums like this, or kankurang, sore eyes will bother you until your eyes split. ... They will not be able to heal if you bring a kankurang there. ... I heard about that from my elders, my father's generation. And I also passed my childhood until I was grown up, I did not see it. If a kankurang came, it would stop at the entrance to the compound. It would not enter the home. ... The bidong is played there. The calabash is played there, but the drums are not played. They say there the jinn does not like it.
>
> *Jinoo le be itolu bulu meŋ i ye a loŋ ko a maŋ lafi wo la, kankuraŋo ye duŋ jee, wala i ye taa jee i ye tantaŋo kosi jee. Katuŋ i ka miraŋo kosi jee. I maŋ balaŋ wo le la, bari ko meŋ ñiŋ Mandinka tantaŋo teŋ, wamba kankuraŋo ye naa, ñaadimoo be i muta la fo i ñaa ye teyi. ... A te kendeyaa noo la le niŋ i ye kankuraŋo dundi jee. ... N ka wo moyi nna alifaalu la, n faamaa ñoolu la, haa. Aduŋ n fanaŋ ŋa dindiŋyaa ke le, fo n kebaayaata, maŋ wo je jee. ... Niŋ kankuraŋo naata, a be daŋna koridaa daa la. A te duŋ na suwokono. ...*

Satedoolu fanaŋ, i ko wolu fanaŋ, tantaŋo buka kosi jee. Haa. Bidoŋo ka kosi jee. Kiijo ka kosi, bari tantaŋo buka kosi. I ko jee jinoo maŋ lafi ala.
(Personal communication, July 17, 2013)

Khadijatou attributes the instrument restrictions in her family compound to the requirements of the particular jinn residing there. Those who went against the jinn's restrictions could face serious consequences, including blindness. I learned about numerous similar examples of compounds that allowed women's instruments such as bidong and calabash, but not drums, during the course of my research. These examples illuminate questions of power and complexities in how people negotiate musical performance practices in particular local contexts in relation to spiritual entities and religious beliefs. Not homogeneous, ideas about gender, Islam, and performance are localized and experienced in distinct ways in different parts of The Gambia as well as within particular compounds and extended families.

Regional health worker Saharu Kante explained, "Even the most … religious, conservative communities, [the bidong] is always allowed. They don't consider it as a music" (personal communication, June 5, 2013). Others likewise observed that kanyeleng frequently played in the compounds of marabouts and imams, where other forms of music were prohibited. The idea that kanyeleng performances may be more acceptable to religious leaders than male drum ensembles is striking considering that some kanyeleng practices are specifically condemned by Islamic scholars. This demonstrates the difficulty in describing ideas about music in relation to Islam where "music" is not a unitary activity but rather encompasses a spectrum of performance forms that have particular associations and significance. Even for different kinds of percussion and dance performances that are all referred to as tulungo in Mandinka, male and female performers and instruments are viewed quite differently. The word tulungo is flexible and can be used to refer to a variety of activities, including children's play as well as music and dance performances (see Chapter 4). The acceptability of women's performances and instruments in contexts where men's instruments are banned suggests that they may be conceptually aligned more with child's play than with the more "serious," and potentially dangerous, male-dominated performances. Even as restrictions on male performers in this context indicate their higher status, these same restrictions serve to empower female instrumentalists by providing them with performance opportunities, income, and communicative influence that are not available to men.

Although people may call upon female bidong and calabash players in lieu of male drummers, this does not mean that drums are the preferred instrument in the absence of restrictions. On the contrary, I found that many women preferred bidong and calabash performances and chose to participate in events featuring these instruments when given a choice. This challenged the assumptions I had about performance preferences in The Gambia, as the following excerpt from my field notes demonstrates. In this excerpt, I describe my experience performing with the APGWA kanyeleng at a celebration for the installation of a new Paramount Chief in Jurunku (North Bank Region) in 2012:

In the evening we went back to the house to rest and then went out again around 9:30. We started performing again in front of the Chief's house. The *kutiro* drum group was performing right next to us, so I was unsure how our group would go over (it gets so noisy with all the groups side by side). But, just as the women had told me ... when the bidong and calabash started playing, I saw a whole group of women leave the drums and join our circle. With the hand clappers, the bidong and the calabash, I can see why they say that it draws a crowd more than the drums. It is louder for one thing, and it seems to encourage more participation, particularly with handclapping.

(December 22, 2012)

This was a pivotal moment for me because up until that point, although I appreciated bidong performance, I still assumed that the drum – performed primarily by men in western Gambia – was the preferred instrument for most audiences. This event made me question the way my own internalized ideas about authenticity (and a preference for non-plastic instruments) were shaping my research. Consequently, I began to focus more attention on bidong performance practice, not as an alternative to the drum or calabash, but as an instrument in its own right. Lessons and discussions with Kejawo Juwara helped me to recognize the unique timbral qualities of the instrument and the virtuosity required to play it well.

Subsequently, many women told me that they preferred the bidong to drums at a dance event. A female health worker from western Gambia explained,

I prefer the bidong to the drums because it's cheaper, you wouldn't pay anyone. And it's nicer for me, and the women enjoy it more. And they, then they are in control of what they are doing, but with the drums, they have to give money to the drummers, they have to pay them at the end of the program, and they are men in control of women's programs.

(Personal communication, August 6, 2013)

In addition to the preference for the sound of the bidong, many women prefer the bidong for financial reasons – it is cheaper than paying a drum ensemble. While some bidong players require payment (though typically less than a male drum ensemble), others may play for free. Just as importantly, having a female bidong player allows women to retain control of their performances rather than following the lead of the male drummers.

Local musical preferences, religious belief, and ideas about gender and maloo combine to place women in a prominent position in many musical performance events in The Gambia. Women negotiate their performance practice in relation to complex ideas about gender, music, and religion that simultaneously restrict their activities and provide opportunities and forms of power that are not available to men. In the next section, I will examine the way women's prominence in the musical sphere has also given them a platform to influence attitudes toward development, health, and gender more broadly. I suggest that efforts to engage female performers in health and development activities must be grounded in understanding of the local perspectives on gender and power outlined here.

Working for the country: gender, global health, and development

Building on Gambian concepts of gender and music participation, an emphasis on women's empowerment and gender equality in international development has created new opportunities for female performers. In response to the strong focus on men during the first two decades of development practice, by the early 1970s scholars and practitioners called for more attention to the role of women in development. In particular, Ester Boserup's book *Women's Role in Economic Development* (1970) spearheaded the women in development (WID) movement, which gained significant momentum during the UN Decade for Women from 1976–1985. In 1970, Sweden was the only donor country to have a WID emphasis, but by 2007, most donor countries had dedicated WID or GAD (gender and development) policies or programs (Swiss 2012: 99). The global emphasis on women's rights and women's roles in development also led to the multiplication of government agencies dedicated to women's issues as well as women's international nongovernmental organizations or "WINGOS" in countries such as The Gambia.

Emerging from American liberal feminist thought, the WID movement has been criticized for its lack of attention to problems inherent in the modernization theory of development and its inability to improve the lives of many of the world's women. Feminist critiques of WID's focus solely on women, rather than the broader social relationships that produce gender inequality, inspired a shift in the 1980s and 1990s away from WID and toward a Gender and Development (GAD) approach and gender mainstreaming. A gender-focused approach has not been achieved in most contexts, however, as many development programs continue to equate "gender" with "women." This is the case in The Gambia, where many funding opportunities and programs target women specifically, rather than considering the relational dynamics of gender that shape the experiences of men as well as women. By neglecting to consider broader social relations of power, such programs can fail to achieve positive change (Schroeder 1999). For example, HIV/AIDS prevention programs in The Gambia have focused extensively on women, with the result being that women are often blamed for the spread of the disease.[6] The majority of HIV/AIDS support group members are women, and there are numerous examples of men divorcing wives when they disclose their HIV positive status. To address this problem, Allatentu Support Group staff have coordinated a series of HIV/AIDS awareness events targeting men specifically. The songs from the *Teriyaa* album have played an important role in these events.

In 1980, in the middle of the UN Decade for Women, the Gambian Women's Bureau was established to work toward gender equality. The newly formed Bureau attracted many of the country's most active advocates for women, including

Isatou Njie Saidy (former Vice President of The Gambia), Binta Jammeh Sidibeh (founder of APGWA[7]), and Dr Isatou Touray (founder of GAMCOTRAP[8] and current Vice President of The Gambia), among others. These women have all continued to work toward breaking down barriers for women and girls through a variety of avenues including forming civil society organizations such as GAMCOTRAP and APGWA.

Binta Jammeh Sidibeh described the responsibility she felt, as one of the first women in the country to graduate from high school and university, to work toward improving the lives of women in her country:

> All the [women] who were educated at that time, they formed an association of university women. You know we were very proud then. … And we have all exceled. … Having gone to that level in that age, in the 70s, that was something. … All eyes were on us. … It was a big challenge. … So I was, since then, really very much interested in women's empowerment, women's education. … That gave me the passion and the commitment.
>
> (Personal communication, March 22, 2013)

Binta's testimony demonstrates the commitment and drive she felt as one of a small number of women to attain advanced education in the 1970s. While influenced by global feminist discourse, the impact of the WID movement in The Gambia was achieved only through the hard work and passion of women such as Binta Jammeh Sidibeh and her contemporaries.

Female leaders such as Binta, familiar with local dynamics of gender and power, translated international concern for WID into local programs involving female performers. Binta asserts that her relationship with the Talinding kanyeleng group, now known as the APGWA kanyeleng, inspired the more widespread involvement of kanyeleng women as communicators in health and development programs. According to Binta, it all started in the early 1990s. The kanyeleng women, led by Niuminding Fatty at that time, approached Binta and asked her to serve as their surrogate mother, a common practice for groups in The Gambia. Surrogate mothers and fathers are usually successful and highly regarded members of the community who help groups by providing financial and social support. Once they started working together, Binta involved the kanyeleng in her development projects. Largely as a result of this collaboration with Binta, the APGWA kanyeleng became one of the most renowned kanyeleng groups in the country. They frequently perform for politics events and health programs of various kinds. As Binta explained, the APGWA kanyeleng have inspired a broader shift in the social position and status of kanyeleng as they have taken on new roles in public health and development work.

While the collaboration spearheaded by Binta Jammeh Sidibeh and Niuminding Fatty was influential, other organizations also engaged female performers in innovative ways in the 1980s and 1990s. Fatou Gaye, now with The Gambia Red Cross, explained that when she was working with the Ministry of Agriculture in the 1980s, Assan Sallah developed new kinds of partnerships with kanyeleng groups to disseminate information about agricultural practices (personal communication, August 6, 2013). Because she found them very effective, Gaye has continued to collaborate with kanyeleng and other female performers in her work at The Gambia Red Cross and other organizations. Rather than being restricted to a particular government ministry or area of focus, engaging female performers as development communicators became widespread across sectors during the 1980s and 1990s. Gambian experts in gender, development, and health sought to develop new approaches that were both locally meaningful and aligned with international development priorities.

An important boost to the "traditional communication" movement came under the 1990s development initiative called the Women in Development (WID) Project. The WID project was a US$15.1 million initiative funded by the World Bank, The Gambia Government, the Kingdom of Norway, the African Development Bank (ADB), the United Nations Development Program (UNDP), the United Nations Development Fund for Women (UNIFEM), and the United Nations Fund for Population Activities (UNFPA). The project was implemented by the Women's Bureau as well as several different government departments, including the Department of State for Health, and NGOs. While performers' roles in communication have a much longer history, the contemporary collaborations between female performers such as kanyeleng and organizations working in the area of health gained significant momentum through the WID project.

The WID project incorporated different communications media in order to promote women's participation. The effectiveness of the "popular theater" component of the project, which involved music, dance, and drama, is emphasized in the evaluation report:

> Popular theater and the local communicator strategy appear to be the most popular methods of communication. Rural women have stated that only through popular theater they have been able to speak their mind and address issues such as men's lack of support for women's heavy workload, their neglect of responsibilities toward the family, the effect of male migration to urban areas on women.
>
> (World Bank 1998: Appendix A)

The WID report underscores several of the features of performance that emerged as particularly significant in my discussions with performers and health workers, notably the importance of participation (see Chapter 6) and performative license (see Chapter 4) in facilitating dialogue on topics of concern to women.

The WID project contributed to a process of professionalization that has made musical performance more appealing for women across social categories. In contemporary Gambia, women increasingly seek out performance opportunities as an income generating strategy in the context of economic hardship. Interestingly, however, even as women seek to earn money through performance, health and development workers often refer to female performers as "volunteers," emphasizing that they do not receive salaries for their work. Similarly, women's groups position themselves as community service organizations that work for the good of the country (*bankudookuwo*) and seek payment from God (*Allah le be n joo la*). The emphasis on volunteerism and community service may also limit male involvement because it is seen as inconsistent with ideas about male roles as providers.[9]

At the same time, although women do not normally receive a salary for their work as performers, they do receive monetary and other benefits, such as "per-diems" that are typically given to participants in health education programs. For example, for attending a three-day workshop in Niamina (Central River Region) in 2013, participants received 200 dalasi each day for a total of 600 dalasi (US$20). This was a significant amount of money in rural Gambia at that time, where a typical monthly salary for an unskilled laborer was 1000 dalasi (US$33) and teachers made around 3000 dalasi (US$100). In other cases, women may receive short-term contracts with a lump-sum payment given for completion of specific health promotion activities. In one instance, upon completion of a training program on hygiene promotion in 2013, kanyeleng women each received a lump sum of 1,700 dalasi (US$56) for their work in disseminating the information they learned in the program throughout their village and surrounding areas. While the income generated through their performances provides an incentive for women to participate, the absence of larger financial incentives and the framing of the performance activities as "voluntary" may also contribute to female dominance in this area. Though men do participate in some groups and are active in development programs, they are far outnumbered by their female counterparts, as is the case in the contexts of musical performance discussed above.

The involvement of primarily female performers as health communicators in the WID project and later initiatives came along with an emphasis on women as the targets of health programs. The focus on women is bolstered both by local ideas about gender roles and priorities of funding organizations. My interlocutors suggested that women's roles in child care and household management made them particularly equipped to deal with family health issues. In addition, both performers and health workers felt that women's strong social networks and communications skills meant that they were more likely to disseminate their knowledge throughout the community, whereas men tended to keep their knowledge to themselves. As influential performer Dodou Njie said, *Niŋ i ye musu kiliŋ karaŋ, i ye kee keme le karaŋ*, "If you teach one woman, you have taught 100 men" (personal communication, February 26, 2013). Similarly, historian Hassoum Ceesay explained that health workers often chose to use female performers in their programs because "they know that if you get them, some of these women's groups, you can rest assured of getting on board almost everybody … the network is very very effective" (personal communication, November 21, 2012).

While women are influential and effective communicators, there are of course limits to what they can accomplish without the support of their male family members. Efforts to improve health must take into account the gendered power relationships that affect individuals' ability to take action in particular areas and may explain apparent failures of health interventions to achieve positive change

(Airhihenbuwa 2007: 105). In 2013, I spoke at length about power and decision making with Amie Bojang from GAMCOTRAP. Amie explained that "At different levels, decision-making is taking place" (personal communication, January 17, 2013). While some women may have the power to make their own decisions regarding family health, others must defer to fathers, husbands, or mothers-in-law. Even though health is often viewed as women's responsibility, a woman's age and position within the family shape her decision-making power. In other words, women's power to communicate in the musical sphere does not directly translate into the power to act.

This discussion offers insight into female performers' transformative labor to sustain continuity and meaning in the face of changing realities in contemporary Gambia. Drawing on opportunities created at the juncture between local and global interpretations of gender and music, kanyeleng groups use performance to reject the stigma of infertility and demonstrate their relevance in contemporary Gambia. Through music, Fatou and the Allatentu Support Band likewise reject the suffering created by HIV-related stigma and emphasize continuity of family and community support networks. These performances are transformative in that they attempt to translate power in one sphere (musical performance) into power in another (public health). Going further, performers seek to transform sung words into action. As I will discuss in the next chapter, however, singers do not have complete control over their sung words, the uses they are put to, and the actions that they inspire.

In his discussion of power and popular culture in Africa, Johannes Fabian describes freedom as "the potential to transform one's thoughts, emotions, and experiences into creations that can be communicated and shared" (Fabian 1998: 20). Power and freedom are not permanent attributes, but rather temporary and incomplete. These dynamics are evident in the work of female performers in The Gambia who use music to negotiate power and achieve "moments of freedom" (Fabian 1998) to communicate their experiences and concerns in the public sphere. Women generate these moments of freedom by creatively working within local understandings of gender, Islam, and shame, while engaging with international movements for gender equality and women's empowerment.

Conclusion

This chapter has brought together multiple perspectives on gender, Islam, and development in order to elucidate the central roles that women play in the areas of both musical performance and public health. Examining the experiences of Niuminding Fatty as well as other musical and community leaders, I have shown that women's roles in music and health promotion are dynamic and influenced by local gender ideologies, religion, and development discourse.

Music participation in The Gambia is unevenly distributed according to gender, age, and caste, reflecting notions of shame and emotional expressivity. Higher status individuals (male gender, older age, noble lineage) are expected to show restraint and avoid boisterous shows of feeling. Partly as a result of gendered expectations concerning expressivity, women and girls form the majority of participants in many music events. At the same time, Islamic discourse in The Gambia limits women's musical activity by emphasizing their domestic responsibilities and framing certain practices, such as kanyeleng rituals, as sinful. Women's power and performances nonetheless take root at the intersection between the local and the global, bolstered by religious discourse privileging women's instruments as well as global health discourse on women's empowerment.

International development programs for women's health and women's empowerment are grounded in ideas about Muslim women's subordination and silence. Yet it is women's experience as noisemakers – their skill in having their voices heard through music – that has enabled these programs to succeed. I advocate for a strengths-based approach that is grounded in recognition of women's capabilities and resourcefulness, rather than assumptions of marginality and powerlessness. Emphasis on Muslim women's vulnerability in international development discourse does not adequately consider local forms of women's social mobilization and "tends to render women's own spaces and their active participation in economic and social processes invisible" (Sieveking 2007: 32). In contrast, I foreground female-dominated spaces of performance as sites for women's agency in the mediation of competing discourses and practices of global health development. In the following chapter, I will continue the exploration of issues of power and agency in women's performances, focusing on Fatou and the Allatentu Support Band.

Notes

1 According to Sheikh Omar Jallow, Yawulu Bande was the name of a prominent Fula leader (personal communication, April 25, 2018).
2 Dawda Jawara was The Gambia's prime minister from 1962 until 1970 when he became the first president. As I discuss in Chapter 6, Niuminding Fatty and the Banjul kanyeleng initially supported Jawara, but they eventually shifted their allegiance to the opposition National Convention Party.
3 The recording of the APGWA kanyeleng singing this song is Track 1 on the website: www.routledge.com/9780367312725.
4 My interlocutors differentiated between Muslim jinns and other kinds of jinns, or spiritual entities. See Soares (2005) for related discussion of concepts of jinns and other spiritual entities in Mali.
5 Not all jinns dislike drumming. I also heard about cases of jinns who loved drums and required them to be played regularly.
6 See F. McNeill (2011) for a related discussion of the way HIV/AIDS programs have caused young women to be viewed as vectors of disease in South Africa.
7 Association for Promoting Girls and Women's Advancement in The Gambia.
8 Gambia Committee on Traditional Practices Affecting the Health of Women and Children.
9 See Deeb (2006) for a related discussion of how community service and volunteer activities are constructed as feminine work consistent with a pious modern identity for Shia Muslim women in Lebanon.

3 Singing *Teriyaa*

Life, death, and HIV-stigma

Introduction

In March 2007, Fatou disclosed publicly through song that she was HIV positive. The launching concert of her *Teriyaa* album, attended by Gambian dignitaries and aired on television and radio stations throughout the country, made Fatou instantly famous. Her energy, health, and beauty challenged stereotypes about people living with HIV and AIDS. For Fatou's NGO sponsors, her concert signified an unprecedented leap toward the de-stigmatization of HIV/AIDS and the dissemination of important information about the disease. In contrast, for government supporters, the concert represented an opportunity to praise President Yahya Jammeh and his self-proclaimed AIDS "cure."

In the previous chapter, I showed that female performers have used the space created by religious discourse, notions of shame, and international concern for gender equality to assert new forms of power and influence. Here, I explore the way Fatou's voice (and body) are caught up in broader conflicts over medical authority. I investigate Fatou's music as a form of transformative labor to maintain continuity in the face of change, linking together personal, community, and societal concerns (Mullings 1995). Specifically, through music Fatou worked to repair and rebuild the social relationships that are torn apart by HIV-related stigma and discrimination. Fatou's transformative labor was deeply personal, reflecting her own experience as an HIV positive woman. At the same time, her project aimed to inspire broader changes in attitudes toward HIV/AIDS at the societal level. Fatou's story demonstrates both the power of transformative labor, and also its limitations, as her body and voice are co-opted to serve powerful others. This chapter examines issues of vulnerability, agency, and the ways in which music is shadowed by death; ultimately, however, I am interested in bringing Fatou's story to life, and in understanding the material consequences of political contestations over health and music in the life of one individual.

Life, death, and music

In interviews, performers in The Gambia often described music and dance as expressions of life and health. They said things like, *Niŋ i ye a je m be tuluŋo la, m be doŋo la, jaato be kendeyaariŋ* ("If you see I am performing, I am dancing, the body is healthy") (Missirah kanyeleng, July 1, 2013). While this may sound obvious (a seriously ill person would not be dancing), it reflects a more significant association between performance, health, and healing. As kanyeleng performer Kanjoo[1] explained, music and dance do not only reflect health and vitality, they also promote health:

> The way you are dancing, your body will be healthy. Illness, if it says it will enter, it will not be quick to find a way. Your body is not still … it is hot, the entering will not be easy.
>
> *I be doŋo la ñaameŋ, bituŋ i jatoo be kendeya la. Kuuraŋo, n'a ko a be duŋ na, a te tariyaa la siloo soto. I baloo maŋ tenkuŋ … a be kandiriŋ, ala duŋo be koleyaa la.*
>
> (Personal communication, July 17, 2013; see
Barz (2006) for related discussion)

Other performers similarly emphasized the health benefits that come from participating in music events by singing and dancing together with other people.

In The Gambia, music is strongly associated with celebratory events such as naming ceremonies for new babies, weddings, and initiation events. As is the case in most Muslim-majority contexts, music is largely prohibited at funerals in The Gambia, and performances are usually cancelled if there is a funeral taking place nearby. My teachers in Lamin and Kembujeh would cancel our lessons whenever there was a funeral. It was considered inappropriate to perform music – a celebration of life – when people were mourning the death of a loved one nearby.

In her songs, Fatou expressed her experience living with a life-threatening disease, but she framed her music as an affirmation of life, consistent with the celebratory performance mode described above. Specifically, she aimed to prevent death by encouraging HIV testing, treatment, and social support. Her songs contrasted with most public health messages in The Gambia at the time, which tended to portray HIV/AIDS as a death sentence and added to the stigmatization of the disease. The association of music (particularly singing and dancing) with expressing health and celebrating life contributed to the power of Fatou's message challenging HIV-related stigma.

While music can provide a potent means to affirm and celebrate life, this does not tell the whole story. Scholarship on music and power in West Africa has elaborated on the Mande concept of *nyama*, and the relationship between song, breath, and bodily fluids (Wise 2006; Hoffman 2001; Conrad and Frank 1995; Hale 1998; McNaughton 1988a; Charry 2000). The Mande word nyama refers to energy, power, or means. Bodily fluids possess nyama. Songs are also laden with nyama, and they are therefore powerful as well as dangerous; they provoke emotion and inspire action (Wise 2006). In his discussion of Mande sung poetry, linguist Charles Bird quotes a Bamana proverb, *nyama be kuma la* ("the energy of action is in speech") (Bird 1976: 98). Bird writes, "When a praise song is sung for someone, his energy to act is augmented, thus forcing him to act, and these acts can lead to his destruction if not appropriately controlled" (1976: 98; see also Charry 2000). Though this use of the term nyama is not common among Gambian Mandinka,[2] the idea that songs have power to effect change is highly relevant for understanding the transformative labor of musicians such as Fatou, and the ways in which words translate into action. The concept of nyama also underscores the potential of song to be both life-affirming and creative, as well as destructive. This duality is embodied in Fatou's performances.

Analysis of Fatou's performances contributes to a growing body of scholarship that examines West African women's songs as important sites for the articulation of power and agency (e.g. Hogan 2008; Sidikou and Hale 2012; Sidikou 2001; Durán1995, 2007; N'Daou 2005; Mack 2004). This scholarship has drawn attention to the way music, and songs specifically, open up opportunities for resistance and transgression, even while working within the confines of patriarchal power structures. Not adequately considered, however, are the consequences of negotiations of power through performance for individual musicians such as Fatou.

Singing about stigma

I met Fatou in 2006 when I was assigned by the US Peace Corps to work with the Allatentu Support Group for People Living with HIV/AIDS in Brikama. At this time, Fatou had just finished recording a song at the one-room studio down the road from her house. The recording was basic – a demo with guitar, drum machine, and keyboard. The song was called "AIDS is Wreaking Havoc," and it described the various ways HIV can be transmitted. When I heard the recording, I was captivated. The tune was catchy and it featured the popular Senegambian mbalax dance style. I thought about what an impact Fatou could have, as an HIV positive woman singing about AIDS. AIDS was a faceless disease, something that affected "other" immoral people, not the people we know. Fatou, as a confident, beautiful young singer, would immediately challenge the stereotypes about AIDS.

Before she composed "AIDS is Wreaking Havoc," Fatou had been sick for years and she did not know why. She had finally decided to get an HIV test at the Medical Research Council (MRC) in Fajara. She went into the nurse's office for her results, and she could tell by the nurse's face that she had tested HIV positive. Then the nurse made a disparaging remark about Fatou to her coworker in English, thinking that Fatou could not understand. Fatou stood up immediately, walked out of the office, and never went back. It took several months before she had the courage to go to the Hands on Care Clinic in Brikama to be tested again. Fatou's husband went with her, and they were counseled by Binta, a young nurse who was caring and reassuring. Even so, Fatou was terrified. Everything she had ever heard about AIDS made her certain that she would die right away. She began to feel better only after talking to Lamin, a counselor from the Allatentu Support Group. She had never talked to anyone who said he was HIV positive before, but Lamin looked perfectly healthy. He was even a little overweight.

Lamin told Fatou that AIDS was no different than any other disease. There were people dying from malaria, cancer, and tuberculosis. Why was AIDS the disease with so much stigma surrounding it? He said it was just people's ignorance that made it that way. After meeting Lamin, Fatou's attitude changed. As she lay in the hospital at Hands on Care, she began to sing. When Binta the nurse came by, Fatou sang to her, adding new verses every day. By the time she was discharged, she was ready to record her first track. Within a few months, she had composed an additional five songs.

Fatou became an active member of the Allatentu Support Group. In 2006, the group consisted of thirty-five members (thirty women and five men) who met regularly to discuss strategies for healthy living and participate in income generating activities. Lamin described the main function of the support group to me: "When you find out you are HIV positive, you are always thinking and worrying. At the support group you share ideas, counsel each other and help each other" (personal communication, December 2006). Fatou's songs emphasized the core philosophy of the Allatentu Support Group, encouraging listeners to talk to one another and learn the facts about HIV in order to stop worrying.

Medical anthropologist Rachel Chapman defines stigma as a "*process* by which hierarchies of social differences are reproduced and challenged, and power dynamics between differently situated social actors are mapped out and contested" (Chapman 2010: 241, emphasis in the original; see also Parker and Aggleton 2003). Chapman's approach to stigma is useful in moving beyond notions of a "spoiled identity" (Goffman 1963), to consider the way stigma reproduces inequality through the process of representation and social interaction. This approach also better captures the ambiguity and sometimes contradictory aspects of stigma, as it is produced and reinforced both symbolically and materially (Boesten and Poku 2009). In The Gambia in the 2000s, global health discourse produced stigma by representing HIV/AIDS as a death sentence and emphasizing individual choice and responsibility for prevention. Stigma was also materialized through poverty, inadequate access to health care, and the social strain of dealing with a life-threatening disease (Boesten and Poku 2009; Turan and Nyblade 2013). In Fatou's case, she faced stigma both as an HIV positive person and as a musician (see Kyker 2016 for related discussion). Fatou came from a marabout[3] lineage, and her family was of higher status than *nyamaaloolu* (artisans) such as jali. As is typical for individuals of non-nyamaaloo background, her family did not want her to become a musician, though they eventually came to terms with her decision.

Fatou did not take the decision to disclose her HIV positive status lightly. When Fatou was recording her songs, she had not yet disclosed her status to many of her closest family members. She came from a loving and supportive family, but she did not want to upset her parents and siblings by telling them she was HIV positive. In preparation for the release of the album, Fatou called together a small group of people to meet with her and her parents to help them to understand the implications of her HIV positive diagnosis, and her plan to sing about her status in songs. Though Fatou appeared self-confident and certain in her decision, it was an emotional and extremely difficult conversation that took place in a secluded room in Fatou's compound. Her family was supportive and loving as they attempted to come to terms with Fatou's HIV positive status and imagine a future for their family in the face of a life-threatening and stigmatized disease.

The *Teriyaa* album was the product of collaboration between Fatou and her husband Musa, the Allatentu Support Group, the National AIDS Secretariat, Action Aid International, and The Gambia Family Planning Association (see Figure 3.1). Allatentu Support Group members participated actively in the launching concert, and at every stage of album production. Although Fatou composed all six songs independently, with contributions from her husband who was also a musician, she offered them to the group for feedback. Fatou also incorporated suggestions from Allatentu members. For example, some lines from the title track "Teriyaa" ("An illness is simply an illness/let's all fight this problem") were suggested by Allatentu members. Fatou also named her accompanying band the "Allatentu Support Band." Just as the Allatentu Support Group included members from various ethnic backgrounds, Fatou sang songs in several different Gambian languages, including two in Mandinka, three in Wolof, and one using a combination of English, Jola, Pulaar, Mandinka, Wolof, and Swahili.[4]

The Allatentu Support Band included guitar, bass, drum set, sabar drums, and Mandinka drums, with me on keyboard and back-up vocals. Musical styles incorporated a variety of West African dance genres, including three mbalax songs in the style made popular by the Senegalese superstar Youssou Ndour, and three songs that musicians referred to as "Afro-Manding" (popular music with Mandinka roots). Band members further classified the three Afro-Manding songs,

Figure 3.1 Original *Teriyaa* album cover, used with permission.

based on the rhythmic feel, as reggae, zouk, and *tubaab* ("European," referring to a slow ballad).

Unifying the album's diverse musical styles, languages, and topics is a positive message that aims to de-stigmatize HIV/AIDS. The anti-stigma message of the album contrasts sharply with songs that had been released by other prominent musicians in The Gambia. Allatentu members were particularly bothered by a song performed by Jaliba Kuyateh, arguably the most popular Gambian jali of his generation. The song was performed in Jaliba's trademark style, with distinctive kora intonation and expressive descending vocal lines, accompanied by the members of his renowned Kumareh Band. The chorus to the song repeated the Mandinka word *saayaa* (death). It portrayed HIV/AIDS as a death sentence and blamed the spread of the disease on adultery and promiscuity. These kinds of messages about HIV/AIDS were still commonly heard in songs I recorded during fieldwork in 2012 and 2013; one example is the performance by the Brikama Nyambai College kanyeleng group discussed in Chapter 4.

The *Teriyaa* songs aimed to challenge the messages expressed by singers such as Jaliba, and to encourage HIV testing, support, and treatment. The emphasis in the Wolof-language song "ARVs" is completely different from more typical HIV/AIDS education songs, such as the one by Jaliba Kuyateh described above, which tend to describe AIDS as a death sentence, and focus entirely on HIV prevention and testing.

Suma reew, suma reew bi Gambia a we nala	My country, my country The Gambia
Reew bi jama la reew bi teranga la, aa lachel gañi	The Gambia is peaceful and welcoming, ask anyone
Lachel gañi, lachel gañi amna fi daraa waw	Ask anyone, ask anyone, yes there is something here
So jogge cha yeneni reew bi, ne ma nge dem Gambia	When you travel from another country to The Gambia
Luko waral, luko waral, luko waral?	What is the reason, what is the reason, oh what is your reason for traveling?
ARV am na si reew bi le	[Because] ART [antiretroviral treatment] is in the country
ARV am na si reew bi	ART is in the country
Nit ñi jaxle tuu ñu jeka jaxle wone da febar bi nuñi amul garab	Before the people were worrying because they said there was no medication for the sickness.
Nun ñu am febar bi, leegi ragal wesuna, jaxle wesuna	Now those of us with the sickness, fear is behind us, worry is behind us
Nañi len ko xeer lichi HIV, kon yaw jarul ngai nobu	Let's fight HIV so that you don't have to hide
Demal seeti sa deret	Go test your blood
Bude li dan ko am, jarum ngai tiit, jarum ngai nobu	If you have it, you don't have to be scared, you don't have to hide
Nda garab bi le am na fi, dinala fach te doosife	Because we have the medication here, you can be treated for free
Nañu len seeti suñu deret li mo si gen da xel mi dal	Let's check our blood, it's better to have peace of mind

Yow mi toogon jogal seeti sa deret, yow mi toogon jogal seeti sa deret	You sitting down, get up and test your blood, you sitting down, get up and test your blood
Leegi jaxle wesuna, mañu len xeer febar bi, kon yow jarul ngai nobu jogal nga dem seeti sa deret	Now worry is behind us, let's fight the sickness, you don't have to hide, get up and go test your blood.
Man mi nga xam ne mangi faju	Me, you know I am treating it
Bul jaxle jogal seeti sa deret	Don't worry, get up and test your blood
Yow mi toogon, bul jaxle jogal seeti sa deret	You sitting down, don't worry, get up and test your blood[5]

The song "ARVs" focuses on treatment, using a celebratory, patriotic tone. The song is reminiscent of political praise songs that listed The Gambia's positive attributes and then thanked President Yahya Jammeh for them. In this case, however, the emphasis is on encouraging HIV testing as a means to access life-saving treatment. The song also evokes a sense of solidarity and support in the fight against HIV/AIDS, challenging the feeling of isolation experienced by many people living with the disease.

The *Teriyaa* album resonated strongly with people living with HIV/AIDS who faced the challenging reality of HIV-related stigma in their everyday lives. Stigma prevented many members of the Allatentu Support Group from disclosing their status to family members. The perception that people with HIV/AIDS (particularly women) had engaged in inappropriate sexual behavior meant that those who did disclose their status often received extremely negative responses including, in some cases, ostracism, rejection, and violence (Cassidy 2011).

A month after the initial recording was completed, the group was busy preparing for the album launching concert. We were also about to begin work on the music videos for each audio track. One morning I came into the Allatentu office and found Fatou and two other people involved in a lively discussion. They informed me that there had been important news announced on the television last night. President Jammeh had found a cure for AIDS, and he would begin treating people the following day.

The next day I spoke to several Allatentu members who were on their way to Banjul to enroll in the President's treatment program. The President had said that he would broadcast the treatment process on TV for transparency. Group member Mariama said that if this was true, she would not go. Her family did not know she was HIV positive and she didn't want them to find out in this way. Another Allatentu member, Isatou, did not agree. She said that if you are cured, it doesn't matter if everybody knows. She said she wanted her three-year-old son to be cured. She would admit the two of them.

For several days the President's HIV/AIDS treatment was not mentioned on the news. I hoped that they would not broadcast the process after all. Then one night my host mother woke me up at around 10 pm. "Your friends are on the tele," she said. That night, and every night after that for many weeks, Jammeh's nine HIV/AIDS patients, including Mariama, were shown to the nation in their hospital beds. In much of the footage the patients, many of whom were women, were naked from the waist up. They were shown being massaged by the president, receiving cups of dark colored medicine, and being prayed over. I thought of Mariama and wondered why she had agreed to enter the State House that day. She was a tall, striking woman, and easily recognized. People asked me about her daily. "So, is it true that Mariama has AIDS?" I always gave noncommittal replies, not wanting to add to her notoriety.

HIV/AIDS treatment in The Gambia

Attitudes toward Fatou and her music were shaped by the fraught political context of President Yahya Jammeh's AIDS treatment program. The album launching concert, discussed further below, was a site in which the voice of an HIV positive woman was foregrounded and endowed with authority, but the event was also overshadowed by broader contestations over political and medical power.

Jammeh's treatment program was ridiculed briefly by international media,[6] and then largely ignored. The treatment was portrayed as just another chapter in the outrageous activities of The Gambia's charismatic, authoritarian leader. In power from 1994–2017, Jammeh's administration was renowned for human rights abuses, repression of political opposition, and control of the media (Saine 2009). Musicians faced strong pressure to express their allegiance to the President through praise songs and performances at campaign rallies. Performers who criticized President Jammeh faced serious threats to their lives and careers, and in some cases had to leave the country. Fatou's performance took place in the context of this "culture of silence" (Saine 2009: 94) in which very few people dared to speak out against Jammeh.

Jammeh's eccentric, authoritarian style of government made it easy to dismiss his HIV/AIDS treatment program as just another example of an idiosyncratic president's delusions of grandeur.[7] More useful, however, is an analysis of Jammeh's treatment that takes into account the particular political and medical landscape in which it emerged, and the reasons why many people with HIV chose to participate. In part, Jammeh's treatment program can be seen as a response to the dominance of global (Western) biomedical science and funding that undermined indigenous medical plurality and national autonomy in The Gambia (Cassidy and Leach 2009b). Useful comparisons can be made with other controversies over biomedical science such as the boycott of polio vaccination programs in northern Nigeria (Jegede 2007) and controversies surrounding HIV/AIDS in South Africa (Fassin and Schneider 2003). Addressing the politics of HIV/AIDS in South Africa under the Thabo Mbeki administration, Fassin and Schneider (2003) highlight the historical and ongoing experiences of oppression, including colonialism, apartheid, and contemporary economic policies, that made distrust of Western science and institutions logical. Analysis of President Jammeh's HIV/AIDS treatment in The Gambia must similarly consider the ways in which the treatment emerged from historically rooted structural inequalities, as well as local perspectives on health, healing, and power.

The first case of HIV was reported in The Gambia in 1986. Since then the numbers have grown to an estimated 26,000 Gambians living with HIV (UNAIDS 2018). In 2000, The Gambia was among the first countries to access large amounts of international funding (US $15 million) for HIV/AIDS programming from the World Bank funded HIV/AIDS Rapid Response Project (HARRP).[8] These funds represented approximately $11 per capita at a time when the Gambian government's entire per capita expenditure on health was only $7.9 annually (UNdata 2000). Four years later The Gambia received an additional $14 million in funds through the Global Fund Round 3 (Cassidy and Leach 2009a: 17). These funds enabled the establishment of a new National AIDS Secretariat (NAS),[9] nine antiretroviral treatment sites, twenty-four HIV testing sites, services for the prevention of parent-to-child transmission (PPTCT), and eight support groups for people living with HIV/AIDS. The influx of AIDS-related funding also supported the production of the Allatentu Support Band's *Teriyaa* album.

The huge inflow of international funding for HIV/AIDS in The Gambia required new institutions, rules, and regulations to control who could access resources for HIV/AIDS programming. Along with the idea that there is money in AIDS-related work, the funding resulted in "a new political economy of resource allocation and a new politics of knowledge" (Cassidy and Leach 2009a: 9). That is, individuals and groups interested in accessing funding learned to subscribe to internationally standardized notions of HIV/AIDS problems and their appropriate solutions. In the process of resource allocation, many people living with HIV/AIDS felt underrepresented and ignored; the main means by which they were able to benefit from HIV/AIDS funding was through support groups. Like other groups vying for HIV/AIDS funding, support groups ascribed to globally standardized biomedical understandings of the disease. This had important implications for concepts of health in a medically pluralistic society (Cassidy and Leach 2009b: 9).

Many Gambians utilize a variety of therapeutic systems to treat illnesses, including biomedical drugs, vaccines, local herbal treatments, and Qur'anic medicine. Gambians living with HIV are no exception. In the context of international HIV/AIDS programming and funding, however, the politics of therapeutic knowledge shifted. In order to access benefits such as food packages, school fees, and "per-diems" (daily allowances for attending workshops), people had to attend an HIV/AIDS clinic regularly and receive biomedical treatment. Although governments give biomedicine preferential treatment in most medically pluralistic African societies (Feierman and Janzen 1992), the case of HIV/AIDS is distinct and uniquely controversial. People living with HIV/AIDS, including Fatou, told me how they went from marabout to marabout in search of a cure for their illnesses, until they finally arrived at the antiretroviral treatment (ART) clinic. While the testimonies of Fatou and other people living with HIV were based on real experiences of the positive effects of starting ART, they also masked a more complex treatment landscape that involved a combination of biomedical and alternative treatments. That is, for many people with HIV, ART did not meet all their needs, and they continued to seek alternative treatments, just less openly.

Jammeh presented his HIV/AIDS treatment as a nationalist and religious project affirming the legitimacy of indigenous knowledge and challenging the dominance of biomedical science and international aid. The President specified that his HIV/AIDS treatment consisted of "seven herbs from the Qur'an," but he did not disclose the exact ingredients even under direct questioning from reporters (Simmons 2007). Supporters claimed that Jammeh's secrecy protected Gambian interests by preventing the medicine from being stolen and sold internationally. Critics argued that this secrecy proved that the treatment was a farce. While international media ridiculed Jammeh's use of the Qur'an in his HIV/AIDS treatment program (Koinange 2007; Simmons 2007), for Gambians accustomed to the therapeutic practices of marabouts, the healing power of the Qur'an was not in question. Indeed, the majority of Gambians use amulets (*safoolu*, pl., *safoo*, sing.) or healing water (*nasoo*) imbued with the ink from Qur'anic verses for the prevention or treatment of various ailments (see Foley 2010).

In addition to his grounding in Islam, Jammeh asserted his legitimacy by emphasizing his position in a long lineage of traditional herbalists and constructing trust in that lineage as a nationalist project. A 2007 article in the government-run newspaper *Daily Observer* explained that Jammeh's treatment was a "secretive herbal medicine notably handed down to him from his forbearers who in their time, were well known and revered herbalists" (Joof 2007: 12). The author went on to criticize Jammeh's detractors for not having faith in "herbal and traditional" medicines indigenous to The Gambia (Joof 2007: 12). The combined appeals to religion, tradition, and nationalism evident in discourse surrounding the President's AIDS treatment endowed it with a sense of power and efficacy, and made it extremely difficult for skeptical Gambians to question its efficacy (Amon 2008: 2). Foreign nationals perceived as posing a threat, such as United Nations Development Program representative Fadzai Gwaradzimba (among others), were expelled from the country. The consequences for Gambians were potentially more serious, as previous examples of detention, torture, and assassination of journalists attested (Saine 2009).

Nationalist rhetoric concerning Jammeh's HIV/AIDS treatment asserted the legitimacy of indigenous responses to a variety of diseases; it also framed HIV/AIDS as an international, racialized battleground. In a televised speech on the national television station in June 2007, Jammeh attributed the international community's negative response to his treatment to the fact that "the virus has been created to kill non-whites and because my medicine has the potential to make them fail their objective of eliminating the black man" (Jammeh 2007). In other cases, Jammeh moved from African/racial nationalism to Gambian nationalism. When Dr. Coumba Touré-Kane of Cheikh Anta Diop University in Dakar (where Jammeh sent blood samples for testing) stated that an undetectable viral load did not prove that a patient was cured, Jammeh attributed her "lack of cooperation" to long-standing rivalry between Senegal and The Gambia (*Daily Observer* 2007).

Jammeh's nationalistic language situated his treatment program in firm opposition to the global biomedical approaches to HIV/AIDS that had entirely dominated and dwarfed alternative approaches to the disease in preceding years.

The apparent usurping of government power by international funding institutions such as the Global Fund and the plethora of development agencies operating in The Gambia contributed to Jammeh's "crisis of legitimacy" (Saine 2009: 94). In this context, the President's AIDS treatment was a strategy to challenge these international structures of authority and assert political power and legitimacy.

The President's treatment program represents an extreme example of the politicization of HIV/AIDS treatment. Nonetheless, it serves to underscore social and political dynamics of healthcare that are more broadly relevant. Contestations over science and medical authority in The Gambia at this time demonstrate the ways in which health seeking behavior is shaped not solely by knowledge and personal choice; rather, the decisions that people make in relation to HIV treatment are fundamentally constrained and shaped by broader political contexts and inequality (Cassidy 2011).

The album launching concert

It was in this tense political and medical environment that Fatou released her album, *Teriyaa*, as the first female popular singer in Africa, to the best of my knowledge, to disclose her HIV positive status through song.[10] For the launching concert of the *Teriyaa* album, Fatou spent hours at the salon getting her hair and makeup done. She also had two dresses made with expensive cloth in the latest styles. The first dress that she wore had extensive embroidery down the front, and long flowing sleeves. She then changed into a second dress, which was made with layers of flowing bright yellow cloth. Fatou's careful fashion choices were consistent with expectations of high-profile female artists, who often changed outfits several times during the course of a performance. Cloth, and fashion more generally, provided an important symbolic representation of feminine power and success (Buggenhagen 2012). Both Fatou's dresses were deliberately modest, floor length with long sleeves. Because of the prevailing stereotypes that associated HIV with immorality, Fatou was always careful to avoid overly revealing attire. Similarly, early versions of her songs included references to condoms. She decided to remove those references so that she would not be accused of promoting promiscuity and extramarital sex (see Chapter 4).

The launching concert foregrounded Fatou's voice, as an HIV positive woman, in an unprecedented manner. President Jammeh had been broadcasting footage of patients in his HIV treatment program since January, but the patients were depicted as passive recipients of the President's therapies. Patients complained that they were shown on public television without their consent, and often naked from the waist up, wrapped in a towel. This went against ideals of modesty for Muslim women, and it was particularly devastating for patients like Mariama who had not yet disclosed their HIV positive status to their friends and family. Fatou's powerful presence on the stage at the launching concert contrasted dramatically with these representations of people with HIV as passive victims.

Fatou's articulation of an empowered HIV positive identity was profound for many people with HIV/AIDS in the audience. Patients undergoing the President's treatment received special permission to leave the treatment center in order to attend the launching concert (an unusual occurrence). Members of the Allatentu Support Group turned up in large numbers at the event, and four women joined Fatou on the stage for several songs. One of the members was participating in the President's treatment at the time, while the other three women were under the care of doctors at the Hands on Care Clinic in Brikama. Their unexpected presence on the stage showed support for Fatou as a fellow Allatentu member and also allowed them to participate more fully in the glamour of the occasion. Isatou, a jalimusoo, took the spotlight more actively by borrowing Fatou's microphone and singing the praises of audience members. As a jalimusoo, Isatou was more skillful and successful than Fatou at soliciting audience donations – a fact that Fatou readily admitted.

The space of the launching concert foregrounded the voices of people with HIV/ AIDS in powerful ways, but it also provided a platform for others to insert their own narratives. The participation of the Minister of Health and Social Welfare in the launching concert encapsulated the underlying tensions embodied in the event. The Minister, a medical doctor trained in Russia, was actively involved in implementing and managing the President's treatment program. Many observers condemned him as a traitor to his profession and claimed that his active endorsement of the President's treatment was politically motivated. I was asked to write a speech for the Minister that he would read at the opening of the event. I drafted a speech that emphasized the importance of working together to improve the lives of people living with HIV/AIDS in The Gambia. While the Minister kept some of my original wording, the majority of the speech he delivered consisted of praises for Jammeh's HIV/AIDS treatment program.

Midway through the concert, the Minister again inserted his own agenda into the program when he mounted the stage to dance with Fatou (see Figure 3.2). This took place during an extended vocal solo by an accompanying singer followed by an instrumental break. The Minister's unexpected and rather long, close dance with Fatou was unusual for Gambian performance events such as this one, which typically feature solo dancing. While the dance was consistent with Fatou's message about de-stigmatizing HIV/AIDS, it also served to emphasize the Minister's power and influence. At this time, he was regularly seen on TV with patients participating in the President's treatment program. By dancing with Fatou, the Minister incorporated her compelling image into a narrative about his own authority in the context of the President's treatment. The duet between Fatou and the Minister of Health and Social Welfare also highlighted the gendered power differentials between them: the foreign-educated government minister, wearing a suit, praising the President, and holding Fatou in a waltz-like embrace; and Fatou, the HIV positive woman dressed in an embroidered African gown, singing about stigma. The Minister's choice to dance with Fatou in a waltz position, like his suit and tie, presented an aesthetic of (Western) masculine power; this contrasted sharply with the aesthetic of feminine power in Mandinka dance, where men and women seldom dance together, and the emphasis is on female bonding.[11]

Figure 3.2 Fatou and the Minister dance at the album launching concert, March 2007, used with permission.

The launching concert was broadcast throughout the country on national radio and television programs. In the weeks and months following the event, the songs of the Allatentu Support Band were widely heard in hospitals, clinics, HIV/AIDS Support Groups, NGO offices, and on government-run radio and television programs. While nongovernmental organizations used Fatou's songs for their educational messages, government-run media turned them into a soundtrack for the President's treatment program. On March 25, 2007, news announcers on GRTS (the government-run television station) stated that Fatou had already been cured by the President, although at the time she stated privately that she would "run away to Senegal" before she would register for the President's treatment. The nightly news on GRTS for the next several months invariably featured updates on Jammeh's AIDS treatment, frequently followed by Fatou's music videos.

Fatou was increasingly recognized on the street as the woman who sang about AIDS, and she faced mounting pressure to join the President's treatment program. She had already begun work on her second album, and some suggested that it would be wise for her to compose a set of songs in praise of President Jammeh. In the week following the launching concert, Fatou began to receive calls from the State House encouraging her to register for the President's treatment. In April 2007, less than a month after the launching of her album, Fatou joined the President's treatment program and ceased taking ART.

Remixing and remembering

During the first week, Fatou sounded happy when she called from the treatment center, even though she said she had not gone there by choice. Fatou knew how I felt about the treatment program, so I wondered whether she was telling me the whole story. I was concerned that she had gone against her will, but I recognized that the powerful combination of political, religious, and traditional authority embodied in the President's treatment gave many participants faith in its efficacy. For the general population in The Gambia at this time, HIV/AIDS was a disease strongly associated with witchcraft and sorcery, and therefore it would be most appropriately treated by Jammeh's Qur'anic and herbal medicines rather than bio-medical treatment. Even for those like Fatou who were not entirely convinced of the efficacy of the President's treatment, participation in the treatment program was seen to have benefits, such as access to nutritional food, and opportunities to gain political favor. Fatou's husband told me that they planned to produce an album of songs about the President's treatment. In The Gambia at this time, presidential patronage was often the most lucrative source of income for performers. At the same time, in the context of political surveillance, violence, and paranoia, performers faced strong pressure to support the President even in the absence of direct remuneration.

Not long after she stopped taking ART, Fatou came down with malaria. She got weaker and weaker, and developed a cough that would not go away. Eventually, she grew so weak that she was transferred to the Royal Victoria Teaching Hospital (RVTH) in Banjul, along with other seriously ill patients from Jammeh's treatment center. These patients told Allatentu staff members that Jammeh no longer treated them, they were denied access to ART, and they felt they had been left there to die. These patients were not permitted to leave the RVTH, and five died before August 2007 (personal communication, support group staff member, July 2007; see also Cassidy 2011). I was told that the family of one patient had helped her to escape from the hospital and they were later harassed by the authorities for going against the President's instructions.

One of the staff members from the Allatentu Support Group visited Fatou in the RVTH at this time. She delivered 1500 dalasi (approximately $45 US) of Fatou's money from cassette sales. Fatou said, "If money could make me well, then I would be well." Foreign visitors were not allowed in this ward of RVTH, but I was desperate to see Fatou and I decided to go ahead and visit. When I walked into the room I barely recognized Fatou. She was a shadow of her former self. Fatou could no longer walk without assistance. There was food next to her bed, but she said that her throat burned too much to eat. Fatou's husband was in the corridor outside preparing amulets and herbal medicines for Fatou that had been provided by a marabout. He was desperate to find something that would help her. Fatou said quietly, "I want to go back to Hands on Care." She said that the patients in the adjoining beds had been dying one by one, and she did not want to be next.

I went outside and talked to Fatou's mother and husband. We talked about how we might get Fatou out of The Gambia in order to get access to ART. I said that if they agreed, I would organize transport to bring her to Dakar, Senegal. They agreed immediately. We knew she could not stay in The Gambia because Fatou would be seen as a threat to the legitimacy of the President's treatment program, and it was also unclear whether any of the HIV clinics in The Gambia would agree to treat her. The future of HIV/AIDS treatment programs in the country was in jeopardy.

During the next few days, I spoke with Fatou's family frequently as we tried to make arrangements for Fatou to travel to Senegal to receive treatment. Some family members were concerned that it would be too dangerous. They said those in charge of her were powerful people. On July 6th, I spoke to Fatou in the morning. She said "We have to put that matter aside for now. I came here already, and I cannot leave." Her voice sounded stronger than the day before. That evening, her husband called and said, "Fatou has left us. It is all over." She had died at 5 pm that evening. They had just finished saying prayers.

In the aftermath of Fatou's death, family, friends, and the entire HIV/AIDs service community, were devastated and angry. There was an overwhelming sense of injustice and frustration at the circumstances surrounding her death, and sorrow that her new songs would never be heard. There was also a sense of determination to find ways to continue Fatou's legacy and to improve conditions for people with HIV in the country, despite the political challenges presented by the President's treatment program.

Catherine Strong and Barbara Lebrun (2015) have written about the way a musician's manner of death shapes the way her entire life and musical work is subsequently interpreted. The close association of the voice with the body can make listening to the voice of a dead person bewildering. In Fatou's case, the political circumstances surrounding her death made it difficult to talk openly about her music. After her death, Fatou's music was seldom played on GRTS, whereas previously it was played almost every day. Fatou's death also changed her message. Whereas she wanted to spread a message about living positively with HIV, her death overshadowed this positive message by suggesting its limitations.

Nonetheless, Fatou's songs continued to be played on a regular basis by health workers, support group members, and others. Jaliba Kuyateh, one of the most respected Gambian musicians alive today, completed a remix of the *Teriyaa* album in 2010. Fatou's husband and members of the Allatentu Support Group invited Jaliba to do the remix as a tribute to Fatou. They chose Jaliba for the remix project both because of his enormous popularity, and also because he had previously released a song about HIV/AIDS that they strongly disliked. They thought that the remix project would be educational for Jaliba and enable him to correct the messages expressed in his previous songs. Jaliba's popularity would also attract listeners and broaden the impact of the album. For the remix, Jaliba, Allatentu staff, Fatou's husband, and I returned to Xalam Studio where the original recording had been completed.

Unfortunately, although the producer had kept the final mix, the individual tracks that had been recorded for the original album had not been preserved. This meant that there were limited options for balancing and blending the tracks in the remix. Jaliba's voice and kora, along with some other additional parts, were layered on top of the original mix. The result is that sometimes Fatou's voice is no longer foregrounded in the mix the way it was in the original. In some cases, it sounds as though Fatou is fading into the background behind the sounds of kora and newly added keyboard parts. In some ways, this serves to enhance an ongoing sense of loss and grief over Fatou's death. That is, hearing Fatou as if from a distance or underwater can provide a sense of longing to hear her more clearly, and this makes her loss all the more palpable. This sense is only amplified by the expressive and emotive vocalizations added by Jaliba Kuyateh in songs such as "Teriyaa" (Friendship). Jaliba is known for the emotional sensitivity of his music, which often moves people to express feelings of sympathy and love. In "Teriyaa," Jaliba responds to Fatou's main vocal line with an expressive descending line on the syllable "oh," which serves to enhance the overall affective impact of the song.

In addition to the new sounds added in the 2010 remix, the music video for the remix similarly featured new footage. Some of the video of Fatou was replaced with footage of Jaliba Kuyateh playing his kora, as well as some new video of members of Allatentu and Peace Corps volunteers dancing. In the video for the remix, they also added a variety of visual special effects, including what appear to be rays of moonlight emerging from the image of Fatou and the other performers in the song "Let Us Fight." Some members of Allatentu appreciated these additions to the visuals because they gave the video a modern, technologically savvy appearance. Others disliked these special effects and thought they ruined the video. In some cases, such as in the video for "Girim" (Orphan), the original video appears to have aged poorly. While the new footage of Jaliba Kuyateh is bright and clear, the old video featuring Fatou is in some cases very dark and off-color. This again contributes to a poignant sense that Fatou is fading from memory.

Through the remix project, Fatou's friends and family aimed to broaden the impact of her songs and to amplify her voice by bringing it into a posthumous duet with Jaliba Kuyateh. The remix was to some extent successful in achieving these goals. At the same time, the layering and mixing of voices and images in the remix reflect the broader processes of contestation over ownership, representation, and meaning that were associated with Fatou's music from the beginning. In some ways, Fatou's voice and image in the remix are overshadowed by powerful men, in a manner reminiscent of the Minister of Health and Social Welfare's intimate dance with Fatou at the launching concert. This does not tell the whole story, however, since the remix project was very much in line with Fatou's message about overcoming HIV-related stigma, rectifying the misguided messages that Jaliba communicated in previous songs.

Even though it was the subject of competing agendas from the time of its release, the *Teriyaa* album continues to be used in ways that are consistent with Fatou's original vision. Even for members of Allatentu who joined after Fatou's death, the album continues to powerfully affect their self-image and understanding of how to live well with the disease. In 2012 and 2013, I attended several support group meetings where, alongside seasoned members, new members watched the *Teriyaa* music videos for the first time. Older members explained to the newer ones that Fatou was a former member of the group. The video sparked conversations about HIV-related stigma and helped members to come to terms with their HIV positive diagnosis.

On singing, death, and meaning

Amie, a member of the Allatentu Support Group, described the importance of Fatou's songs as follows:

> Other musicians are there who address HIV, but their ways of singing are not the same. Because having someone with HIV standing up to show everyone. … She had this disease. The others are just thinking about it in their heads and singing about it. … She knew it, the way it was in her body.
>
> *Musisian doolu fanaŋ be jee meŋ i ye a loŋ ko i ka HIV denkiloo ke. … bari a denkiliñaa maŋ kiliŋ … niŋ meŋ mu liviŋ with HIV, wo le loota ka yitandi moolu bee la. … Wo doolu, i ka i mira i kuŋo teŋ, i ye denkiloo ke doroŋ. … A ye a loŋ, a be a jaato kono ñaameŋ.*
>
> (Personal communication, January 3, 2013)

Amie's perspective underscores the connection between words, voice, and the bodily experience of disease in Fatou's music. This is particularly important in the context of HIV/AIDS programming, where people with HIV are always spoken for, but seldom heard. The connection between the voice and the body has been theorized by Roland Barthes who writes that the voice of another person provides an indication of "their way of being, their joy or their pain, their condition; it bears an image of their body" (Barthes 1985: 255). The ways in which people responded to Fatou's voice, and her narrative about HIV/AIDS, were grounded in ideas about her HIV positive body. Her experience of illness is also evoked in certain inflections of her voice, including occasional breaks, hoarseness, and expressions of emotion. The listener *hears* her pain. For many people who knew her as well as some who did not, listening to Fatou's voice on the recording inspires strong emotional reactions and poignant reflection on her mortality.

Fatou's music was appealing in part because of her striking image and personality. She was tall and beautiful, and her image challenged the stereotype of the emaciated, near-death HIV/AIDS sufferer. At the same time, Fatou had been struggling with health problems for years, and even after she finally received her HIV diagnosis, it took months for her health to stabilize. Fatou's songs are powerful in part because they express the experiences of an individual who was acutely aware of her own mortality. The celebration of antiretroviral therapy (ART) in many of the songs on the album is genuine, because ART enabled Fatou to go from being close to death, to living a normal life. It is particularly poignant in retrospect, but even though Fatou's songs are primarily a celebration of life, they are also shadowed by the specter of death; they demonstrate the vulnerability of the human body and voice in the context of contestations over political and medical authority.

Conclusion

Fatou's story suggests that the feminist adage "the personal is political" may be particularly true for song, where internal movements of an individual's vocal cords become public expressions of private emotion, complete with marks of imperfection and illness (see Albright 2010). Made public, the audible articulations of an internal organ are then politicized and subject to contestations of power. Fatou was aware of the power of voice to connect the personal and the political. Through her songs, she sought to insert embodied knowledge of disease into public debates on HIV/AIDS. Knowing through personal experience that HIV was more than a medical problem, Fatou used song as a form of transformative work to rebuild relationships ruptured by HIV stigma. She did not anticipate, however, that these same songs would be caught up in larger struggles over medical authority. In the end, Fatou's voice made her simultaneously powerful, empowering, and powerless: powerful because her songs enabled her message to be widely heard; empowering because that message gave hope and strength to people with HIV in The Gambia; and powerless, because her voice was ultimately desired and used by others in ways she could not have foreseen. In the next chapter, I will explore in more depth the dynamics of performative license that enabled Fatou, and other musicians, to address challenging topics such as HIV-related stigma through music.

Notes

1 With the exception of Fatou and other public figures, all the names used in this chapter are pseudonyms.
2 According to Roderic Knight "the belief in the nyama is not so widespread among the Gambian Mandinka, probably as a result of the strong acceptance of Islam" (1973: 44).
3 Marabouts are Sufi Muslim clerics and experts in therapies based on the Qur'an that are often used in combination with herbal medicines.
4 Three of the six songs from the *Teriyaa* album ("Teriyaa," "HIV Be Keering" and "Girim") can be downloaded from the "eResources" tab on the website: www.routledge.com/9780367312727.

5 Transcription and translation from Wolof to English by Awa Jatta and Cheikh Fall. Wolof orthography is adapted from the *Peace Corps The Gambia Wolof-English Manual* (1995).
6 See, for example, Koinange (2007) and Simmons (2007).
7 See, for example, Mbai (2007), "Inside the State House with Teeth Bite: Dr Mbowe says Jammeh is mad!"
8 Unlike Global Fund initiatives that followed, HARRP funds were loans rather than grants, requiring repayment with interest (see Cassidy and Leach 2009a: 16).
9 Prior to the establishment of NAS in 2001, the National AIDS Control Program (NACP) directed all HIV/AIDS programming in the country.
10 The popular singer Philly Lutaaya of Uganda disclosed his HIV positive status before dying of AIDS in 1989. He is credited with de-stigmatizing HIV/AIDS and paving the way for more Ugandans to "live positively with HIV" (Barz 2006: 72). Members of the Allatentu Support Group took inspiration from Philly Lutaaya and saw Fatou as continuing his legacy.
11 There are, of course, dance contexts where men dominate, including male circumcision dances, hip hop, and reggae, as noted in the Introduction. Masculine power is also displayed in performances that feature male drummers, and where eroticism is evident in the relationship between the drum and the female dancer's body.

4 "Let's insult the soldier's mother"

Performative license and communication

Introduction

Returning to The Gambia in the years after Fatou's death was a search for understanding, moving with and beyond a personal grief over a lost friend toward new songs and new ways of knowing. It is perhaps fitting that this search propelled me into the music, laughter, and ritual of kanyeleng who are experts on grief and, like Fatou, experts on singing the unsayable. I found, however, that while Fatou sang about HIV/AIDS *despite* her stigmatized status as an HIV positive woman, kanyeleng sang about sensitive health issues in part *because* of their special social position as *moo bee sanango* (everyone's joking cousin). In this chapter, I examine the varied ways that women use song to communicate about difficult topics, leveraging stigma and marginality into new forms of power.

Exactly six years after Fatou's death, I attended a performance in the village of Taibatou in eastern Gambia in July 2013. From Basse, I crossed the river in a small boat and drove to Taibatou on a motorcycle with the Community Health Nurse, Omar, who was hard working and widely respected in the community. A popular kanyeleng group made up of performers from Taibatou and the neighboring village of Kerewan performed at the local health center. The performance showcased the group's characteristic rich, strong vocal quality and lyrical cleverness, which had earned them recognition not only from the Ministry of Health and Social Welfare, but also from President Jammeh and his APRC party. Two of the kanyeleng accompanied the singing on *kutiro* drums, which they played with two hands rather than one hand and one stick, which is typical of male drum ensemble technique. The group performed a song about malaria with the chorus *ali ŋa dandaŋolu seneyandi* (let us clean our areas), in which they urged listeners to clean their compounds and get rid of standing water that could become a breeding ground for mosquitoes. Then the lead singer, Jawno Kijera, switched to *saataroo*,[1] a narrative style of heightened speech, and announced:

Kuuraŋo, niŋ i be kibaaroo dii la hadamadiŋo la	Illness, if you will give information to a human being
I si a dii ala neeneeroo kono	You should give it to them in a pleasing manner
I si a dii ala saayisaayiyaa kono	You should give it to them in mischief
I si a dii ala jeloo kono	You should give it to them in laughter
A si ite la kumoo moyi	They can hear your words

This song articulates a kanyeleng perspective on the power of playful performance in enabling human beings to hear and understand words (*kumoo moyi*). The Mandinka verb *moyi* used in the kanyeleng's song can refer to either hearing or understanding, depending on the context. In this case, both meanings apply; the kanyeleng are asserting that playful performance can facilitate hearing, by bringing people together to listen, and understanding, by encouraging engagement and dialogue.

Female performers in The Gambia demonstrate myriad ways in which music opens up space for embodying, articulating, and communicating forms of knowledge that would otherwise remain cloaked and unsaid. It is not a coincidence that these forms of knowledge that find outlet and expression in musical performance are often gendered as feminine in the context of a patriarchal and patrilineal society. Kassim Koné, drawing on James Scott's theory of domination and resistance, describes Mande discourse on *baadinyaa* (matrilineal relatedness; *badenya*, Bamana) as a "hidden transcript, the critique of patrilineal authority offstage" (Koné 2002: 22; see also Scott 1985). Like Koné, I am interested in the way women use concepts such as baadinyaa in their songs to foreground matrilineal ties and challenge systems of patriarchal power. Musical articulations of women's "everyday resistance" (Scott 1985) in The Gambia are anything but hidden, however; women perform resistance and transgression *on*-stage, in the public sphere. Female performers exploit what I call performative license to make their voices heard, challenge authority figures, and address sensitive health topics. Perspectives on license also offer insight into the mechanisms of women's transformative labor to maintain coherence and meaning in the face of change.

Leroy Vail and Landeg White define "poetic license" as an aesthetic feature of African oral poetry that enables "freedom of expression which violates normal conventions" (1991: 43). Expanding on Vail and White's work, I define performative license not as freedom of expression (license to speak), but rather as license to hear and be heard. This approach to license is grounded in the perspectives of health workers and performers in The Gambia, such as the members of the Taibatou/Kerewan kanyeleng group and the Allatentu Support Group. Examining license in terms of communication and reception, rather than primarily expression, foregrounds both the relational experience of performance and its effects in the world. The notion of performative license pushes beyond the metaphor of text in the concept of "poetic license" to foreground the way performance can elicit subtle or sometimes more dramatic transformation of both performers and listeners, shaping their realities rather than solely reflecting prior experiences (Wong 2004; Waterman 2019).

A significant body of research has explored music as a tool for articulating dissent and resisting dominant power structures in African contexts (e.g. Vail and White 1991; Schumann 2008; Becker 2005; Thorsén 2004; Panzacchi 1994), in some cases neglecting the ways in which music is also used to serve the interests of the powerful (see Dave 2014; Stokes 2004). As evident in the case of Fatou and the Allatentu Support Band, the same features of music performance that provide a platform to express marginalized perspectives are also appropriated by the powerful to reinforce their authority. If license is about the freedom to hear and be heard, then that freedom "comes in moments" (Fabian 1998: 21) and is incomplete. Performative license is not inherently progressive or democratic, but rather can serve a variety of conflicting interests, sometimes simultaneously. The license to hear and be heard affects not only what topics can be addressed through song; it also shapes relations of power, and perceptions of self and other.

The singer: marginality as flexibility

Scholarship on African music has tended to attribute poetic license to the singer (particularly griots in the Mande area) rather than the song (Vail and White 1991: 75). Here I shift the focus to non-griot women and situate performative license at the intersection between the singer, song, and listener.

Words can be powerful but also dangerous. As a result, Mande norms of communication place value on verbal restraint and ambiguous language that can be interpreted in multiple ways (Dave 2014; M. Roth 2008; Hoffman 2001; Conrad and Frank 1995). Social expectations about who should speak (or sing) about particular topics and who should remain silent intersect with gender and caste categories and notions of shame, as shown in Chapter 2. Concerns about the power and danger of words are only amplified when communication touches on sensitive topics relating to sex, death, disease, or stigma.

As "masters of words" as well as music (Hale 1998), griots have a special ability to manage the power of speech, to communicate effectively, and to inspire action. At the same time, because griots are reliant on the patronage system, they often refrain from outspoken critique of the powerful (Janson 2002). As Lucy Durán (1995) has shown in her research with Malian *wassoulou* singers, non-griot performers may have greater freedom to comment on social issues than griots who are restricted by their hereditary roles and patronage relationships.

As I demonstrated in Chapter 2, knowledge relating to maternal and child health is often viewed as women's responsibility, partly as a result of women's roles in the domestic sphere, and partly because of the way women have been targeted by public health programming. At the same time, according to gendered notions of shame (*maloo*), women are (in theory) expected to be more communicative, emotional, and musically inclined than men.[2] While these ideas have in some ways normalized women's involvement in health communication, female performers must still negotiate sensitivities around publicly addressing difficult health topics such as those relating to sex and death (see F. McNeill 2011). Performers creatively exploit communicative strategies, such as the use of jokes, polysemic language, and varied modes of delivery, to manage the power and danger of words (see Hoffman 2001: 12). As I will elaborate below, to some extent the medium of song provides an accepted forum for women to hear and be heard. However, the extent to which particular performers feel able to address sensitive topics through song (and how they will be heard and understood) varies.

Women sing about sensitive health topics in a pluralistic medical context, where people typically make use of diverse forms of health knowledge, prevention, and treatment for any given ailment. At the same time, understandings of health and healing are deeply intertwined with notions of Islamic authority and efficacy. The most widely trusted healers are often marabouts, who are usually older men respected for their knowledge of Islam and the healing properties of the Qur'an. Even when people pursue biomedical treatment for an illness, they often emphasize that their health outcomes are in the hands of God and practice prayer as an important part of therapy (Foley 2010). Singing in this medical and religious context, female performers frame their information about health problems and their treatments within this broader Islamic worldview, and work to present themselves as pious Muslim women.

In this context, women facing reproductive challenges and women with HIV have drawn on the flexibility that comes with marginality to assert creative power (see Furniss and Gunner 2008), using the medium of song to redefine social positions and articulate their perspectives on sensitive health issues.[3] As I will demonstrate, however, despite the similarities in the marginality experienced by kanyeleng and women with HIV, there are also differences in the extent to which they feel able to address sensitive topics through song.

Kanyeleng license: vultures and joking cousins

Women facing infertility or child deaths have the opportunity to engage with an established support network through the institution of kanyelengyaa. Although women with HIV have created their own support groups,[4] these groups operate outside the public eye and do not gain legitimacy through drawing on traditional knowledge and power the way kanyeleng groups do. While infertility is stigmatized, kanyeleng are widely respected because of the perceived efficacy of their rituals in promoting fertility and preventing child deaths (see Saho 2012). Because kanyeleng groups are an accepted, highly visible social organization, they represent in some ways the opposite of the experience of women with HIV who must hide their status and seek support in secret. It is therefore not surprising that there are dozens of kanyeleng groups involved in health communication in The Gambia, whereas Fatou has been the only woman (to my knowledge) with HIV to sing about health publicly.

In this section, I use two kanyeleng songs as a lens through which to understand the unique combination of ritual knowledge and play that underlies kanyeleng performative license. The first song, "Vultures," was performed regularly by kanyeleng groups in western Gambia:

Duwoolu, ntolu mu duwoolu le ti o	Vultures, we are vultures oh
Niŋ ŋa moyi daa o daa, a niŋ boroo	Whenever we hear/smell it, we run
	We will beg [pray to] the king
M be manso daani la, wo niŋ duwaa	[God] with prayer

As is typical of kanyeleng songs, this one has multiple layers of meaning. On one level, the metaphor of the vulture reflects kanyeleng's scavenger habits; they are known for their exceptionally large appetites and their ability to devour food that others would find unappealing, such as dirty leftovers. Kanyeleng boast that, like vultures, they wander around and as soon as they smell food or hear the sounds of music, they run to partake.

There is more to the vulture metaphor than scavenging, however. The figure of the vulture appears frequently in Mande proverbs and praise songs for warriors and hunters, where it serves as a symbol of intelligence, competence, courage, and sometimes sorcery (Frackowski 1989; Durán 1995; McNaughton 1988a, 2008). As Patrick McNaughton writes about the well-known Mande praise song "Vulture," "[W]arriors have been willing to go to great and dangerous lengths to earn the right to have it sung in their honor" (2008: 239). In this context, when kanyeleng describe themselves as vultures in their song, they are highlighting not only their scavenging behavior, but also the deeply rooted knowledge and wisdom that underlies their performances. In line with kanyeleng practices of ritual inversion of gender roles, it is fitting that they have taken on a metaphor historically associated with masculine power and heroism and made it their own. The double meanings associated with the metaphor of the vulture points to the unique constellation of attributes that underlie kanyeleng performative license and enable them to effectively engage with difficult topics through song.[5]

In Mandinka, the word for vulture (*duwoo*) is very similar to a word for prayer (*duwaa*). The song incorporates a play on words in that the kanyeleng describe themselves first as vultures and then as people who will "beg [pray to] the king [God] with prayer" (*m be manso daani la, wo niŋ duwaa*). The integration of references to the vulture (a symbol of kanyeleng scavenging behavior and ritual knowledge) alongside references to prayer is typical of kanyeleng songs, as demonstrated in Chapter 2. Kanyeleng songs speak on multiple levels, suggesting in some ways their humility and piety and in others their flagrant disregard for social norms and authority. As I will argue in Chapter 6, these elements of kanyeleng practice should not necessarily be seen as contradictory or incoherent; they are interwoven and powerful in kanyeleng efforts to promote fertility and family health.

The way kanyeleng play with words in songs like "Vultures" is part of a broader orientation toward creative play and joking in their performances. A distinctive song associated with the APGWA kanyeleng group provides further insight into this unique feature of kanyeleng practice. The song repeats the words "let's insult the soldier's mother" (*ali ŋa soojaroo baa neŋ*) in call-and-response fashion. After hearing the kanyeleng refer to the song often in casual conversations as well as in performances in 2013, I asked Khadijatou Mass and Nyali Damba about the origin of the unusual lyrics. They said that Khadijatou had composed this song on a tour of the country with Binta Jammeh Sidibeh several years previously.

Nyali and Khadijatou explained that on their tour the group came to a ferry crossing. They wanted to cross the water to go to Janjanbureh Island, which is a large island in the middle of the Gambia River. Binta Jammeh Sidibeh had already crossed with her vehicle and was waiting on the other side. The armed soldiers who were guarding the ferry crossing told the kanyeleng that their vehicle was too heavy for the ferry and they would not be permitted to cross. Khadijatou responded by getting her bidong out and placing it on the ground. She found two sticks underneath a nearby tree and began to play, spontaneously singing a song with the words, "Let's insult the soldier's mother." Khadijatou led the song, and the other group members followed in call-and-response style. Instead of being insulted, the soldiers laughed and danced so vigorously that their hats fell off onto the ground. When the group finished singing, the soldiers told them, "Go ahead and cross. Your vehicle is not too heavy." Once they had crossed, when one woman asked how much they should pay, the soldiers said, "You don't owe us anything."

This incident illustrates the way kanyeleng women perform their disregard for authority and, far from being punished, obtain benefits in exchange for their insults. When traveling with kanyeleng, episodes like this were not uncommon. By entertaining drivers and fare collectors with songs and jokes, kanyeleng often received free transport and had all the passengers laughing and sometimes singing along.

Khadijatou explained that the soldiers at the ferry crossing responded the way they did because "A kanyeleng is everybody's joking cousin" (*kaɲeleŋo mu moo bee sanaɲo le ti*). The Mandinka term *sanawuyaa* (lit. cross-cousinage) describes special joking relationships between people who may or may not be biologically related (see Davidheiser 2006; McNaughton 2008).[6] Sanawuyaa may be defined based on family, ethnicity, professional group, or region of origin. For example, a sanawuyaa relationship exists between Fulas (Fulbe) and Jolas, between grandparents and grandchildren, and between people from Kiang and Badibu (regions on opposite sides of the Gambia River). In some cases, sanawuyaa relationships may be extended through association, or even completely made up. When two individuals are related through sanawuyaa, they are able to joke and insult each other without causing offense. Thinking of kanyeleng as "everybody's joking cousin" helps to explain their unique license to insult and draw attention to topics that would normally be off-limits.

Joking kinship is a flexible tool that can be used in a variety of contexts to defuse conflict and to promote communication, but not all joking relationships are equal. Kanyeleng, in particular, are known for their ability to address topics that even other joking partners would avoid. For example, Gambian development worker Baai Jaabang collaborated with kanyeleng in conflict mediation across the border in the Casamance region of Senegal, which has experienced an ongoing, low-level armed conflict since the 1980s. Jaabang explained that the kanyeleng's unique social position as well as their skill as musicians and comedians enabled them to engage the conflicting parties in the Casamance in ways that others would not dare (personal communication, December 6, 2012). Similar dynamics are evident in health communication programs where kanyeleng are able to directly address topics relating to sexual and reproductive health that other communicators omit or avoid.

Sanawuyaa also provides insight into broader ideas about play and license in this part of West Africa. *Tulungo,* the Mandinka term for percussion and dance events, literally means "play" or "game." The linguistic liaison between play and performance is not uncommon globally and particularly in African and African-diasporic contexts (R. Stone 1988; Modic 1996; Turner 1982). A common Mandinka proverb states *tuluŋo buka sobeya tiña* (play does not spoil seriousness) (see Hoffman 2001: xxv; Kamara 2016). This Mandinka perspective on play is aligned with scholarly research demonstrating the "seriousness of play" for promoting creativity and for negotiating social relationships and identities (Turner 1982; Arnoldi 1995; Bateson 1972; Conquergood 1992; Dudley 2008; Huizinga 1950; Carty and Musharbash 2008). Joking and play facilitate communication, "creating meaning or creating the very contexts through which shared meaning becomes possible" (Carty and Musharbash 2008: 215).

According to discourse and practices of sanawuyaa, play is understood as relational, flexible, and improvisatory, which makes it a potentially potent resource for social change. By asserting joking relationships, performers and health workers construct a sense of kinship and responsibility. The norms of joking relationships demand that joking partners not take offense. Rather than creating static, predefined relationships, joking interactions are defined by flexibility, or what Dennis Galvan refers to as "everyday creativity" (2006: 811), which provides a context in which participants can address serious topics that might otherwise be avoided. Gregory Bateson's (1972) notion of play as a "framed" activity is useful here. "Framing" refers to features of the way information is presented ("metacommunication") that tell us how to interpret that information (Bateson 1972). Because joking kinship, and performances more broadly, are presented within an interpretive frame of play, they enables participants to communicate relatively freely without offending others. This is particularly true for kanyeleng, who creatively exploit their status as "everyone's joking cousin" to address sensitive topics that others avoid.

Fatou's songs: in spite of stigma

While kanyeleng engage in health communication in part because of their special joking cousin status, in this section I explore why Fatou sang about HIV/AIDS in spite of her marginalized social position as an HIV positive woman. I examine understandings of the nature of song and musical experience that may explain why Fatou sang what she had not yet said.

Fatou had to work hard to reframe her HIV positive status from an obstacle to a resource in the context of HIV/AIDS programming. More so than kanyeleng women, she had to manage her image carefully to avoid reinforcing negative representations of women with HIV as immoral carriers of pollution (Mbonu et al. 2009). After being diagnosed with HIV, some women choose to start wearing a *hijab* (Islamic headscarf) when they did not previously wear one.[7] For some women with HIV, wearing a hijab likely reflects an inward turn toward religion as a source of succor in the face of hardship. For others, it is a more outwardly oriented strategy to distance themselves from the negative representations of women with HIV as immodest and sinful, and to assert their morality and shame (*maloo*). In Fatou's case, she did not wear a hijab – it would be unusual for a singer to wear one because of the association with maloo – but she had to carefully manage her image and the messages in her songs so as not to reinforce these negative stereotypes. In contrast to the revealing outfits preferred by many mbalax stars, Fatou chose long-sleeved, modest clothing. She incorporated references to her husband in her songs and performed alongside him in the music videos in order to present herself as a faithful, committed wife. Fatou also carefully chose her words and refrained from mentioning controversial topics, such as condoms.

A member of Allatentu, Jalimusoo Isatou[8] always impressed me with her eloquence and insight. I asked Isatou about the *Teriyaa* album and why Fatou sang about her HIV positive status, despite widespread stigma, when she had not spoken about it even to many of her close friends and family. In response, Isatou explained that sung words are different than spoken words. She said that singing requires courage and calm concentration, which are understood in Mandinka as involving the *jusoo* (heart or liver). In order to sing, the performer's *jusoo* must be dry *(jusoo ka jaa*, i.e. courageous) and standing still *(jusoo ka loo*, i.e. calm/focused). Isatou elaborated:

> When you are singing a song, your mind follows only the path of the song. ... You listen with care. ... You don't look at this, you don't look at that. Your mind is not on anything else. Your mind is standing only on your song. That is why your singing words and your chatting words do not touch each other [i.e. are completely different].
>
> *Niŋ i be denkiloo laa kaŋ, ko meŋ ko ite la hakiloo ka tara looriŋ donkiloo dammaŋ la siloo ... i ye a lamoyi hakiloo la ... i buka ñiŋ juube, i buka ñiŋ juube, hakiloo buka tara kuukoteŋo. Ite la hakiloo ka tara looriŋ ila donkiloo damma le to. Wo le ye a kendi ila jaliyaa kumoo aniŋ kacaa kumoo buka maa noo ñoo la.*
> (Personal communication, December 3, 2012)

As Isatou explains, singing requires courage and concentration of a different sort than casual conversation. In following the path of the song, the singer must let go of other concerns and inhibitions to fully express the musical and textual material in interaction with listeners. Isatou's description of the focused experience of singing is aligned with Mihaly Csikszentmihalyi's (1990) concept of *flow*, which describes an enjoyable state of total absorption and involvement in an activity in which normal awareness of time and everyday experience is suspended. Isatou suggests that the intense focus experienced in performance creates a special space for a singer such as Fatou to articulate ideas through song, such as the details of her HIV positive status, that she would not express in other contexts.

Isatou emphasized the transformative potential of song not only for the singer, but also for the listener. She explained that sung words can enter the body of the listener and inspire actions that would have previously been inconceivable:

> The words enter inside you. You will take out 200 [dalasi]. You will find that the song that is being sung, you also like that song a lot. The performance that is happening, you are enjoying that a lot. You can see that among us Mandinkas, if words enter inside you ... some also take off their shirts and give them to the

singer. They can open the lid to the trunk, take out a complete outfit and give it to them. But if performance is not happening, they would not take that action.

Kumoo dunta ila. I be a je la i be keme fula bondi la. I be a tara la ko meŋ donkiloo meŋ be fo kaŋ, i fanaŋ be lafiriŋ wo denkiloo la baake. Tuluŋo meŋ be keeriŋ i be lafiriŋ wo la baake. I si a je ntelu, Mandinkoolu kono, niŋ kumoolu doolu dunta i kono, i si a je doolu fanaŋ ye ila dendikoo wura ye a dii jalo la. I si kunewo daa yele, ye kompleto bondi ye a dii ala. Bari niŋ jaliyaa te keeriŋ fereŋ, i te wo maa ñaa ke la.

(Isatou, personal communication, December 3, 2012)

Song performances transform both the singer herself as well as her listeners, inspiring acts of bravery and generosity that would otherwise be unthinkable (see Charry 2000, Bird 1976; Knight 1973; Janson 2002). Isatou held that sung words are powerful and dangerous not primarily because of their literal meaning, but rather because of the way they enter the physical body of the listener and elicit strong emotional responses. While griots are particularly skilled in transforming themselves and others through music, the intense focus and transformative potential of song performance described here also affect non-griot performers.[9] That is, the concentration and commitment required to perform a song successfully change a singer's mental state and enable her to share information that she might normally withhold. At the same time, emotional responses and active participation are provoked in the experienced listener.

As a singer follows the path of the song, in a sense that song takes on a life of its own. As it is no longer solely the expression of an individual singer, a song can become simultaneously deeply personal and depersonalized. This duplicity was evident in attitudes toward Fatou's songs, and may be particularly true for recorded music where the sound is no longer dependent on the presence of the physical body of the singer (see Strong and Lebrun 2015). On the one hand, discussions of the *Teriyaa* album emphasized the authenticity of expression in the songs, which were seen as sonic manifestations of the physicality of Fatou's body and her experience of disease. On the other hand, occasionally people asserted that she was just pretending. They suggested that she was just playing the role of an HIV positive person for payment. While this attitude reveals a skepticism about the existence of HIV/AIDS, it also provides insight into the interplay between notions of authenticity and façade in responses to performance. In Fatou's case, it was as though she were simultaneously revealing herself through song, but also hiding behind song.[10] Song provided a medium for her to communicate aspects of experience that she had never publicly disclosed, as well as a shield to deflect criticisms from her based on the stigma associated with HIV.

If this duality (being real but not real at the same time) is a broader feature of performance as a form of meaning generation, imagination, and play, then this gets to the heart of why Fatou sang what she had not said. Working with Fatou almost daily during the preparation of the album, I hold that she sang about her status not primarily for financial gain or fame, but rather because song allowed her to push beyond one-dimensional portrayals to be heard differently as an HIV positive woman. Drawing on research with griots in Mali, Barbara Hoffman discusses Mande norms of communication in which "the medium of expression largely determines how the content of communication will be understood" (2001: 11). In Fatou's case, the medium of mbalax and Afro-Manding dance music gave her songs a positive framing that freed her to create meaning on multiple levels and to recast her image in celebratory rather than derisive terms. It enabled her to express, through the poetry of the lyrics and the positive associations of dance music, an optimistic reframing of what it meant to be HIV positive and an emotional connection with listeners. It was not easy for Fatou to sing about her experience as an HIV positive woman, but through song it was easier for her to break through stereotypes to be heard and understood in new ways. Of course, as I demonstrated in Chapter 3, the ability of Fatou's songs to open up new ways of understanding HIV/AIDS also made them compelling, and contested, in the context of politicized disputes about therapeutic authority.

On hearing and being heard

I have suggested that performative license is about the (often momentary) freedoms to hear and be heard that emerge at the intersection between song, singer(s), and listener(s). This section will illustrate the way songs about health topics build on broader dynamics of performative license that have long enabled West African women to have their voices heard, articulate frustrations with gender inequality, and influence public opinion (see Sidikou and Hale 2012). At the same time, I will show how differences between Fatou's motivation and social position and those of kanyeleng performers translate into significant differences in their songs.

Performers maintain a sense of continuity with the past by adapting familiar musical and lyrical features of song, even as they transform their practices to address new topics and meet the expectations of health organizations. To demonstrate, in this section I will examine four songs associated with the lenjengo dance rhythm. I refer to each of these examples as different songs, but they are actually variations on what I call the "popular lenjengo melody" because I heard it performed particularly frequently.[11] When singers compose new songs based on this melody, they typically adapt the rhythm as necessary to match the lyrical structure, while maintaining the basic melodic organization of four descending phrases and the lenjengo rhythmic feel.

The first song, "Father Has Killed Me," I heard performed regularly by children as well as adult women (kanyeleng and others) at community events:

Oh, Baba ye nte faa le	Oh, Father has killed me
Oh, Baba ye nte faa le	Oh, Father has killed me
A taata nna kuruwo talaa n koomaa	He went and divided my kola nuts behind my back
A taata n dii keebaa kotoo la	He went and gave me to an old man

This song expresses a young woman's discontent with her father over her engagement to an old man. Kola nuts are offered to a woman's father as the first part of a marriage negotiation. The distribution of the kola nuts indicates acceptance of the marriage proposal, in this case without the approval of the bride-to-be. In some versions of this song, the English term "sugar daddy" is used in lieu of the Mandinka *keebaa kotoo* ("old man"), which implies that money is the motivating factor in the woman's engagement. I heard this song performed several times a week by neighborhood children in Lamin during my kutiro drum lessons. I also heard this song performed occasionally at community celebrations. Typical of the repertoire in female-dominated performance contexts, this song illustrates a young woman's sense of frustration in a patriarchal society where arranged marriages are common. While a woman would not typically criticize her father publicly, song offers a space for her to express her feelings of resentment and distress over an unwanted engagement.

A second song, "Let It Be Sweet," also based on the popular lenjengo melody, describes a tension between participation in performance and a woman's domestic responsibilities:

Tantantiyo, tantaŋo maa a ye diyaa	Owner of the drum, touch the drum let it be sweet
Tantantiyo, tantaŋo maa a ye diyaa	Owner of the drum, touch the drum let it be sweet
Biriŋ ŋa ila tantaŋo moyi kumoo la	Since I heard your drum sounding
I m'aa jee, nna soosoo jaata taato	Don't you see, my sauce dried up on the fire

The Mandinka word *tantango*, though I have translated it as "drum," is actually a more general onomatopoetic term for a drum-like instrument (e.g. bidong or calabash). In this song, the singer expresses her enthusiasm for the tantango, which has interfered with her domestic responsibilities. She was enjoying the music so much that she burned her sauce. These lyrics serve as a compliment for the percussionist whose skill enables listeners to temporarily forget the everyday tedium of domestic chores, in a context where cooking and other domestic labor is strongly associated with notions of feminine responsibility and womanhood. Through songs such as this one, participants articulate everyday challenges associated with gendered labor responsibilities.

A third example is the song "Don't Call Me Meero," based on the same popular lenjengo melody. This song reflects the perspective of an older woman:

Boysoolu, kana fo ñe meero	Boys, don't call me "Meero"
Boysoolu, kana fo ñe meero	Boys, don't call me "Meero"
Niŋ i ko ñe meero m be na kotoo la	If you call me "Meero" I will become old
I ye a fo ñe Bai baamaa	Call me Bai's mother

Meero is a respectful term for an older woman. For some women such as my friend Binta, however, being called Meero signified an undesired progression toward old age. Rather than being called Meero, Binta would rather be referred to as "Bai's mother." I heard this song performed on numerous occasions, and it always inspired laughter and light-hearted teasing. Lyrics such as these illustrate the way women use songs to explore ambivalence about aging and social relationships within the family. In the context of everyday greetings, women would not ordinarily correct someone who addressed them as Meero. The song, however, provides a site for communicating their concerns about aging and their changing generational position.

This same popular lenjengo melody has been adapted to address a variety of health topics. One example is a song performed by the Brikama Nyambai College kanyeleng at the Regional Health Directorate in Brikama in September 2013. Led by Jainaba Saho, renowned for her strikingly beautiful voice and melodic variations, the group addressed the topic of *nyaka* (female genital cutting).[12] The movement to eliminate nyaka in The Gambia represents female genital cutting both as a health issue and a human rights issue for women and girls. As I will discuss further in Chapter 7, nyaka was made illegal in The Gambia in 2015, but the practice continues and is a persistent topic of controversy. Nyaka is a highly sensitive topic concerning beliefs about the ideal female body, personhood, and deeply rooted notions of womanhood and sexuality. Music has long played an integral part in nyaka ceremonies, as well as in the movement to end the practice.

The Nyambai College kanyeleng's nyaka song[13] communicates the perspective of a protective and loving mother:

Cati oh, kana kumboo	Youngest child, don't cry
Ɗansinba, kana a samba	Circumciser, don't take her
Ɗa a naanee kodoo niŋ saroo la	I encouraged her with money and watermelon
Nte maŋ lafi a ye kumboo	I don't want her to cry

The song expresses a mother's desire to save her youngest child (*cati*, pronounced "chati") from the trauma of cutting. A mother's relationship with her youngest child is often seen as protective and indulgent. In this song, the kanyeleng are advocating for the elimination of nyaka in a subtle and personal way, grounding their message in notions of motherly love and protection.

Songs such as this one have played an important role in facilitating open dialogue about sensitive, gendered practices associated with nyaka that were not normally the subject of public deliberation. By using this familiar lenjengo melody, the kanyeleng framed their critique of nyaka as part of a broader repertoire of songs articulating women's perspectives and critiques of gender norms.[14] Because of the proliferation of songs based on this melody (and others like it), the nyaka song is in some ways unremarkable. Prior to the banning of the practice in 2015, however, this popular lenjengo melody was also commonly heard at nyaka celebrations (*nyakaboyo*) recognizing newly cut girls (as well as other community events). These events celebrated the girls and also recognized their proud mothers, who often became quite emotional during performances I attended. Through the lyrics and the familiar melody, the kanyeleng's song evokes the feelings of motherly love and pride that were perhaps the most emotionally meaningful part of these nyaka celebrations and redirects them to support their message about preventing cutting. The song is effective, I suggest, because it starts with the basic emotional motivation for nyaka (wanting to take care of your child), and reframes it to suggest that looking after your child means *not* letting her be cut.

As this nyaka song illustrates, performative license is not a "thing" that can be pinned down, but rather the contingent and often temporary result of creative skill and knowledge expressed through song in reference to other songs and everyday contexts of performance. This dynamic process of creative license is also evident in the way women have adapted familiar lenjengo and musuba songs to address HIV/AIDS, another topic that is bound up with notions of morality and appropriate forms of sexual behavior for women. Most of the performance groups I worked with had songs about HIV/AIDS as part of their repertoire, reflecting the prioritization of this disease in global health programming over the past several decades.

For example, the Nyambai College kanyeleng included a song about HIV/AIDS[15] during their performance at the Regional Health Directorate in September 2013. The song was accompanied by bidong and calabash playing the musuba rhythm. In her saataroo (heightened speech) sections, Jainaba Saho provided detailed information about how HIV is transmitted, including sharing of knives/razor blades in circumcisions, childbirth, and sexual intercourse. She also explained that condoms can prevent transmission between sexual partners. Typical of HIV/AIDS awareness programs, this song emphasized prevention and portrayed the disease as a death sentence, in marked contrast with the emphasis on treatment and care in the songs of Fatou and the Allatentu Support Band.

Eh yeh, n si a kele ko feŋ jaw ba	Eh yeh, we must fight it like a very bad thing
Eh, kuuraŋo meŋ ka naaful tiyolu faa	Eh, the disease that kills wealthy people
Kuuraŋo meŋ ka wuluulalu faa	The disease that kills parents
Ɖa kele ko feŋ jaw ba ...	Let's fight it like a very bad thing ...
AIDS kuuraŋo funtita ñiŋ bankoo kaŋ	AIDS has come out in this country
Dokitari baalu aniŋ noosoolu ye n karandi	The big doctors and nurses taught us
I ko AIDS, i be ala kumoo kacaa la lopitaanoo to	They said AIDS, they will talk about it at the hospital
Bari i te daŋna lopitaanoo to	But they will not stop at the hospital
I be funti la satewo kono le ...	They will go out into the village ...
Niŋ kee niŋ musu ye laa ...	If a man and a woman lie together ...
Niŋ ali maŋ wo tu noo jee	If you cannot abstain
Ali si fankanta condom la	You can protect yourselves with a condom

Condom use is a controversial topic in The Gambia. Middle-aged women such as the members of this kanyeleng group would not normally discuss sex publicly, and advocating for condom use in particular is often seen as encouraging sexual promiscuity and immorality. Kanyeleng songs such as this one can be useful in broaching the contentious topic of condoms and allowing health workers and others to engage in further dialogue.

Momat Jallow, former Program Manager with the Directorate of Health Promotion and Education, explained that kanyeleng were able to address topics in their songs that health workers were unable to talk about directly. He said,

> If I want to ... go to the community, and talk about sex in that way I may be harassed or even driven away. But the kanyelengs they can go change it into songs, and women can be laughing and getting the message at the same time.
> (Personal communication, January 31, 2013;
> quoted in McConnell 2016)

As Bala Saho writes, "in a society where talking about sex in public is seen as immoral and shameful, the [kanyeleng] can do so without sanctions" (2012: 117). Whereas health workers are reluctant to discuss sex openly, kanyeleng are experienced and comfortable addressing topics related to sexual and reproductive health. By presenting information in the frame of playful performance, kanyeleng enable listeners to relax and engage in dialogue.

While Fatou's *Teriyaa* album has been used in similar ways to open up dialogue in health education programs, there are significant differences between the kanyeleng song about HIV/AIDS and the *Teriyaa* songs. Whereas the kanyeleng represented HIV/AIDS as a death sentence and did not mention antiretroviral medication, Fatou used her own status to emphasize positive messages about testing and treatment. Another difference is that while the kanyeleng included condoms in their discussion of HIV prevention, Fatou focused only on abstinence and fidelity. An excerpt from her Mandinka-language song "HIV/AIDS Be Keering" (HIV/AIDS Is Real)[16] illustrates Fatou's approach:

HIV/AIDS be keeriŋ ne	HIV/AIDS is real
Ali m bee si fankanta	Let's protect ourselves
Ite be a soto la ñaadii le?	How do you get it?
I be a soto teŋ tiŋ ne	You get it like this
Niŋ AIDS be ila, i ye taa i penku	If you have AIDS and you get an injection
I taata i ye doo penku la	They go inject someone else
I taata yeloo dii doo la	They go give blood to someone else
I taata doo tiimooso	They go tattoo someone else
Musoo si a dii noo a diŋo la	A woman can give it to her child
Niŋ a be a suusundi	When she is breastfeeding
Musoo si a dii noo a diŋo la	A woman can give it to her child
Niŋ ye a tara kono be ala	When she is pregnant
Aniŋ niŋ a be wululaa	And when she is giving birth
A be keeriŋ ne	It is real
Futu ñooma i si a dii	Married couples/sexual partners
noo ñooma	can also give it to each other
Ali m bee si fankanta	Let's all protect ourselves

M be ali yaamari la	I will advise you
Ali ŋa taa yelejiibe la	Let's go test our blood
...	...
Fankanta kurutoo fele nti, moone buka fara noo	Protection pants here, an unexpected thing cannot rip them off
Niŋ meŋ ye muso soto, i si daŋ i musumayaa	If you have a wife, be faithful to her
Niŋ meŋ ye kewo soto, i si daŋ i keemaa yaa	If you have a husband, be faithful to him
Niŋ e maŋ wo noo duŋ, nko i si fata ma fereŋ	Otherwise, abstain completely
I ka nte meŋ je teŋ	Me who you see here
HIV le be nte wo la	I am HIV positive
Niŋ i maŋ laa ala	If you don't believe
HIV le be nte wo la	I am HIV positive
Moolu ko i maŋ laa	People say they don't believe
HIV be keeriŋ ne	HIV is real
HIV/AIDS be keeriŋ ne	HIV/AIDS is real
Ɖa fankanta	Let's protect [ourselves]
Niŋ i maŋ laa ala	If you don't believe
A be keeriŋ ne	It is real
I si nte jiibe	You can look at me
A be keeriŋ ne	It is real

Unlike the kanyeleng performers, as an HIV positive woman, Fatou felt unable to raise the topic of condom use in her album. In earlier versions of her songs, Fatou included information about condoms, but she eventually decided that advocating for condom use would reinforce the association of HIV/AIDS with immorality and undermine her credibility as an HIV positive woman. Instead, Fatou emphasized abstinence and fidelity. Her skillful use of the Mandinka language enhanced this message. For example, in the song "HIV Be Keering," she incorporated the Mandinka proverb *fankanta kurutoo felee, moone buka fara noo*, which always inspired appreciative chuckles from listeners. Literally, the proverb means "protection pants here, an unexpected thing cannot rip them off." The deeper meaning is about the importance of prevention and planning for the future. This proverb is used in a variety of contexts to suggest that preventing adverse outcomes is preferable to dealing with those outcomes should they arise. While Fatou incorporated the proverb to lend weight to her message about abstinence and fidelity, its meaning is open-ended and multilayered. By using this popular proverb, Fatou is placing her messages about sexual practices and HIV/AIDS prevention within a familiar framework of Mandinka wisdom and polysemic language, thereby making the message less threatening.

Gregory Barz (2006) has written about the importance of local languaging practices in facilitating dialogue on HIV/AIDS in Uganda. In the case of Fatou and the Allatentu Support Band, they specifically rejected local language terms for HIV/AIDS such as the Mandinka *saata kuuraŋo* (deadly disease) and *jeene kuuraŋo* (adulterer's/prostitute's disease) because these terms reinforced stigma. Instead, Fatou used the English "HIV/AIDS," selectively combining biomedical language with "deep Mandinka" language (i.e. proverbs laden with wisdom) to reframe discourse on the disease. This languaging process opened up possibilities for dialogue and communication.

Whereas kanyeleng groups typically perform live, recordings offer a useful, portable tool for breaking the ice and promoting dialogue on sensitive topics such as HIV/AIDS. Allatentu Support Group educator Nyima explained that during their HIV/AIDS awareness events, they start by playing all six songs on the *Teriyaa* album:

> We can play this music first … the messages are sung in Wolof, Mandinka, and English. … You will see that people are happy because they danced first, they danced, they danced, they danced. After they come to sit again, they listen to the message. … The cassette was saying it first. Now when we also say it, they can hear it. … So you will see that person is fast to understand.
>
> *N si musiko ñiŋ folo kiliŋ play … kuma kaŋo a ye a fo, Suruwa kaŋo, Mandinka kaŋo, Angilikaŋo. … I be a je la ko, moolu ka kontaŋ, katuŋ i ye i doŋ ne folo, i ye i doŋ, i ye i doŋ, i ye i doŋ. After i ye naa sii kotenke, i ye lamoyi a ka kumakaŋo meŋ fanaŋ fo. … Kaseto folo be a fo kaŋ. Saayiŋ niŋ ntolu fanaŋ ŋa a fo, i si a moyi. … So i be a je la, wo maari ka tariya ka fahamuroo soto.*
> (Personal communication, January 24, 2013)

Nyima emphasizes the way recorded music facilitates hearing and understanding by making participants comfortable, encouraging participation through dancing, and presenting the information in an enjoyable format. The *Teriyaa* album has been used in similar ways in education programs run by other health organizations, as well as on radio and television programs.

Allatentu staff explained that when they begin education programs by playing the *Teriyaa* songs, participants are more engaged and often have questions based on the information they hear in the songs:

> When we go to sensitizations like this, *Teriyaa* helps us a lot. Before we talk, we play *Teriyaa*. … When we finish, questions come from all sides. Because the cassette first causes them to not be afraid. … It makes them not afraid of people. It makes them not afraid of stigma. … The cassette does all that. … It is very important.
>
> *Niŋ m be taa sensitizationo teŋ,* Teriyaa *ka m maakoyi baake le. Jaŋ niŋ m be diamu la folo, n ka* Teriyaa *play. … Niŋ ŋa m bandi doroŋ, ñininkaroolu ka naa le, karoo bee la. Because kaseto ñiŋ folo folo ka tinna moolu si naa hañi. … A ye i hañindi moolu la. A ye i hañindi stigma la. … Kaseto ka wo bee ke le. … A kumayaata baake le.*
> (Allatentu member, personal communication, January 3, 2013)

The experience of Allatentu educators illustrates the way recorded music can provide license to hear and understand topics relating to HIV prevention and care. After listening to the songs, people typically ask many specific questions about where they might go to access HIV testing and treatment in different parts of the country. The *Teriyaa* songs inspire people to get tested for HIV because they realize that there is treatment and support available. The music helps listeners to overcome their fear of the disease and take action to learn their status.

In addition to the more formal contexts of HIV/AIDS education programs, Allatentu members have also used the *Teriyaa* album informally to educate people in their social networks. For example, Sally told me that on several occasions when she wanted her friends to get an HIV test, rather than talking to them directly, she simply lent them the album. On one occasion, Sally was concerned about her neighbor, a middle-aged man with a severe cough that would not go away. She gave the *Teriyaa* DVD to his wife and asked her to play it in their home. Several days later, the husband came to Sally and asked her to accompany him to the clinic to get an HIV test. The test came back negative, but it turned out the man had tuberculosis, which required urgent treatment. Other Allatentu members told me they played the DVD for friends who ended up testing positive for HIV. They agreed that it was easier and more effective to educate friends and neighbors indirectly, through the *Teriyaa* songs, rather than speaking to them directly. Here again, the songs enabled listeners to hear and understand information about HIV testing and treatment, whereas Allatentu members saw direct conversations as too confrontational.

Teriyaa has also had a powerful effect on Allatentu members themselves, helping them to hear and internalize messages about living positively with HIV. As discussed in Chapter 3, although antiretroviral treatment is widely available, many Gambians still consider an HIV positive diagnosis to be a death sentence. The stigma associated with the disease discourages people from getting tested, and it also prevents people from disclosing their HIV positive status to their partners. In 2007, some Allatentu members who were eligible for antiretroviral treatment chose not to receive medicine rather than disclose their HIV status to a single family member (a precondition for treatment at this time). Still today, many Allatentu members have not disclosed their status to family members.

The anti-stigma message of the album is powerfully articulated in the lyrics of the title track "Teriyaa," examined further in Chapter 5, which urges the listener to support friends or family members who are HIV positive: "Do not leave her, she is your friend, do not throw her away, she is your friend." This message has been transformative for members of Allatentu who told me that the music "takes away loneliness" and "makes the soul [*niyo*] happy." One member, Mariama, who joined the support group after Fatou's death, said that the *Teriyaa* songs had completely changed her outlook on life. The music allowed her to hear, understand, and engage in discussion about how to live positively with HIV/AIDS. Mariama said when she first started coming to the support group, she was withdrawn and confused about her future. Then one day when Mariama was at the support group office, one of the Allatentu members turned on the *Teriyaa* DVD.

> *Teriyaa* made me think. When I first came [to the support group], I came confused. I didn't have time for people. When I came, I would be sitting by myself. … If someone talked … it went in here [one ear] and out here [the

other]. … But one day, I was just sitting, they put this *Teriyaa* cassette there. I listened until *Teriyaa* finished. … Just listening to Teriyaa, it completely took my mind of this disease. … *Teriyaa* is the reason we don't worry about this disease anymore.

Teriyaa *le ye n miirandi. Nna naa folo, wo waatoo n confusiriŋ naata. N niŋ moolu buka taim soto. Niŋ n naata, n ka tara siiriŋ n faŋo. … niŋ moo ye diamu … a ka duŋ jaŋ a ye funti jaŋ. … bari luŋ kiliŋ doroŋ, m be siiriŋ doroŋ, i ye ñiŋ* Teriyaa *kaseto ke jee. Ɗa a lamoyi fo* Teriyaa *banta. … Biriŋ ŋa ñiŋ* Teriyaa *wo lamoyi, a ye n hakiloo bondi saasaa faŋo kaŋ ne fereŋ.* Teriyaa *le ye a tinna ntolu buka saasaa mira kotenke.*

(Personal communication, August 20, 2013; quoted in McConnell 2015)

The testimonies of Mariama and other support group members illustrate both the damaging effects of disease-related stigma, and the role of musical performance in helping people with HIV to regain hope and an optimistic outlook on life. Mariama's testimony also elucidates performative license, framed as the license to hear and understand. When she first joined the support group, Mariama was not able to hear and take in the comforting words of those around her. It was only in Fatou's songs that she was able to understand the words, internalize them, and imagine a positive future as a woman with HIV.

The examples discussed here illustrate diverse ways in which songs facilitate license to hear and be heard, enabling women to articulate their experiences and engage with challenging topics relating to sexual and reproductive health. Performers adapt musical forms that have long been used to critique gendered relations of power to address health issues important to women such as nyaka and HIV/AIDS. These songs have implications not only for health knowledge, but also for social roles and attitudes. For people with HIV/AIDS in particular, songs have played a vital role in promoting a sense of self-worth and confidence, shifting away from narratives of deficiency and immorality, toward understanding and care.

Conclusion

In this chapter, I have argued that performative license is best understood not solely as freedom of expression, but more broadly as license to hear and be heard. Performative license is shaped by the social position of the performer, but also by broader features of song and musical experience. Whereas Fatou exploited the special features of song performance to disclose her HIV positive status despite widespread stigma, kanyeleng performers draw on their special "joking cousin" status and ritual knowledge to address topics such as condoms that others avoid.

The momentary freedoms to hear and be heard that emerge in performance can open up space for reimagining and reconfiguring social realities, such as the damaging effects of HIV-related stigma. Testimonies from health workers, musicians, and people with HIV provide varied examples of the way music enables people to engage with difficult information that, when presented in a different format, might be rejected. These testimonies are informative for a strengths-based approach to health promotion in The Gambia that recognizes the unique capabilities and expertise of local performers, challenging dominant public health narratives that frame West African culture as an impediment to health promotion.

I end this chapter with the words of Dr. Isatou Touray who explained that music can "create an environment where [people] feel comfortable in discussing. …You have actually captured their mindset because this [music] is something that resonates with their lived realities" (personal communication, January 17, 2013). The notion of resonance in this context suggests an opening up, a response in the present that is grounded in one's past, in familiar ways of relating, hearing, and being heard through music. In the next chapter, I will look more closely at the way women use music to build social connections and negotiate competing moral economies of health.

Notes

1 Not exclusive to kanyeleng, the term saataroo (lit. narration or explanation) is widely used to describe a free-flowing style of song or heightened speech. See Knight (1973) for discussion of saataroo as practiced by jali vocalists in The Gambia.

2 Drawing on research in Mali, Barbara Hoffman suggests that these understandings of gender reveal "a striking similarity between [the] characterization of women's position in Mande society and aspects of the social position of griots and other nyamakalaw [artisan groups]" (2002: 16).

3 Similar dynamics are evident in the work of *tshilombe* musicians in South Africa whose "marginality, coloured by their self-attributed 'madness' … allows them to be openly critical where others would not dare" (F. McNeill 2011: 182).

4 While most HIV/AIDS support groups have a mixed gender membership, the vast majority of members tend to be women. MUTAPOLA voices is a support network specifically for HIV positive women (see Campbell 2017).

5 In her thorough discussion of kanyeleng (spelled *kanyaleng*) involvement in development communication, Carolyn Hough (2006) references the vulture metaphor as evidence of negative attitudes toward kanyeleng. I suggest that this is an oversimplification, since the vulture metaphor is used to emphasize intelligence and courage in addition to the association with scavenging.

6 The Mandinka term sanawuyaa identifies a kind of relationship that is common among many ethnic groups in the region, including the Wolof, Jola, Serer, Serahule, Fulbe, and Bamana. Similar joking relationships are found in many regions of sub-Saharan Africa.

7 Women who wear the *hijab* are referred to locally as *ibadu* (servants of God), and they are expected to have more shame (*maloo*) and to be pious and restrained when it comes to music and dance (see Janson 2013: 57).

8 With the exception of Fatou, all names of Allatentu members and other people with HIV/AIDS are pseudonyms.

9 Isatou used the term jaliyaa to describe the music of Fatou and the Allatentu Support Band. She explained that when someone becomes a musician, they also take on aspects of a jali identity, even if they were not born into the profession. This demonstrates flexibility in the way people interpret status categories in contemporary Gambia, and the limitations of the idea that there are clearly differentiated "jali" and "non-jali" spheres of music making.

10 This relates to Judith Butler's discussion of the way potentially threatening alterity is more acceptable when it is presented onstage, or framed as performance (1988: 527).

11 One example is Track 5 available for download at www.routledge.com/9780367312725.

12 Female genital cutting (FGC) is also referred to as female genital mutilation or female circumcision. It involves the removal of all or part of the external female genitalia. See Hernlund and Shell-Duncan (2007), Hernlund (2003), and Shell-Duncan et al. (2011) for discussion of the complex international politics and power dynamics of the movement to eradicate female genital cutting in The Gambia.

13 This song is Track 5 on the website: www.routledge.com/9780367312725.

14 A useful contrasting example comes from Fraser McNeill's (2011) research with peer educators in South Africa who have adapted preexisting songs to address HIV/AIDS, with varying degrees of success.

15 This song is Track 6 on the website: www.routledge.com/9780367312725.

16 This song is Track 4 on the website: www.routledge.com/9780367312725.

5 When money dances
Songs of health and wealth

Introduction

Nyali's daughter gave birth to her first child in April 2013. One week later, I performed with the APGWA kanyeleng group at the baby's naming ceremony in Talinding. Kejawo played the lenjengo accompaniment rhythm on the bidong, and Fatou[1] led the song, singing into a loudspeaker to ensure that all the guests would be able to hear her words. The remaining members of the group sang the response part.

Baadinyaa, ali ŋa ñoo naanee	Baadinyaa, let's encourage each other
Baadinyaa sandaŋ kodoo te m bulu	I don't have money that can buy baadinyaa

In a tight circle of women singing and clapping, Nyali's daughter handed crisp five-dalasi notes to Fatou one by one. Other women entered the circle dancing and singing, waving money in the air. One after another, they handed the money to Nyali's daughter, who then passed it to Musukebba who was collecting money for the group in a black plastic bag. Nyali entered the circle smiling infectiously, wearing a bright turquoise outfit with a matching headwrap. She began to hand money to the performers. A jalimusoo standing nearby reached out her hand and Nyali gave her a five-dalasi note. Nyali then pasted a five-dalasi note to Kejawo's head, which was damp from perspiration.

As if overcome by an impulse to dance, Kejawo changed her bidong pattern from the accompaniment rhythm to the lenjengo dance rhythm, moving her body from side to side. The guests began to leap in the air, throwing their arms up and back and stamping their legs. Several dancers held five-dalasi bills, waving them in the air and laughing. A young woman ran into the circle from the back and began to dance vigorously, her headscarf falling to the ground.

A few days later, as usual during my drumming lesson in Lamin, the neighborhood kids joined me and Haruna to sing and dance lenjengo. The children sang a song with the lyrics *baadinyaa la kanoo eh eh, baadinyaa la kanoo, ŋyoo mutoo* (Baadinyaa love, baadinyaa holding on to each other[2]). Laughing with delight, a two-year-old girl Sona[3] began to give us candy wrappers, one by one, that she had collected in a tin can from the nearby garbage pile. The other children joined in, waving the candy wrappers in the air, throwing them up and watching them fall down onto our drums. Haruna said the children were giving us good luck; we would be blessed with real money soon.

Singing, dancing, and monetary exchange during the Talinding naming ceremony, and during my drum lesson in Lamin, reflect an approach to musical performance that emphasizes baadinyaa. This chapter uses the theme of baadinyaa to tease out the way women negotiate conflicting notions of health and value through musical performance. The concept of baadinyaa, frequently referenced in song texts and everyday conversation, demonstrates the importance of maternal power and influence in a patrilineal and patriarchal society (Koné 2002). Baadinyaa[4] literally refers to the relationship between children of the same mother in a polygynous context, but it is used more generally to refer to positive social relationships between people who may or may not be biologically related. It serves as a signifier for social cohesion, community, and positive relationship.[5] In Mande social theory, baadinyaa contrasts with *faadinyaa* (lit. father-childness), which describes the competitive relationship between children of the same father but different mothers in a polygynous context. Just as is the case with baadinyaa, faadinyaa is also used more broadly to describe relationships based on competition, jealousy, and individual ambition. Baadinyaa and faadinyaa provide a lens into Mande social theory and principles that guide behavior (McNaughton 2008: 101).

Faadinyaa refers primarily to competitive relationships between men, because it is male descendants who inherit wealth from the father, whereas women marry and relocate to their husbands' compounds. While women also experience the competition, jealousy, and ambition characteristic of faadinyaa, these qualities are associated with masculinity and male power. Baadinyaa, on the other hand, refers to a relationship between people of any gender that is defined by allegiance to the mother, associated (in theory) with the feminine qualities of nurturing and social cohesion (Koné 2002; C. Roth 2014). Although baadinyaa represents a challenge to notions of patrilineal authority, references to baadinyaa are not at all hidden in The Gambia. Rather, they are constantly asserted, in public and in private, onstage and off, whereas faadinyaa is seldom mentioned. The prevalence of references to baadinyaa in songs is not an indication that competition and conflict are absent; on the contrary, baadinyaa discourse provides an important tool for managing ever-present tensions, asserting social allegiances, and negotiating shared values.

Discourse on baadinyaa and faadinyaa constructs gender as relational and performative, rather than as an essential characteristic of biological sex (see Koné 2002), consistent with theories of gender developed in the foundational work of Judith Butler (1988). For example, in Mande culture, a man may be called "wife" by his older sister's husband; similarly, a woman can be called "husband" by her brother's wife (Koné 2002). Baadinyaa and faadinyaa are best understood not as static social facts, but rather as a dynamic set of discourses and practices that people draw on to assert their relatedness to others in the face of challenges and often conflicting notions of wellness and value.

Baadinyaa provides insight into a Mandinka moral economy that involves negotiations of ethics, obligation, and power (Kea 2013). Following Sayer, I define moral economy as "norms and sentiments regarding the responsibilities and rights of individuals and institutions with respect to others" (2000: 79). In the foundational work of E. P. Thompson (1971) and James Scott (1976), the concept of moral economy was used to investigate conflicts between the market economy and non-market ("moral") systems of exchange embedded in social relationships. This approach suggests an oppositional relationship between "traditional" moral economy and "modern" capitalism, obscuring the moral values that also underpin the market economy (Kimambo et al. 2008). Like Kazuhiko Sugimura, I approach moral economy not as a "remnant of the past" but rather as a "response to a changing present" (2008: 9). References to baadinyaa in songs, interviews, and everyday interactions, are moral statements about social responsibility and care for others in the context of economic austerity, authoritarian national politics, and inadequate access to medical care.

In the first part of this chapter, I explore the way women use song, dance, and monetary exchange to negotiate social relations and maintain baadinyaa, understood as women-centered networks of social support. I suggest that performances are important sites for the composition of wealth-in-people and wealth-in-knowledge (Guyer and Belinga 1995). In the second part of the chapter, I show that performers emphasize baadinyaa in their health-related songs as a way to maintain coherence and meaning, reinterpreting the individualist behavior-change model of health communication through the lens of indigenous systems of communication and relationality.

Following the money: music and baadinyaa

The song performed at the Talinding naming ceremony, "You Can't Buy Baadinyaa," asserts the value of human life and human relationships. The message of this song was often repeated in music performance contexts, health education events, and everyday interactions. For example, when I asked my drum teacher Haruna how much I should pay for lessons, he told me that baadinyaa was more important than money. I should pay whatever I could afford. With this statement, Haruna was prioritizing a long-term relationship over short-term gain. At the same time, by asserting a baadinyaa relationship, he was invoking expectations regarding generosity and sharing. Haruna's emphasis on baadinyaa made me more generous than I would otherwise have been. The song "You Can't Buy Baadinyaa" presents a similar paradox. The song lyrics emphasize the value of baadinyaa, which cannot be purchased with money. And yet, the APGWA kanyeleng sang this particularly song strategically because they knew it was especially effective in inspiring large monetary donations in performance events. Kejawo explained that the song often evoked strong emotional responses and even tears from listeners because it made them think of loved ones who they had lost. By emphasizing the meaninglessness of financial wealth in the absence of caring relationships, the song seemed to inspire a desire to transform cash into social capital in the immediate performance context.

Practices of monetary exchange in performance are referred to in Mandinka as *sooroo* (offering), which is distinct from *jooroo* (payment) (Charry 2000). In tulungo percussion and dance events, sooroo normally takes place during the beginning section of a song described as the *ngaanyaa* section. Ngaanyaa is a verb that means "to show off" or "to show pride." While money is being shown off in this context, practices of sooroo also reflect pride in social relationships rather than solely material wealth. Furthermore, from a religious perspective, gift giving is seen as a source of blessing or God's grace (*baraka/barako*)(see Soares 2004). Contemporary practices of sooroo demonstrate continuity with, as well as intensification of, longstanding approaches to musical patronage and reciprocity (Charry 2000; Ebron 2002; Janson 2002). Informal kinds of monetary exchange exist alongside more formal types of remuneration and musical commoditization in contemporary Gambia.

Monetary exchange in performances has been theorized as an expression of Mande caste relationships and griot-noble interaction (M. Roth 2008; Schulz 1997; Janson 2002). Yet the non-griot performances discussed here demonstrate broader practices of exchange that generate income for performers and enable participants to negotiate social solidarities that are not defined primarily by caste identities and relationships. The transfers of money in women's performances are not solely commodity exchange in which further social obligations are absent; nor are they adequately described as an "exchange of tokens" to build relations of reciprocity (M. Roth 2008: 7). Women's performances challenge the oppositional dichotomy between capitalism and local moral economies (see Hull and James 2012; Guyer 2004), as different economic ideologies intersect and are reinterpreted through musical interactions.

In addition to participating as a performer in APGWA kanyeleng events, I also frequently video recorded their performances. When I first started in 2012, I often focused the video camera on the dancers and instrumentalists, but the group members redirected me. They told me to focus instead on the exchange of money, the sooroo. This helped me to understand that sooroo is not only monetary exchange; it also represents a central site of musical and social meaning making. Sooroo gives weight and significance to a singer's words (M. Roth 2008). The exchange of money is an important form of participation and also one way that performers judge the success of an event. This is partly because the money represents much needed income in the context of economic hardship, but also because the exchange of money reflects the degree to which the performance was successful in achieving social goals of promoting baadinyaa. In other words, in women's performances, money as a material object and symbol is "used to structure and organize the very forms of sociality – based on bonds of affect and sentiment – that it is usually held to disrupt" (Stokes 2002: 147; see also Parry 1989).

In women's performances, when money dances, it challenges divisions between the social, the economic, and the aesthetic. At small neighborhood events like the naming ceremony in Talinding, it is expected that money should be donated in crisp, clean, small-denomination bills (5 or 10 dalasi; 10 dalasi is about 25 US cents).

While wealthier individuals may give large-denomination bills, this is unusual in small neighborhood events. Giving 100 dalasi in five-denomination bills takes time and therefore draws attention to the generosity of the giver. To get the necessary small-denomination bills, guests frequently make change from the money that the performers have already collected. When I first began performing with the Lamin *bolonkono kafoo* (upcountry group), I made the mistake of donating dirty, ripped, and large-denomination bills during performances. Finally, one of the group members took me aside and told me to go exchange my dirty twenty-five-dalasi bill for clean five-dalasi bills. This helped me to recognize the importance of the aesthetic and performed character of sooroo. Sooroo is a social dance that should be beautiful; filthy money undermines the aesthetic value of the performance.

The aesthetic of newness evident in the crisp, clean money obtained from the bank especially for the occasion is also apparent in fashion. Performance events enable women to display their latest outfits. For many celebrations, women are expected to have a new asobi (matching outfit) tailor-made for the event. The asobi serves as a visual marker of celebration and group solidarity. It also puts financial pressure on women who may feel obliged to spend outside their means in order to participate in group events.

Monetary exchange in performances is not unidirectional. During the kanyeleng performance in Talinding, Nyali, the grandmother of the child whose naming ceremony was taking place, gave a significant amount of money to the musicians, and she also received money from guests at the event, an example of what Molly Roth describes as "triangular giving" (2008: 102). Guests at a music event exchange money between themselves that normally gets passed on to the hosts who then give it to the musicians. In this way, the exchange is not solely a way to pay the musicians. It is also a way to demonstrate support for the hosts of an event, and to publicly show generosity, with the understanding that this may be repaid in some form in the future.[6] The exchange of money in performance connects to broader ideas about value in the Senegambia region, and in particular the notion that in order to "generate value, wealth must not stagnate ... it must circulate" (Buggenhagen 2012: 90; see also Maher 2016: 94). In performance contexts, small-denomination bills are often literally circulated multiple times as people continue to make change from the bills collected from others' donations. In this way, the circulation of money in musical events creates a web of obligation and responsibility that extends far beyond the performers themselves.

The small-scale movements of cash and bodies in music events is bound up with larger movements of money and people around the globe. The stripping of the public sector and poor agricultural productivity have inspired large increases in the out-migration of Gambians to Europe and North America. The migration of men, in particular, has important implications for the social and economic structure of households, which are increasingly run by women and dependent upon remittances from abroad. Beth Buggenhagen's (2012) research with Senegalese women demonstrates that the increasing importance of remittances in the Senegalese economy has inspired a growth in extravagant gift giving at ceremonies. In other words, and this is also true in The Gambia, the increased circulation of money at the micro-level in performance contexts parallels the macro-level global circulation of money created through this economy of remittances. The inflation of gift giving in ceremonies also means that women feel pressure to participate and reciprocate in ways that are beyond their means.

Performers use songs about baadinyaa and associated sociomusical interactions strategically in the face of ever-present competition and economic pressures. In the naming ceremony performance in Talinding, there were other musicians, including griots and kanyeleng, soliciting donations while the APGWA kanyeleng were performing. A woman who cooked for the event also attempted to intercept the flow of money from Nyali's daughter to the musicians. She came up and reached out a hand as a way to say, "I am working hard and I am also entitled to compensation." Events typically feature multiple individuals and groups who compete for limited resources. While the concept of faadinyaa provides an important reminder of the prevalence of conflict as well as social solidarity in musical performance contexts, contestations over power and allegiances usually occur using the language of baadinyaa (Jansen and Zobel 1996). The discourse of baadinyaa is powerful in leadership and conflict resolution because it highlights relatedness and responsibility between conflicting parties. This is heightened by the strong moral connotations of "goodness" and virtue associated with baadinyaa (Skinner 2010: 23). In musical performance contexts, the emphasis on baadinyaa is a strategy that performers use to mediate and manage social tensions and to bring together the knowledge and resources necessary for action. This plays out in community events of various kinds, including health education programs.

In the challenging economic environment of contemporary Gambia, remuneration for musicians is increasingly competitive. When I attended events with Haruna, he often complained that kanyeleng groups were stealing resources that rightfully belonged to others. This is because kanyeleng were historically focused on fertility-related practices and did not normally receive monetary compensation for their performances. Haruna said that in the past when he performed with kanyeleng groups, the kanyeleng would give all the money to the drummers. Today, however, kanyeleng expect to take an equal share. Some griots also criticized kanyeleng for incorporating praise singing into their performances and taking payment that should have gone to griots.

Complex rules about who should give money to whom in music events are linked to a hierarchical social system and complex relationships defined by specific obligations and responsibilities (Charry 2000; Knight 1973; Hoffman 2001). Rules are somewhat fluid, however, and monetary exchange in performance events is an important site where relations of power and social obligations are negotiated (Hoffman 2001: 1). Jalimusoo Sambou Suso explained that kanyeleng solicit gifts (*daani*) from jali, since jali are often considered to be of higher status. In some situations, however, jali may solicit gifts from kanyeleng, depending on the particular relationship and context (personal communication, July 25, 2013).[7] Sambou Suso's perspective confirms what I observed in performance contexts. Interestingly, high profile jali musicians such as Jaliba Kuyateh and Sambou Suso receive monetary gifts publicly, but in private people frequently ask them for money, recognizing their high status and financial success. In the APGWA kanyeleng performance in Talinding, complexity was also evident in the way performers donated as well as received money. This is because the event was hosted by the family of one of the kanyeleng (Nyali), so the group members had an obligation to contribute to the event, even though they were also receiving money as performers.

Monetary donations in performances are often inspired by praise singing, referred to as *jamundiroo* or *jairoo* in Mandinka. Praise singing takes a variety of forms, but it typically involves the recognition of an individual's positive attributes, with reference to family lineage, ethnic group, and region of origin (Janson 2002; Knight 1973; Charry 2000; Dave 2014; Newton 2006). Though praise singing is strongly associated with griot performers, singers of all kinds incorporate praises to please the people present, to encourage sooroo, and to position themselves in relation to powerful individuals. Performers often recognize that griots are the most skilled in praise singing, however, and many non-griot performers do not attempt to sing griot-style praise. These different approaches to praise singing were evident in the *Teriyaa* launching concert described in Chapter 3. During this event, Fatou sang the praises of special guests at the event in a non-griot style, which is also apparent on the album itself. This was mostly preplanned and delivered in the same straightforward textual and melodic style that characterized the other parts of the songs, with none of the melodic embellishments that are typical of griot praise singing. These were evident in the performance of Jalimusoo Isatou who made an unexpected guest appearance during the event. While many people did give monetary donations to Fatou when she was singing, Isatou was more effective in encouraging sooroo. This is evidence of the way monetary exchange practices and praise singing continue to be strongly associated with the professional identities of griots, even as non-griot performers like Fatou take on prominent roles in new popular music styles.

As the displays of wealth in ceremonies have intensified in West Africa, praise singing and associated practices of sooroo have increasingly been subject to critique (Dave 2014; Charry 2000; M. Roth 2008; Schulz 2000). In Mali, Eric Charry (2000: 343) notes that in the main concert venue in Bamako, monetary donations to praise singers got so excessive that they were prohibited entirely. In The Gambia, performers such as Jaliba Kuyateh have argued that griots need to move away from excessive praise singing and focus instead on addressing the social and health problems facing the country (personal communication, February 6, 2013). The reality is, however, that many performers, including kanyeleng and the members of the Allatentu Support Band, incorporate praises alongside their messages about health as a way to frame health problems in accordance with local notions of social responsibility and hierarchy. For many people, praise singing remains important musically, socially, and economically. Praises remind individuals of their histories and social connections with others based on family ties, patron-client relationships, and regions of origin. Praise songs are also morality songs that remind recipients of their responsibilities to others and affirm ideals about appropriate behavior modeled on the actions of their ancestors.

While praise singers are critiqued for bolstering the position of the powerful (see Dave 2014), the discourse of baadinyaa in praise songs provides a powerful tool to remind leaders of their responsibilities. In other words, the language of social cohesion and solidarity establishes a basis for future collective action, whereas outspoken critique and conflict can undermine any sense of responsibility to the group (Jansen and Zobel 1996). Performers influence the powerful in part through praise songs that draw on notions of baadinyaa as social obligation, and use that to imagine an ideal world in which their leaders are generous, responsible, and honest. This also carries over into health education contexts, where practices of monetary exchange and praise for health workers, community leaders, and politicians allow for the negotiation of values and social allegiances.

Songs of praise and baadinyaa reflect West African philosophies of "wealth-in-people" and "wealth-in-knowledge" (Guyer and Belinga 1995). In precolonial West Africa, the principal measure of status, power, and prosperity was people rather than material wealth (Frank 2004: 231; Jacobson-Widding and van Beek 1990; Guyer 1995; Janson 2002: 9). The importance of people in defining wealth and security remains significant in contemporary Gambia where economic instability makes individual livelihoods precarious. In this context, strong social connections provide a safety net that enables people to survive challenges such as illness, poor agricultural productivity, or the death of a breadwinner. The emphasis on baadinyaa and social practices of monetary exchange in performance reflect this broader orientation toward wealth-in-people.

Women's performances also represent an important site for the social (and musical) composition of "wealth-in-knowledge" (Guyer and Belinga 1995). Jane Guyer and Samuel Belinga argue that in precolonial Equatorial Africa, "social mobilization was in part based on the mobilization of different bodies of knowledge, and leadership was the capacity to bring them together effectively" (1995: 120). This reflects a process of knowledge "composition" rather than "accumulation" (Guyer and Belinga 1995: 120). The concept of wealth-in-knowledge is useful in reframing understandings of specialization and access to knowledge in the Mande area of West Africa. That is, even though certain specialized knowledges are passed down within specialist lineages, a broader social theory of knowledge must account for the flexible and complex ways in which individuals and groups compose knowledge from various sources and apply it in their lives. Individuals have unique capabilities and access to knowledge (including embodied musical knowledge), which are shaped by their caste position, family, region of origin, and life experiences. Part of what makes musical performance powerful, according to my interlocutors, is the way it brings many individuals with differentiated knowledge and abilities together in one place, working toward a common goal (McConnell 2016).

What I am suggesting here is an intersection between Guyer and Belinga's (1995) notion of the social composition of knowledge and *musical* composition in performance contexts, which similarly depends on effectively combining individual capabilities, voices, and bodies to produce collective sounds and movements. Kanyeleng explained that their performances were efficacious in promoting fertility and child health because they brought together the particular knowledges and abilities of different group members. Where one member's knowledge of ritual, prayer, and musical performance fell short, another member's knowledge would be efficacious.[8] Furthermore, through the social process of musical composition in performance and ritual, kanyeleng aim to strengthen relationships of baadinyaa, which in turn can facilitate the composition of wealth-in-knowledge. This has broader implications for health-related performances, where women bring together knowledge from various sources to articulate an understanding of healthy living that resonates with local lived experiences and worldviews.

In musical performances in The Gambia, women dance with each other, with money, and with knowledge. Songs of baadinyaa and practices of monetary exchange in performance suggest a paradox and, to quote Barbara Hoffman, "where there is social paradox, there are usually questions of power at issue" (2001: 5). That is, through their performances, women engage with seemingly contradictory ideas about value, knowledge, and power. Singing about baadinyaa and dancing with money, women are negotiating power, moving across the fissures between differentiated knowledges, economic systems, and gendered hierarchies. In the next section, I will explore the way the theme of baadinyaa and associated practices of monetary exchange carry over into health communication contexts where performers use music as a form of transformative labor to navigate conflicting moral economies of health and maintain a sense of coherence and meaning.

Performing moral economies of health

I often asked performers why they sang so many songs about baadinyaa. Maimuna,[9] a kanyeleng woman from Farafenni, explained that baadinyaa was an important tool for health promotion. She said,

> Baadinyaa, it keeps health among people. That in itself is enough. That is why … it has a benefit … it is our work.
>
> Baadinyaa, *haani moolu kono, a ka jaatakendeya sabatindi jee. Wo damma faŋo kañanta le … a ye nafaa soto … nna dookuwo le mu.*
> (Personal communication, May 4, 2013).

Baadinyaa is described as both a goal in itself as well as a resource for promoting health. This is because interpersonal conflict and jealousy (failures of baadinyaa) make people vulnerable to health problems in multiple ways. "Marabout sickness" occurs in situations of conflict when one party engages a marabout to bring harm on the other party. People may also fall victim to witches, known as *buwaalu* (witches) or *suutamoolu* (night people) in Mandinka. Witches are known to "eat" people while they sleep, producing a variety of physical and psychological symptoms in their victims that cannot be cured through biomedical treatment. In addition, a breakdown in social support can negatively impact health by decreasing individuals' access to resources such as nutritional food, health care, and information.

Notions of collective responsibility and social support associated with baadinyaa are often at odds with the moral economy of global health programs in The Gambia, which emphasizes individual behavior change and values some diseases and some lives over others (see Polzer and Power 2016; Kimambo et al. 2008). In their critique of dominant models of global health practice, João Biehl and Adriana Petryna argue that "An unattended-to inequality of lives is at the core of a Western moral economy in which an ethics of suffering and compassion … compromises a politics of rights and social justice" (2013: 17). Global health discourse naturalizes inequality when it fails to articulate the historical, political, and economic factors that produce ill health in Africa. These include exploitative economic relationships that keep African countries poor, the ongoing effects of structural adjustment programs implemented under the auspices of the World Bank and the International Monetary Fund, and the misuse of funds by autocrats such as Yahya Jammeh. According to the moral economy of global public health, however, illness is attributed instead to the poor choices of individuals. In this context, music performance can provide a privileged site for navigating conflicting understandings of health and value, as women assert the relevance of baadinyaa and associated ethics of care and solidarity even as they engage with public health messages regarding disease prevention, behavior change, and individual risk factors.

Important concepts in the moral economy of global health development in The Gambia are reflected in the Mandinka terms *yiriwaa* and *nyaatotaa* ("progress" and "forward movement," respectively), which are widely used in health promotion programs. Like the English term "development," these words have strong positive connotations to do with progress and modernity (Esteva 2010; Airhihenbuwa 2007). These terms are associated with women's economic empowerment initiatives emphasizing small business development and entrepreneurship. In addition, they are connected with neoliberal health discourse which represents health as a personal responsibility and ill health as a moral failing of the individual (Polzer and Power 2016: 12; Dutta 2015). Gambian discourse on development also reflects people's awareness of the wealth concentrated elsewhere in the world, and their desire to partake in the benefits of globalization and free market capitalism. This is evident in the strong pressure young people face to emigrate in order to seek economic opportunity elsewhere.

Women's performance groups frequently include yiriwaa in their name (e.g. Brikama Nyambai Yiriwa Kafoo; Kembujeh Women's Yiriwa Association). Singers regularly refer to yiriwaa and nyaatotaa in their songs in order to place their messages within the framework of economic development priorities consistent with the donor organizations that they are working with. For example, in health education contexts many groups sang variations of songs with the words *londoo nafaa mu yiriwaa* (the benefit of knowledge is development), or *ntolu la nyaatotaa, ali ŋa dindiŋolu maakoyi* ([for] our development, let's help the children). In these songs, development has a strong moral inflection, suggesting virtue and responsibility and framing health as a development challenge. The first excerpt in particular (the benefit of knowledge is development) was adapted to a wide variety of health topics. I heard renditions that focused on Ebola, HIV/AIDS, and malaria. In these songs, performers often incorporated praises for health workers who were lauded as generous, hardworking bearers of health knowledge who saved many lives. These praises were often based on real appreciation for Village Health Workers, Community Health Nurses, and others who provided much needed care and information in remote areas. Praise singing in these health education contexts was also consistent with broader practices of praise as a tool for generating both income and social allegiances.

Discourse on Ebola in the context of the 2014–2016 West African outbreak offers a dramatic illustration of friction at the contact zone between moral economies of global public health and local moralities of care. Beginning in southern Guinea, the Ebola outbreak quickly spread to the neighboring countries of Sierra Leone and Liberia, eventually causing a total of 11,310 deaths in the three most affected countries (CDC 2016). Small numbers of cases were also documented in Nigeria, Mali, Senegal, United States, United Kingdom, Spain, and Italy. The Ebola outbreak threw into sharp relief the devastating consequences of the neglect of basic health infrastructures in West Africa and the problems with top-down approaches to health communication (Leach 2015; Wilkinson and Leach 2015). The international response to the outbreak was slow, failed to adequately engage local communities, and employed coercive approaches that caused "huge social harm" in the three most affected countries of Guinea, Liberia, and Sierra Leone (Pellecchia et al. 2015: 9). Particularly challenging was the way Ebola prevention programs specifically targeted social practices of care seen as moral obligations, such as looking after the sick and washing the bodies of the deceased. The coercive approach to Ebola containment contributed to fear and conflict between health workers and communities, the most dramatic example being the killing of a team of health workers and journalists in southeastern Guinea in 2014 (BBC 2014).

In this climate of fear, as Ebola spread to neighboring Senegal and nearby Mali, health workers in The Gambia rolled out an Ebola Preparedness Plan with support from the World Health Organization (WHO), the United Nations Children's Fund (UNICEF), and the United Nations Development Program (UNDP). The Gambia did not have any documented Ebola cases, but it was considered to be at high risk because of its proximity to affected countries. Songs were an important component of the Ebola communication strategy in The Gambia developed by the Directorate of Health Promotion. With Buba Darboe, elsewhere I have written about the importance of the emotional content of Ebola songs in "transform[ing] fear into social mobilization" (McConnell and Darboe 2017: 29). Here, I use an Ebola song by kanyeleng from Taibatou and Kerewan (eastern Gambia) to demonstrate the way women negotiate disparate moral economies of health through performance. This song was recorded by Buba Darboe from the Directorate of

Health Promotion on October 26, 2014. With their characteristic powerful vocals and evocative lyrics, the Taibatou/Kerewan kanyeleng sang:

Ali ŋa taa kibaaroo nooma	Let's go after information
Kibaaroo mu feŋ kumaa ti	Information is an important thing
Hadamadiŋo la ñaatotaa ti	For the progress of human beings
Ali ŋa naa nna ñanto nooma	Let's go after our rights
Niŋ ŋa nna ñanto nooma	If we go after our rights
Muna n si nna hakoo nooma	We should go after what is morally ours
Jaraloo mu ñanto le ti	Medical treatment is a right
Tankandiroo mu ñanto le ti	Prevention is a right
Kibaaroo ñiŋ fanaŋ mu ñanto le ti ...	Information is also a right ...
Niŋ moo ye i saba moo la	If a person surpasses you in people
I niŋ a te kañ ...	You are not equal ...
Ebola mu kuuraŋ baa ti oh	Ebola is a big disease oh
Niŋ i taata Guinea Conakry	If you go to Guinea Conakry
Fo i taata Sierra Leone	If you go to Sierra Leone
Liberia be meŋ kumboo la	That which Liberia is crying about
Gambia nkoolu be tankandiroo la	Gambians are preventing
Ali ye a lamoyi niŋ hakiloo la	Listen with intelligence
Ebola kuuraŋo mu saasaa le ti	Ebola disease is an illness
Ali kana suboo bee domo	Don't eat all meat
Wulokono suboo te domotaa ti	Bushmeat is not for eating
Niŋ moo ye i saba moo la	If a person surpasses you in people
I niŋ a te kañ ...	You are not equal ...
Woto hadamadiŋo mu feŋ ne ti duniya kono	Therefore, a human being is something in this world
Allah faŋo la jooraŋo mu hadamadiŋo ti	A human being is God's own tool
Hadamadiŋo mu feŋ kumaabaa le ti	A human being is a very important thing
Ali ŋa kata,	Let's try
Ɗa ń buloo kafu ñooma	Let's join hands
Ɗa nna miroolu tenteŋ	Let's winnow our ideas
Ɗa hakiloo suusaa ñoola	Let's put our minds together
Ɗa ñiŋ kuuraŋo kele ...	Let's fight this disease ...
Niŋ moo ye i saba moo la	If a person surpasses you in people
I niŋ a te kañ	You are not equal
Noosoolu be yamaroo la	Nurses are advising
Dokitaaroolu be yamaroo la ...	Doctors are advising ...
Ali ń bee ŋa yamaroo meŋ	Let's all hear the advice
Ali ye a lamoyi niŋ hakiloo la	Listen with intelligence
Ali kana a taa niŋ jusoo la	Not with anger
Ali ye a taa nna denkiloo to	Take it from my song
Niŋ moo ye i saba moo la	If a person surpasses you in people
I niŋ a te kañ	You are not equal
	(Quoted in McConnell and Darboe 2017)

The kanyeleng group's musical dexterity and creative use of language in this song elicited appreciative laughter and smiles of approval from a large audience at the Regional Health Directorate in Basse in eastern Gambia. In the middle of the song, the lead singer incorporated praises for several of the health workers in attendance who responded by giving her monetary donations, including the large denomination 100-dalasi bill. For the remainder of the song, the kanyeleng proudly waved the money in the air as they danced and sang.

Public health discourse attributed the devastating Ebola epidemic in West Africa to harmful traditional practices such as eating bushmeat and washing the bodies of the deceased (Leach 2015). Prevention messages in The Gambia and throughout the region emphasized prompt reporting of suspected cases, hand washing, avoiding handshaking, and avoiding contact with wild animals. According to the moral economy of Ebola prevention, individuals were responsible for following these guidelines in order to protect themselves and those close to them. The Taibatou/Kerewan kanyeleng group received thorough training on Ebola prevention, and in this song and others they provided detailed information about Ebola symptoms and urged listeners to go quickly to the hospital for treatment. The kanyeleng also drew on notions of progress and development, emphasizing the importance of information provided by health experts (doctors and nurses) for "the progress of human beings."

At the same time, the Taibatou/Kerewan kanyeleng interpreted Ebola through the lens of local moral economies of health, emphasizing collective responsibility, the value of human life and relationships, and moral rights to health care. The chorus to the song is a Mandinka proverb about the importance of human relationships and wealth-in-people: *Niŋ moo ye i saba moo la, i niŋ a te kañ*. Literally meaning "if a person surpasses you in people, you are not equal," the proverb asserts the value of people and baadinyaa relationships. The underlying message is that someone who shows care, generosity, and commitment to others will be rewarded. That is, an individual with a strong social network is better able to access the resources and information necessary to overcome challenges. The song also further emphasizes the value of human life with the words "A human being is God's own tool/ A human being is a very important thing." In this way the song implies that protecting the lives of human beings (i.e. by preventing Ebola) is a moral good, framed in religious terms.

In this song, the kanyeleng describe medical treatment and information as rights, using the terms *nyanto* and *hakoo*. The term *nyanto* is roughly translated as "right," but it suggests not only a sense of entitlement (i.e. a benefit that one has access to), but also obligation (i.e. something that one *should* access). The related term *hakoo* has a strong moral overtone, suggesting a sense of ethical entitlement and obligation. In contrast to individualist public health discourse on Ebola, however, the kanyeleng portray the obligation as a collective one. The kanyeleng sing, "Let's join hands/ Let's winnow our ideas/ Let's put our minds together/ Let's fight this disease." In this way, they represent Ebola as a shared responsibility, a problem that is best solved through cooperation, bringing together the collective knowledge of the group to find meaningful solutions. Ultimately, however, the message of the Taibatou/Kerewan kanyeleng's song is not specific to Ebola. The song suggests a broader statement about rights to health care and information in an environment where many Gambians lack access to even the most basic health services and where Ebola is not necessarily the number one priority (McConnell and Darboe 2017). The song reflects people's frustration with the patchy and uneven distribution of health care in the country, with some diseases and some regions prioritized while others are neglected.

The kanyeleng's emphasis on access to health care in this song is aligned with the strengths-based approach that informs this book. Regarding the West African Ebola outbreak, medical anthropologists Doug Henry and Susan Shepler write "If ... we are truly concerned about the health and wellbeing of African populations ... then humanitarian assistance cannot be for just this one disease, but must attend to its aftermath, and the investment in infrastructure necessary to prevent future suffering" (2015: 21). The effective prevention and containment of future outbreaks depends upon building strong health care infrastructure in West Africa and engaging the knowledge, creativity, and resourcefulness of local communities (Leach 2015).

Songs addressing other health issues reflect a similar process of negotiating conflicting moral economies of health in creative ways. One example is the song "It Is Malaria"[10] performed by the Nyambai College kanyeleng group at the Brikama Regional Health Directorate on two occasions in 2013 (August 21 and September 22). The main message of this song is that malaria is caused not by witchcraft but by a mosquito-borne parasite. The song urges the listener to seek prompt medical treatment for a child with symptoms of malaria. On both occasions, the song was led by Jainaba Saho. Performed with the lenjengo dance rhythm, the song featured the following chorus, performed in call-and-response style:

Eh, buwaa m'aali toora, malaria le mu	Eh, a witch is not tormenting you, it is malaria[11]
Musudimbaalu oh, buwaa m'aali toora malaria le mu	Mothers, a witch is not tormenting you, it is malaria

In the September 22 performance, Jainaba Saho performed a saataroo (narrative solo in heightened speech). The rest of the group responded with the chorus after each phrase.

Malaria kuuraŋkesoo, niŋ a ye dindiŋo maa ala kumoo ka siyaa, bairi balakandoo meŋ ka tara a kuŋ keŋo la, wo le ka dindiŋo diamundi	The malaria parasite, when it touches a child their words become many, because the fever that is in their head, that makes the child talk [i.e. they become delirious]
Wo le ye a tinna n ka yaamaroo dii moo jamaa la: niŋ dindiŋo baloo kandita, i ye taa lopitaanoo to	That is why we give advice to many people: if a child has a fever, go to the hospital
I si a je n si malaria ñiŋ kuuraŋkesoo faa dindiŋo bala jaŋ niŋ a be semboo soto la a bala...	You can see we can kill this malaria parasite in the child before it gets strong...
Dindiŋo be a fo la ko, niŋ malaria seleta kuŋ keŋo la ... dindiŋo baamaa si taa moroolu yaa	The child will say that, if malaria goes up into the head ... the child's mother can go to the place of the marabouts

A ko a ye, jiiberoo ke ñe katuŋ n diŋo saasaata niŋ a ka kaari too fo	She says to him, look for me because my child is sick and they said so-and-so's name
Niŋ a ye wo fo doroŋ, baa si a fo a ye ko, koto, musoo meŋ be nna maafaŋo, a si ke noo wo le ye n diŋo maa	If she says that, the mother can tell him, my elder, a woman who is in our area, it is possible that she touched [harmed] my child
Noosoolu ye a je ko siñooma walindi, a ye siñooma kuukundi, aniŋ malaria mu feŋ ne ti meŋ i ye a loŋ ko a manke suutankoo ti	Nurses see that it has brought a problem between neighbors, and malaria is something that is not [caused by] night people [witches]
Wo le ye a tinna i ye a fo dimbaalu ye taa lopitaanoo to	That is why they say mothers should go to the hospital

The August 21 performance also included the following lines:[12]

Meŋ be taa niŋ naa la, ila fiiro tiñaata, wala ila dookuwo tiñaata, wo le ye a tinna jaatakendeya moolu ko ŋa dandaŋolu seneyandi ... malaria kuuraŋkesoo la	Those who are going and coming [to the hospital], their business is ruined, their work is ruined, that is why the health people say let us clean our areas [to prevent the spread] of the malaria parasite

This song asserts that malaria is an illness caused by a mosquito-borne parasite. Jainaba urges the listener not to assume that symptoms are caused by witches (*buwaalu*), also known as night-people (*suutamoolu*). In this way, the message is consistent with the biomedical understandings of illness emphasized by the Ministry of Health and Social Welfare. Jainaba explains that a child with a high fever may become delirious and falsely accuse someone of witchcraft. Such accusations can cause delay in accessing malaria treatment. She then goes on to explain that failure to seek prompt medical attention at the health clinic will result in economic losses to the family. In this way, the impact of the child's illness on economic development of the family is emphasized, as well as the responsibility of the mother to seek prompt medical care for the child.

While some aspects of the Brikama kanyeleng's song are consistent with individualist behavior-change discourse in public health, the song also emphasizes notions of social responsibility and baadinyaa. In her saataroo section, Jainaba Saho explains that assumptions of witchcraft are damaging for two reasons: First, because they prevent a family from taking the child immediately to the health center to get treatment, and second, because they rupture social relationships between friends and family. When a friend or family member is falsely accused of witchcraft, baadinyaa ties (i.e. relationships of care) are broken needlessly, and this has long-term consequences for the individuals and families concerned. The song proceeds from the assumption that witchcraft does exist, but asserts that it is not implicated in this particular illness. In this way, Jainaba Saho interprets the biomedical message regarding prompt attention for malaria symptoms and integrates it into a song that underscores the importance of baadinyaa. The loss of income due to illness is represented as damaging for the well-being of the family as a whole as well as their relationships with others. These messages are reinforced by the lenjengo dance rhythm and melody used in the performance, which are associated with the theme of baadinyaa, so frequently the subject of songs at life cycle celebrations.

The songs of Fatou and the Allatentu Support Band demonstrate a similar process of juxtaposing and negotiating competing moral economies of health, integrating an emphasis on baadinyaa alongside messages grounded in a biomedical public health model. *Teriyaa* includes songs that provide detailed information about how HIV is transmitted. The songs stress individual responsibility for HIV prevention, and the importance of HIV testing and antiretroviral medication. At the same time, the album reflects the prevalent view among the members of the Allatentu Support Group that HIV-related stigma was more damaging than the disease itself. Stigma here represents a breakdown in baadinyaa because it ruptures caring relationships between family and friends. Allatentu members particularly appreciated the title song on the album, "Teriyaa" (Friendship),[13] which highlights the importance of loyalty and support between friends and family in the face of HIV/AIDS:

Teriyaa nna wo Teriyaa, Teriyaa kanoo maŋ di nna wo Teriyaa	Friendship, oh friendship is not an easy thing
Kabiriŋ ate maŋ kuraŋ, ate le mu i terimaa ti	When she was not sick, she was your friend
Niŋ HIV ya mutaa, hani bee i terimaa le mu	Now that she is HIV positive, she is still your friend
Kana bula, hani bii i terimaa le mu	Do not leave her, she is still your friend
Kana fayi, hani bii i terimaa le mu	Do not throw her away, she is still your friend
I ka nte meŋ je teŋ, HIV le benna	Myself, I am HIV positive
Duŋ n kee maŋ a soto, aduŋ a maŋ n bula	My husband doesn't have it, and he did not leave me
Woto musoolu wo m be ali yaamarila	Women oh, I will advise you
Niŋ alila kewoolu ye ñiŋ sotoo, al kana i bula	If your husbands have this, do not leave them
Dun kewoolu fanaŋ duŋ	And men also
Niŋ ila musoolu ye nin soto, ali kana i bula, ali kana i tu jee	If your wives have this, do not leave them, do not leave them there
Ali futuu musoolu le mu, a niŋ ali futuu kewoolu le mu, ali kanaa ñoo tu jee	They are your wives, your husbands, do not leave each other
Teroolu fanaŋ kana ño tu jee	Friends also, do not leave each other
Teriya nna wo Teriyaa, Teriyaa kanoo maŋ di nna wo Teriya	Friendship, oh friendship is not an easy thing
Kuma folo meŋ fota ama, wo le ye a too kuyaa	The first words that were used gave it a bad name
Doolu ko "saata kuuraŋo" le mu	Some called it the "dying disease"
Doolu ko "jeene kuuraŋo" le mu	Some called it the "prostitute's/adulterer's disease"
Aduŋ a maŋ ñan wo la	And it should not be called by these names
Kuuraŋo mu kuuraŋo le ti	An illness is simply an illness
Ali m bee ye ñiŋ kuu kele	Let's all fight this problem

The song "Teriyaa" addresses the social context of HIV/AIDS, urging listeners to support their friends and family members who are HIV positive. "Teriyaa" challenges the association of HIV/AIDS with immorality and death, asserting that it is just a disease like any other. This approach contrasts with the dominant narratives of HIV prevention, which implicitly or explicitly blame HIV positive individuals for their condition. The large treatment gap in access to ART in African countries reflects a moral economy that has prioritized prevention over treatment, despite evidence that treatment is highly effective in reducing HIV transmission and decreasing ongoing costs to the health care system (Nattrass 2004; Jon Cohen 2011). As Petryna and Biehl write, the moral economy of HIV/AIDS turns "some into innocent victims worthy of care and others into villains to be disregarded or condemned" (2013: 28–29; see also Fassin 2013). One problematic example is the practice of providing antiretrovirals to prevent mother-to-child transmission of HIV, while neglecting to treat the mother's ongoing HIV infection (Fassin 2013).[14] Since 2016, revised WHO guidelines recommend universal treatment for people with HIV, but just 29 percent of Gambians with HIV are on ART (UNAIDS 2018). In contrast, 68 percent of mothers with HIV receive treatment to prevent mother-to-child transmission of the virus (UNAIDS 2018). As Didier Fassin (2013) argues, this discrepancy reflects an underlying moral economy that values the lives of unborn children more than their mothers, who are more often blamed for their HIV positive status.

The song "Teriyaa" reflects the experience of Fatou and other members of Allatentu who faced ostracism, rejection, and even violence because of their HIV positive status. The strong concern for social support and relationships in "Teriyaa" demonstrates the primary motivation behind the album for Fatou and the other members of the Allatentu Support Group. Even as they engaged with public health discourse regarding individual responsibility, abstinence, blood tests, and biomedical treatment, they saw HIV/AIDS primarily as a social failing. In this sense, Fatou's songs depart radically from more typical HIV/AIDS awareness messaging aligned with a moral economy of individual risk and prevention. Instead, Fatou's songs focus extensively on social support, treatment, and care, identifying the breakdown in baadinyaa resulting from HIV-stigma as the principal problem.

Embedded in songs about health such as these are layers of meaning that reference public health discourse as well as local understandings of the social basis of illness. The notion of moral economy is helpful in foregrounding the norms and values that underpin health discourse and the negotiations of power involved in women's performances. Local moral economies are not unchanging artifacts embedded in performances but rather mechanisms of survival and meaning making in the context of political and economic change (Tsuruta 2006). Female performers draw on themes such as baadinyaa to emphasize social responsibility and care, even as they articulate messages about behavior change and individual responsibility. Despite the differences in the epidemiology of Ebola and HIV/AIDS, similar problems can be observed in the global response to these two epidemics. Both epidemics have caused devastating loss of life that could have been ameliorated with faster responses, long-term strengthening of health care infrastructure, and better engagement with the knowledge and resourcefulness of local communities. Coercive, top-down approaches, such as those implemented in the responses to Ebola and HIV/AIDS, can inspire resistance and resentment on the part of local communities whose practices of intimacy and care are demonized and targeted for elimination. In the Gambian context, many health workers have recognized that involving musicians offers an important means to promote community involvement and meaning making. By emphasizing baadinyaa and associated notions of love and care, female performers play an important role in making health information resonate with local lived experience. Musical performance is perhaps particularly suited for this purpose because of the existing association of melodies and rhythms with themes such as baadinyaa.

Conclusion

The concept of baadinyaa, so often emphasized in songs, provides an interpretive lens through which to investigate multi-layered practices of monetary exchange, notions of social health, and approaches to knowledge construction in The Gambia. Practices of sooroo in performances demonstrate the way women have adapted the material and symbolic value of money to serve multiple purposes. Money is used as a tool for asserting social allegiances even as it remains important as a source of livelihood for performers. Women use songs about baadinyaa, and related musical practices such as praise singing, to build wealth-in-people and wealth-in-knowledge. Attending to local concepts and practices such as those associated with baadinyaa can inform a strengths-based approach that goes beyond narratives of failings and lack to emphasize indigenous cultural practices that promote resilience in the face of change.

Women's performances in The Gambia are a site of collision between notions of collective responsibility and relatedness associated with baadinyaa and the moral economy of global health, which values particular diseases and individuals over others (Kimambo et al. 2008), and emphasizes individual behavior change rather than structural change to provide sustainable primary health care over the long term (Polzer and Power 2016). Musical performance represents an important site of transformative work in which these ideas about health and value are negotiated to maintain a sense of continuity and meaning. Female performers engage with global health discourse emphasizing linear, individual-focused behavior change initiatives but transform it through the prism of baadinyaa and broader social determinants of health. In the next chapter, I will further develop this argument by focusing in on the social dynamics of musical participation as an intervention in interdisciplinary debates regarding community participation in global health programming.

Notes

1 No relation to Fatou of the Allatentu Support Band.
2 *Nyoo mutoo* literally means "holding on to each other," but it also implies social cohesion or looking after each other.
3 Not her real name.

4 Baadinyaa can be broken down to "baa" (mother), "ding" (child), and "yaa" (state of being), yielding "mother-childness."

5 Baadinyaa is the Mandinka spelling of a term which is widely used in Mande languages and has been addressed in a significant body of scholarship, much of it conducted in Mali (Bamana spelling: *badenya*) (C. Roth 2014; Bird and Kendall 1987; Koné 2002; Jansen 1996; Conrad and Frank 1995; Skinner 2012; Wooten 2009; McNaughton 2008).

6 Panzacchi (1994) notes that bank notes in Senegal smell of perfume because they get passed around so much by women at ceremonies.

7 While leatherworkers (*garanke*) are viewed as being of higher status than jali (see Knight 1973), I witnessed kanyeleng from leatherworker families soliciting donations from jali. Additionally, jali who were known to be financially successful were often expected to donate money even to people from *sulaa* families. These examples demonstrate flexibility in social expectations and obligations, rather than a fixed hierarchical structure.

8 Kanyeleng also explained that *baraka* (blessing or grace) is unevenly distributed, meaning that God may hear some prayers more than others. See Soares (2004) for a discussion of *baraka* in relation to broader understandings of differentiated power or favor from God.

9 Not her real name.

10 The recording of this song is Track 7 on the website: www.routledge.com/9780367312725.

11 The English-language term "malaria" is used rather than the Mandinka term *kajee*. The use of English-language terms such as malaria and HIV/AIDS may reflect the extensive attention that health educators have given these particular diseases, as well as (in the case of HIV/AIDS) a rejection of language that contributes to stigma.

12 Jainaba Saho expressed similar ideas in the September 22 performance, but due to lack of clarity in the recording, I have combined the two performances here.

13 This song is Track 2 on the website: www.routledge.com/9780367312725.

14 Trials of programs to prevent mother-to-child transmission were shown to worsen the mother's prognosis by causing her to develop resistance to antiretroviral drugs (Lallemant and Jourdain 2010).

6 Stealing power
Embodiment and participation in kanyeleng performance

Introduction

In 1970, The Gambia's Prime Minister, Dawda Jawara, asked for help from Niuminding Fatty, the head of the Banjul kanyeleng group. Jawara and his People's Progressive Party (PPP) were leading a campaign to declare The Gambia a republic. Jawara wanted to become the country's first president, replacing Queen Elizabeth II as head of state, but he needed help. A previous referendum on the issue in 1965 had failed when it did not achieve the required two-thirds majority. The leader of the opposition United Party, Pierre N'jie, was organizing the "no" campaign, and the outcome of the referendum was uncertain. Jawara brought an offering of kola nuts as a sign of respect for the kanyeleng and asked them to support him in the upcoming referendum (NCAC and Fatty 2003).

In an interview with the National Centre for Arts and Culture in 2003, Niuminding Fatty described how she called the Banjul kanyeleng together to pray for Jawara's victory (NCAC and Fatty 2003). She asked their drummer Sutay to play the drum first thing in the morning to send a message to all the kanyeleng from Banjul. When they heard it, the kanyeleng gathered in a clearing on the outskirts of town. When they arrived there, they removed all their clothes except for their underskirts. They sang, danced, and prayed for Jawara to be successful in the election. They repeated this every morning during the run up to the referendum. They also took to the streets, singing songs in support of Jawara and the PPP (Sheikh Omar Jallow, personal communication, April 25, 2018). In the end, their prayers were answered. With ninety percent of registered voters participating, over seventy percent voted "yes," and The Gambia was declared a republic. Dawda Jawara became the country's first president on April 24, 1970 (Hughes and Perfect 2006).

After his success in the referendum, Jawara called the Banjul kanyeleng to the Statehouse to celebrate (NCAC and Fatty 2003). The kanyeleng women sang and danced for Jawara and his wife, Lady Chilel. In her 2003 interview, Niuminding explained that in the middle of the festivities, she stepped out, announcing that she needed to urinate. On the way to the bathroom, Niuminding noticed that Jawara's underwear was hanging out to dry on a clothesline. She looked around to make sure no one was watching, and then she grabbed one pair of underwear from the line. She went into the bathroom and put them on under her short wrap skirt, pulling them high up to her waist so they wouldn't fall down. Then Niuminding went back out to join the other kanyeleng, singing and dancing in front of President Jawara and Lady Chilel (NCAC and Fatty 2003).

Niuminding declared that Jawara's was not the only underwear she stole (NCAC and Fatty 2003). She also claimed to have stolen the underwear of Sheriff Dibba, then Vice President, when the kanyeleng group went to his compound to perform. Niuminding boasted that for years she continued to wear both pairs of underwear in kanyeleng events all over the Banjul area. She danced with the two pairs of underwear until they were completely worn out and torn.[1]

Niuminding explained, "That is why I am famous. ...The fame of this theft is still with me until the day I die" (*Wo le ye a tinna n darajata. ...Wo suñaaroo darajo, n niŋ wo le mu haani bii fo janiŋ m be faa la*) (NCAC and Fatty 2003). The legendary pilfering of Jawara's underwear made Niuminding notorious and respected among kanyeleng for her thieving skills, which are an important part of a kanyeleng identity. Kanyeleng thievery is seen to give health and strength to kanyeleng children. Blatantly stealing food, clothing, or whatever else strikes her fancy is a strategy that a kanyeleng woman uses to look after her family, prevent illnesses, and allow her children to live into adulthood. Along with music, dance, ritual, and prayer, stealing and trickery are part of the day-to-day performance of *kanyelengyaa* (being a kanyeleng) (see Hough 2006).

Niuminding's renowned underwear theft is in some ways typical of kanyeleng comic narratives about joking and trickery. Jawara's underwear also tells a larger story about power, combining in characteristic kanyeleng fashion the personal with the political and linking the intimate private sphere with the public expression of authority. Jawara used the kanyeleng group's spiritual and social power to bolster his authority and allow him to succeed in the 1970 referendum, becoming the first President of the Republic. After the referendum, by stealing (or claiming to steal) the President's underwear, Niuminding was also taking some of his power and fame for herself.[2] According to Niuminding, Jawara and his wife were aware that she was wearing his underwear. They tried to get them back from her, but eventually gave up and let her go (NCAC and Fatty 2003).

The act of stealing and then wearing Jawara's and Dibba's underwear combined kanyeleng practices of thievery, cross-dressing, and ridiculing authority. It is significant that Niuminding claimed their *underwear*, the apparel that is used to cover the male genitalia. By putting this most intimate of garments on her own female body, Niuminding was wearing and refashioning the masculine authority of Jawara and Dibba for her own purposes. By singing, dancing, and clapping her hands with the President and Vice President's underwear, Niuminding was simultaneously ridiculing them and embodying aspects of their power.

And Niuminding was fearsome. I knew none of this intimate history when I joined the APGWA kanyeleng group in 2012. But after years of performing with the kanyeleng group she founded, hearing Niuminding's songs, and reading transcripts of her interviews at the National Centre for Arts and Culture, her formidable character shines through. The story of Niuminding's legendary underwear theft opens a window into the bigger questions of embodiment and power which are the focus of this chapter. How, I ask, can kanyeleng understandings of sound, body, and participation, inform a strengths-based approach to health promotion? Going further, how might kanyeleng models of musical interaction reframe power relations in health development programs?

Elsewhere I have critiqued the notion of participation as it is used in public health programs involving music (McConnell 2017). I have argued that ethnomusicological perspectives on music participation provide an important alternative to dominant paradigms of communication evident in "edutainment" programs (Okagbue 1998). In this chapter, I broaden this discussion to address issues of power and corporality with specific reference to kanyeleng musical performance practices and understandings of the body. I argue that embodied musical participation enables kanyeleng to steal power – to communicate, mobilize, and enact change.

Kanyeleng, food, and the body

"Kanyeleng are shameless," Alanso[3] told me with pride. "You are a kanyeleng, so you should not feel shame." With those words, she pushed me forward into the crowd. "I want you to record the young boys when they enter the *luwo* (the dancing circle)." Steeling myself, I held my camera close and wove through the crowd, trying to make myself as inconspicuous as possible.

Alanso held the megaphone up to her mouth and began to sing, *Dansiŋ baa lee? Oo baa fele* (Where are the mothers of the initiates? Oh, here they are). She stopped and announced loudly, "I've been farting this whole time! Can you smell it?"

We had spent the afternoon eating *benachin* (spiced rice) and *panketos* (donuts). For kanyeleng, food and music go together. In addition to performing, kanyeleng are often invited to cook for events in return for a small payment. Kanyeleng are experts in overeating and hoarding of food. They often leave an event with containers, bags, or pockets full of leftovers. Laughing, Kejawo explained kanyeleng love of food with a song: *Kini biri biri, kini le ka moo sabu moo ma* (Food brings people together). When you eat together and sing together, you become family. You create baadinyaa.

"Give this to your son Dandang," Alanso told me as she filled a bucket to the brim with leftover benachin and cassava. "It will make him strong." Alanso and the other members of the group had taken my son under their wing and given him the name Dandang. He was a kanyeleng child, because he was born after I joined the group. For them, he was the product of their prayers for me to be blessed with a big baby boy. One child was not enough, though. Despite my protestations, Alanso and the others told me regularly that Dandang needed a younger sister.

The kanyeleng were proud of Dandang. When we walked through the village, they told everyone we met that he was a kanyeleng child. They described, in a highly embellished kanyeleng style, the way I had become a kanyeleng, the way we sang, danced, and ate together, and slept in the same bed when we traveled for performances.

In these various everyday performances of kanyelengyaa, kanyeleng concepts of the body were foregrounded. Sometimes uncomfortably, it was often *my* body that was on display, used to demonstrate the efficacy of kanyelengyaa. Kanyeleng discourse emphasizes bodily functions such as eating, farting, having sex, giving birth, and breastfeeding. Kanyeleng discuss normally private physical experiences publicly and concern themselves with sensory experiences that are normally unspoken. This concern with multisensory, embodied experience is evident in kanyeleng performance practices and norms of interaction in music events.

Kanyeleng describe their shameless behavior as humbling themselves before God. If God sees their desperation for a child, he will surely have pity on them and answer their prayers. At the same time, the emphasis on physical experiences of eating, singing, and dancing, represents an expression of aliveness in the face of grief and loss. For kanyeleng, embodying sound and movement together with others is an assertion of participation in a world that would exclude them. The musical norms and expectations associated with kanyeleng performances facilitate kanyeleng goals of social inclusion and integration of the marginalized infertile woman's body. Going further, kanyeleng performances are a site of transformative labor in which women build meaning and power through musical sound and movement. This transformative labor enables kanyeleng women to sustain a sense of continuity and value despite infertility or child mortality. For kanyeleng, these various embodied practices of music, eating, and joking are a healing praxis with direct positive effects on their health and the health of their children. As was the case with Niuminding and Jawara's underwear, the moving and sounding female body steals power and steals health.

Health promotion and participation

In April 2018, The Gambia Ministry of Health and Social Welfare coordinated a public awareness campaign on open defecation. Supported by UNICEF, the Ministry hoped to make The Gambia the first country in Africa to eliminate the practice of defecating in open spaces or waterways rather than using a toilet. While the majority of Gambian households have latrines, the campaign targeted areas of the Lower River Region and the Central River Region where open defecation was still practiced. The Ministry aimed to increase the use of latrines and hand washing in order to minimize the spread of disease.

Buba Darboe, the Program Manager for Health Communication at the Ministry and my long-term collaborator, explained that the open defecation program was challenging. People found the topic embarrassing and demeaning. In addition to the problem of resources and labor power to build latrines, local beliefs about defecation prevented people from using latrines even when they had access to them. For example, in some areas, there were taboos about children and elders sharing a toilet, and it was believed to be dangerous to use the latrine at certain times of the day. The complexity of local beliefs about toilet practices, and questions of resource allocation, were not always adequately captured in international discourse on open defecation, however. In some ways, understandings of open defecation exemplified aspects of the modernization theory of development, casting local communities as ignorant and backward, in need of outside assistance in order to differentiate between cleanliness and filth, and private and public domains (see Doron and Raja 2015). Perhaps most importantly, the emphasis on open defecation seemed out of touch to some Gambians with whom I spoke who were rightly concerned about other issues such as inadequate access to medicine, an ongoing doctors' strike, and dangerously high levels of air pollution in the urban areas due to burning at the Bakoteh dumping site. In this context, Ministry staff were the intermediaries, tasked with implementing a program that reflected international development concerns (led by UNICEF) rather than local health priorities.

Recognizing the challenging nature of the open defecation program, the Directorate of Health Promotion and Education took a creative approach, engaging performers of various kinds to translate messages about open defecation into a locally meaningful format. Performers included kanyeleng groups, popular jali Pabobo Jobarteh, rapper ST Brikama Boyo, and comedian Kitabu.[4] The Ministry had T-shirts made for the program that featured a large image of excrement on the front with the words "I belong in the toilet!"

I accompanied the performers and Ministry staff on a tour of the country to raise awareness about open defecation in targeted rural areas. The tour was the culmination of a series of consultations with local communities, with the goal of making sure that every family had access to a sanitary latrine. On the morning that the tour was scheduled to begin, the flatbed truck that was hired to transport the musicians broke down. As a result, it was almost time for evening prayers by the time we finally turned off the paved South Bank road and drove through the forest to the village of Sibito not far from the Casamance border. The thick, humid heat of the day began to dissipate as the sun dropped below the trees and we drove up to the village meeting place next to the mosque. The community members had been waiting for us all day. When we drove up, children ran to greet us, jumping up and down in excitement. A large crowd quickly formed.

While we were waiting for the performers to set up, a local kanyeleng group arrived. They started singing and dancing, to the delight and excitement of the assembled crowd (see Figure 6.1). They were dressed in ragged caftans (likely stolen from male family members), and one woman wore a black and white baseball cap jauntily perched atop her bulky braids. Standing in the center, a rotund woman held a dented green bidong (20-liter plastic jerry can) that she played with one stick to set the tempo. The kanyeleng began to sing in Pulaar (the main language in Sibito), and the crowd joined in, clapping their hands in sync with the bidong. One of the women entered the circle to dance, met with shouts of laughter and encouragement. The bidong player placed her instrument on the ground, and the clapping intensified as other dancers entered the circle, jumping high in the air and stamping their feet in the dust, raising their arms to one side and then the other. Women standing in the circle clapped their hands, moving side-to-side along with the dancers, babies bouncing on their backs. Others took out their mobile phones to record the performance to show friends later. It occurred to me

Figure 6.1 Sibito kanyeleng group performing, March 2018, photograph by the author.

that for the kanyeleng group and the Sibito community, this event was about much more than open defecation; it was a celebration, a chance to connect with friends, laugh, sing, and dance.

By the time the visiting musicians were ready to start, it was almost completely dark, and the stars had come out. Speeches from the Ministry staff tactfully reiterated the purpose of the program (to eliminate open defecation) and apologized for their delayed arrival. With his renowned Kaira band, Pabobo performed a Mandinka-language song about open defecation composed specifically for the program in the popular kora mbalax style, combining virtuosic kora playing with the driving rhythms of mbalax. Then ST Brikama Boyo came up on the stage. He performed his insightful, often humorous Mandinka-language rap with Pabobo's band backing him in an impromptu collaboration.

Meanwhile, a journalist was recording the program for broadcast on the national radio and television service. She set up a large floodlight for video recording, which was the only lighting at the event. To capture a variety of footage, she periodically turned the floodlight from the performers on the truck to the crowd with the kanyeleng women and then back again. The kanyeleng were dancing and singing with enthusiasm along with ST Brikama Boyo and Pabobo. Every time the light shone on the kanyeleng, the crowd went wild. They clapped, shouted encouragement, and danced energetically. When the light turned back to the performers on the truck, the crowd quieted down. This happened continuously throughout the performance.

There are a few reasons the crowd may have responded more actively to the kanyeleng than to the visiting musicians. Firstly, the kanyeleng were familiar faces. They lived in Sibito and were well known to the community. This level of familiarity may have made people feel more comfortable and encouraged participation. In the same vein, the visiting performers were singing in Mandinka, a language that many residents of this predominately Fula (Fulbe) village did not speak fluently if at all. The language barrier likely enhanced a sense of unfamiliarity and dampened the level of active participation.

I suggest, however, that the most important influence on the crowd's response had to do with norms of participation. Pabobo and ST Brikama Boyo were excellent, highly skilled musicians who were greatly appreciated by the community, but their performances were more presentational in style. This means that although there was some audience-performer interaction, there was not an expectation that the audience would actively participate in music making, though monetary donations were encouraged. In contrast, the kanyeleng performers expected and demanded participation from the group. As a result, whenever the floodlight shone on the kanyeleng and showed them clapping their hands, singing along, and dancing, the crowd joined in with enthusiasm. When the light moved away from the kanyeleng, the level of audience participation diminished.

The level of participation should not be equated with enjoyment, nor with the quality of the performance. The visiting musicians on the truck were among the most popular in The Gambia, and the audience clearly enjoyed their music. They showed this through smiling faces and nods of appreciation. The difference had to do with expectations regarding participation and interaction. When the kanyeleng were visible, they encouraged the audience to be actively involved in the performance rather than passively listening. This difference is, I suggest, linked to kanyeleng music practices which emphasize embodied participation and have implications for power and action. For the kanyeleng, the event was about more than open defecation; it was a platform for social engagement.

Ethnomusicologists have theorized musical participation as complex, multi-faceted, and context-specific (see Russell and Ingram 2013). My approach to participation here is informed most directly by the work of Thomas Turino (2008), Charles Keil and Steven Feld (1994), and Christopher Small (2011). I discus Mandinka-language concepts here, but many of these have parallels in other local languages (e.g. Pulaar, Wolof) and associated musical practices. Kanyeleng performance is tulungo, a game. It implies interaction, give and take, and perhaps laughter. These features differentiate it from jaliyaa, the art of jali, which is music for listening, serious and virtuosic (McConnell 2017; Knight 1974; Charry 2000). Tulungo can also be differentiated from *musiko*, a term which is often associated with artistry, or *artistyaa* (being an artist), and recorded versions of songs. These distinctions are not absolute. Pabobo's kora mbalax does encourage dancing, and ST Brikama Boyo actively encourages audiences to sing and dance along with him. However, there remains a clear distinction between audiences and performers, and the level of participation tends to be significantly lower than in kanyeleng tulungo events.

Tulungo is participatory music, in which everyone present is expected to be actively involved (Turino 2008). This does not mean everyone does the same thing. In tulungo, there are varied musical roles that accommodate different kinds of participants: song leaders and song holders, handclappers, percussionists, and dancers. In tulungo performances, anyone can lead a song. Call and response enables people to easily join in with a simple, repeated refrain, while more complex text and melodic embellishments can be added by the song leader. If participants are not clapping, kanyeleng admonish them, yelling out *ali buloolu kosi* (clap your hands!).

The Mandinka verb *duu* (to be thick, tense, or heated) is used to describe successful events featuring high energy participation (McConnell 2017). The "thickness" of the crowd of participating bodies also typically corresponds to the "thickness" of the sound (see Turino 2008; Keil 1987). When heterophonic vocal lines and interlocking handclapping patterns are thick and dense, the dancing is sweet (*doŋo ka diyaa*) and may go on for hours. It is as though the excitement and euphoria of sound and movement impels participation. One by one, dancers enter the circle to stamp their feet, lifting their knees and arms high in the air, emerging breathless and smiling. Overcome by the urge to move, dancers push others out of the way as they enter the circle, impatient to have their turn. A shawl thrown around the neck of a friend is a sign of respect and an invitation to enter the circle and dance. Such an invitation should not be refused. This combination of what Turino (2008) calls simultaneous (i.e. singing and clapping together) and sequential (i.e. dancing one by one) participation (see Figure 6.2) produces continual variation and maintains interest and challenge for individual performers.

In kanyeleng tulungo, performers exploit the polyrhythmic feel of dance pieces such as lenjengo and musuba to encourage participation. As is common in

Figure 6.2 Members of the Brikama Nyambai College kanyeleng group dancing, September 2013, photograph by Chris Honeycutt.

African polyrhythmic music, these Mandinka dance pieces feature interlocking two-against-three patterns that are accentuated by handclapping as well as the bidong and calabash parts (see Charry 2000; Knight 1974). The prevalence of two-against-three cross-rhythms can suggest "metrical ambiguity" (Charry 2000: xxvii), but in most cases there is one overriding metrical feel that tends to be based on a four-beat pattern corresponding to the movements of the dancers' feet (e.g. four beats, twelve pulses (often written as 12/8) or four beats, sixteen pulses (often written as 4/4)) (see Polak 2010). On the micro-level, "cyclic variation of subpulse durations" gives a piece such as lenjengo its particular rhythmic feel, as Rainer Polak has demonstrated for Malian jembe drumming (2010: par. 1). In lenjengo performances, the three subpulses within a beat are arranged in a long-short-short pattern (the result of the composite performance as it unfolds over time) (Morford 2019). This pattern is more marked during the slower-tempo opening section of a lenjengo performance, sometimes referred to as the *ngaan-yaa* ("showing pride") section or *lenjengdingo* ("little lenjengo").[5]

Bidong and calabash playing technique is not standardized, but performers share an orientation toward responsivity, adapting their playing to respond to a dancer's moves. Percussionists also vary the tempo of their playing to accommodate the preferences of particular dancers. While the calabash pattern usually stays fairly constant in performances, the bidong part (much like the *sabaro* drum in a *kutiro* ensemble) is continually varied in response to the movements of dancers and according to the style of the individual player. When a dancer enters the circle, the bidong player typically abandons the basic pattern and instead plays sparse, syncopated solo passages to accentuate the dancer's movements. For a percussionist, the ability to encourage dancing and to respond to preferences of particular dancers is more important than virtuosity, though the most skilled performers combine both responsivity and technical brilliance.

To sum up, kanyeleng performances encourage participation through their flexibility and adaptability. Flexibility is evident in the duration of song and dance cycles, which tend to continue for as long as people are participating. If people are dancing, the percussionists match their playing to the tempo and style of the dancer. If no one is interested in dancing, then the percussionists often stop playing the dance rhythm and wait for someone to lead a song. What Turino has called "'feathered' beginnings and endings" (2008: 59) facilitate participation in kanyeleng tulungo, because participants can join in and drop out when they feel like it rather than having to worry about synchronization with others. Flexibility is also evident in instrumentation, with percussionists joining in and dropping out as they like, and instruments improvised with whatever materials are on hand.

Whereas the absence of standardization in kanyeleng performance is sometimes interpreted as a sign of the weakening of tradition or a lack of professionalism, kanyeleng assert that their flexibility is in fact a sign of the strength of their tradition and the power of their performance. For kanyeleng, flexibility and the capacity to facilitate participation – to inspire hands to clap, voices and bodies to move together – is more powerful than virtuosity or a beautiful singing voice. As Sheikh Omar Jallow explained, Niuminding was a terrible singer, but an exceptional composer and social organizer (personal communication, April 25, 2018). Of course, there are many kanyeleng with beautiful voices, like Jainaba Saho whose bell-like, agile voice inspired wonder in listeners. What I mean here is that, like other kinds of participatory music, it is participation rather than abstract, aesthetic beauty that is the point of kanyeleng performance. In the Sibito event described above, the kanyeleng used the gathering as an opportunity for playful social engagement rather than virtuosic displays or didactic messages about open defecation.

So far, my discussion has implied that performances can be easily categorized as either participatory or presentational. In reality, however, most live performances lie along a continuum between fully participatory and fully presentational (Turino 2008: 87). Using participation as a theoretical lens demands not simplistic categorization of music, but rather attention to the diverse contexts and modes of engagement with music as a social practice. In other words, a participation lens breaks apart the notion of a unified thing called "music" and shifts the focus to situated social meanings and questions of power. While these issues of power and meaning are a longstanding concern in ethnomusicological research, they are often not adequately considered in health and development programs involving music.

Kyra Gaunt has suggested that the notion of "participatory discrepancies" should be taken to describe not only the "slightly out of syncness" (Keil and Feld 1994: 96) of musical sounds, but also the friction and inequalities of social participation. Taking my cue from Gaunt, as well as the path-breaking work of Charles Keil and Thomas Turino, among others, I propose that ethnomusicological theories of participation provide a useful lens through which to interpret health performances, attending simultaneously to micro-level dynamics of participation in music, as well as macro-level dynamics of participation in broader discourses and practices of development.

Empowerment and the participation continuum

If participation is the point, then how is this reconciled with the specific communication goals of public health campaigns such as the open defecation program? The answer is that kanyeleng often adapt their performance practice to meet the expectations of health organizations, while simultaneously maintaining an emphasis on the social goals of participation. In some cases, such as the Sibito performance described above, kanyeleng insert their participatory practices within the framework of more presentational events. In other cases, kanyeleng respond to the expectations of health workers by making their performances more presentational as they seek to clearly convey information about a particular health topic (McConnell 2017).

Prior to the 2018 open defecation awareness tour, the Ministry organized a high-profile launching event in Brikama. A performance by the Sanyang kanyeleng group at this Brikama program demonstrates the process of negotiation that often takes places in health promotion contexts as kanyeleng attempt to meet the expectations of health workers and make their performance appealing for listeners not actively involved in music making. The launching event attracted a significant audience from the local area, and the program was also broadcast on national television and radio stations. People were seated on plastic chairs arranged in a C-shaped formation facing the podium where speakers stood as they addressed the crowd. The kanyeleng began their performance in a closed circle (*luwo*) next to the podium. Then one of the women pulled the others back so they were standing in a line and thus more easily visible for the seated audience members. This clearly felt unnatural for some of the members of the group who gradually turned to face the other group members, unconcerned that their backs were facing the audience. The result was a hybrid, semi-circle formation rather than the closed circle typical of kanyeleng community events.

As they have stepped into the arena of health promotion, some kanyeleng have changed their attire as well. Instead of wearing the men's clothing or ragged apparel typically associated with kanyeleng, the Sanyang group wore the matching T-shirts with images of excrement that had been printed specially for the event, along with their kanyeleng beaded hats and necklaces draped over one shoulder. For some groups, new clothing choices reflect kanyeleng efforts to remake their identities and overcome the stigma associated with kanyelengyaa. Groups like the APGWA kanyeleng perform in asobi, matching outfits often tailored specifically for the occasion, in order to provide a visually appealing performance and emphasize their professionalism.

In order to convey their messages about open defecation, the Sanyang kanyeleng group also incorporated elongated saataroo sections in heightened speech. This is a typical strategy that kanyeleng use in health promotion contexts (see McConnell 2017). Saataroo sections give the lead singer a chance to communicate detailed information about a health topic, in this case the importance of good hygiene and sanitation, while maintaining the call-and-response format. Saataroo practices are flexible. While some singers perform short saataroo sections of rapid-fire speech to fit within the song's phrase length, in other cases singers perform lengthy saataroo sections that span multiple phrases or sections of phrases. When the lead singer finishes her saataroo, the rest of the group joins in with the response part.

The changes that kanyeleng have made to their performance style in health promotion contexts have not completely erased the participatory norms of kanyeleng events. In the Sanyang group's performance, there was significant audience participation as people came up to dance, sing, and give monetary donations. As I showed in Chapter 4, kanyeleng compose songs on health topics by adapting existing lenjengo and musuba melodies. Because these melodies are widely known, listeners can quickly join in on the response part. Likewise, because kanyeleng use rhythms like lenjengo and musuba that are strongly associated with community dances, they often inspire listeners to get up and move. The result is a hybrid form that maintains important participatory aspects even as kanyeleng make other features more presentational.

The way musicians such as kanyeleng negotiate participation in the space of performance holds relevance for larger questions of participation, power, and health development. I suggest that participatory kanyeleng performance has the potential to foster empowerment, or more specifically, the stealing and sharing of power. Here, I build on a growing body of scholarship showing that music engagement can be important in overcoming disease-related stigma (Barz and Cohen 2011; Barz 2006; Batt-Rawden, Trythall, and DeNora 2007; Ansdell 2014; McConnell 2015), building positive social determinants of health (Sunderland et al. 2018), disrupting Eurocentric models of communication (Majalia 2011; McConnell 2016), promoting social mobilization to respond to health problems (de Quadros and Dorstewitz 2011; Frishkopf 2017; R. Stone 2017), and engaging with the power structures of global health discourse and funding (Judah Cohen 2011; Reed 2011).

Concern for participation and engagement in music scholarship parallels broader interdisciplinary debates on participation in global health practice. In 1978, the Alma-Ata declaration called for the "full participation" of individuals and communities in health care, working to overcome entrenched disparities in health outcomes worldwide. Since then, participation has become a buzzword in health development programs, as organizations attempt to respond to ongoing critiques of outsider-driven interventions that do harm to indigenous knowledges and lifeways (Obregon and Waisbord 2012; Dutta 2008). The ideas of Paulo Freire have been particularly influential in informing participatory approaches to development, including the theater for development movement which addresses real-world issues faced by community members through participatory performances in which there is no audience-performer distinction (Boal 1979; Harding 1998). In practice, however, so-called "participatory" programs often fail to move beyond the dominant model of top-down, individualist behavior-change communication (Okagbue 1998; Obregon and Waisbord 2012; Morgan 2001). Despite their emphasis on community participation, public health programs frequently exemplify what Freire calls the "banking concept of education," which casts the learner as a passive recipient of information, an empty container to be filled (1973: 72).

Theater for development scholars have shown that many performance-based programs fail to realize their stated participatory goals because they are product-oriented and directed by outside "experts" with specific, predetermined agendas (Plastow 1998; Okagbue 1998). In such programs, participatory performance practices are transformed into hierarchical, presentational forms that do not hold the same potential for community engagement in producing positive social change. This corresponds to a broader problem in international development whereby powerful concepts such as "participation," "community," and "empowerment" are co-opted to serve the interests of political authorities or international donors (Morgan 2001). As ethnomusicologist Kathleen Van Buren argues, although music has the potential to encourage participation and dialogue in development programs, "some performances may be no better than banking systems of education – even if the narrative is wrapped in creative disguise" (2011: 82). In such performances, the learner "is spectator, not re-creator" (Freire 1973: 75). Such programs reflect a behavioralist orientation, where health and development problems are viewed primarily in terms of poor individual choices, disembedded from broader structures of power.

Whereas fully presentational performances involve one-directional communication, participatory performances can open up space for dialogue, speaking back, hearing and being heard. Of course, the thick textures that often characterize participatory performances don't always make it easy to hear, but in that noise, I suggest, is the power of movement, friction, and change. Clarity of messages in presentational performances may mask the undercurrent of alternative views, different ways of singing a melody, or different ways to tell a story (or different stories). Participatory norms of performance make room for those "discrepancies" (Keil 1987), and this is how kanyeleng steal power. While the notion of empowerment implies that the power is being bestowed benevolently from the outside, I use the term stealing power intentionally to suggest that kanyeleng are taking power when it would otherwise be denied them. They are taking power through participation together with others, and through their bodies by wearing clothes they are not supposed to wear, eating food they are not supposed to eat, and stealing the President's underwear. This power is an embodied power, emerging through dance and voice.

To summarize my argument here, health and development programs involving music must be rooted in local perspectives on music making and social norms of participation. If not, they risk being ineffective, or worse, producing unintended negative consequences. Arild Bergh and John Sloboda (2010) discuss such an unintended negative consequence resulting from the work of an international NGO in Sudan. With the goal of empowering performance groups and promoting income generation, the NGO helped performers to purchase resources such as instruments and costumes. A woman from the area explained that,

> Now singing and dancing has become limited to those who are recognized as members of the bands. The rest of the people have been turned into spectators. This has limited the extent of enjoyment of the rest of people as it has become like a stage where they perform and we, the public are the spectators.
> (Quoted in Bergh and Sloboda 2010: 9)

While access to resources and costumes may have benefited the bands involved in this program, the program unwittingly undermined the participatory performance norms in this community. Programs such as this one may have long-term consequences in terms of shifting understandings of who can or should make music and decreasing the overall level of active engagement with music in the community.

I am not suggesting that this has occurred in The Gambia. The country is home to a diverse range of participatory and presentational performance practices, from kanyeleng tulungo to jaliyaa to hip hop. What I do see, however, is inadequate concern for *musical* participation in development programs specifically espousing "participatory approaches." In some cases, kanyeleng may be invited to participate when programs do not have funding to hire a big-name performer like Pabobo or ST Brikama Boyo. The underlying assumption is that fame and resources might result in greater communicative efficacy. If the goal is simply to disseminate a set message as widely as possible through mass media, then this may well be the case. If, however, the goal is to develop dialogue, community engagement, and mobilization, then participatory performance such as kanyeleng tulungo may well be the better choice. Hybrid formats, such as the one kanyeleng have developed for health promotion programs, may also offer the "best of both worlds" in providing a clear message through extended saataroo sections, while also encouraging participation through call-and-response singing, handclapping, and dancing.

Power and social bonding: variations on participation

The notion of a participatory-presentational continuum is helpful in recognizing diversity in the forms and meanings of participation. Participation is not a fixed quality of musical sounds, but rather an emergent, creative process for individuals and groups. While this chapter focuses primarily on kanyeleng performance, recorded music such as the *Teriyaa* album offers opportunities for different kinds of participation and engagement. As discussed in Chapter 3, the album itself was the product of participation and negotiation between various actors, including members of the Allatentu Support Group, donor organizations, musicians, dancers, videographers, and producers. For Fatou and other support group members, *Teriyaa* was an attempt to participate in national discourse and programming on HIV/AIDS, from which they felt largely excluded. Just as kanyeleng used music to steal power, Fatou sang to steal back some of the power of international HIV/AIDS knowledge and funding, with the ultimate goal of empowering people living with HIV. Of course, her message was used in sometimes conflicting ways by supporters of Yahya Jammeh and his AIDS cure, which ultimately undermined her ability to access ART treatment and contributed to her death. Nonetheless, not unlike the way Niuminding Fatty stole power through linking private and public domains, for Fatou as well, her private, embodied experience of disease (expressed through her voice, the most personal of instruments) was a central aspect of her public influence, as well as her vulnerability.

When compared with live tulungo events, recorded music such as the *Teriyaa* album forecloses some forms of participation and opens up others. Audiences engaged with Fatou's *Teriyaa* songs primarily in their recorded form, as they were disseminated on radio, television, and through sales of cassettes, CDs, and DVDs. This does not mean that listening was disembodied from social contexts, however; rather, the social contexts of listening were fragmented and multiplied (see Kjus 2018). The recorded version could be heard in the safe space of the support group, where people with HIV/AIDS could feel comfortable singing and dancing together without being overheard by nosy neighbors. At the same time, the recordings were exchanged through social networks in ways that were more private and individualized, as opposed to the public contexts of live performances in The Gambia, where any passerby may (and often does) join in. In some ways, recorded music is more aligned with a one-directional model of behavior-change communication: recorded songs communicate a set message and do not ask for listeners to speak back. As the *Teriyaa* example shows, however, diversity in the settings and forms of engagement with recorded music can spawn diverse forms of participation.

In the face of the stigma and social rupture associated with infertility, or diseases such as HIV/AIDS and Ebola, musical participation of various kinds can be particularly powerful in rebuilding a sense of social connection and well-being. Gregory Barz's (2006) research with people living with HIV/AIDS in Uganda illustrates that music serves as both communication and therapy, enabling people to overcome stigma and "live positively" with the disease. Similar dynamics are evident in the activities of HIV/AIDS support groups in The Gambia, where actively singing and dancing together to the songs of Fatou and the Allatentu Support Band creates a sense of social belonging. Interestingly, the songs of Ugandan Philly Lutaaya are also frequently played in Gambian HIV/AIDS support groups, demonstrating a transnational exchange of ideas about how to live positively with HIV. Support group members engage with these ideas not just through listening, but also by singing along with songs such as Lutaaya's "Alone and Frightened," creating a sense of shared experience and belonging through a hybrid format combining participation with recorded music (see Turino 2008: 28).

What I am trying to suggest here is a multilayered understanding of music engagement and health, recognizing the importance of social connectedness that emerges through musical and lyrical meanings as well as embodied participation. A performance by the APGWA kanyeleng at the 2013 launching of a polio vaccine campaign will provide further insight into this process. At this event, the kanyeleng performed a song about polio based on a song they frequently sang at community events such as weddings and naming ceremonies. The lyrics to the original song (as performed by the APGWA kanyeleng) included the phrase *ali baading cokoo* (let's join children of the same mother). The song urges people to come together and look after one another like children of the same mother. As the kanyeleng explained, this is a song about baadinyaa that "praises love" (*ka kanu le jamu*). The polio version of the song featured the lyrics *polio ka naa ali ŋa ala ñaato kuntu* (polio is coming, let's stop its progress). By using a familiar melody associated with the theme of baadinyaa, the kanyeleng encouraged listeners to participate and engage with others, and indeed many members of the audience came up to sing and dance along with the APGWA group (see McConnell 2017). I suggest that the impact of kanyeleng performances like this one depends on intersections between musical meanings accumulated over time, such as the memory of a wedding celebration or baby naming, as well as in-the-moment participation and the heightened concentration on the music and on the group (Turino 2008).

Research has demonstrated that participatory music can play a powerful role in creating a sense of social connectedness, or what Turino calls "sonic bonding" (Turino 2008: 3; W. McNeill 1995; Blacking 1977). The lyrical emphasis on caring relationships in the large repertoire of baadinyaa songs corresponds to a feeling of closeness that can emerge when singing, dancing, and playing together with others. As Turino writes, "The signs of this social intimacy are experienced directly – body to body – and thus in the moment are felt to be true" (2008: 3). Again, this feeling is not inherent in the music, but something that is negotiated in the social environment and felt through embodied experience. The gendered dynamics of musical participation along with lyrical emphases on baadinyaa mean that, in the Gambian context, this process of social bonding is often embedded in women-centered networks and forms of power. Kanyeleng steal power not only through voice and lyrics, but also through the body with a stance that says "I belong," a refusal to be small and polite, and an unapologetic presence that is actively engaged with others. Embodied participation in kanyeleng performance is a form of collective imagining, building alternative futures through song and dance (see de Quadros and Dorstewitz 2011).

Conclusion

Attending to the diversity of modes of participation and embodiment in music can inform understandings of social participation and questions of inequality. Even as particular features of musical sound are associated with participatory forms, music engagement is ultimately a process of negotiation between individuals in a group. Complex dynamics of musical participation offer fruitful insight into indigenous models of social engagement in The Gambia that can inform a strengths-based approach to health promotion. Live performances exist on a spectrum between fully presentational forms with complete separation between performers and listeners, and fully participatory forms in which everyone present is actively involved in music making. Furthermore, recorded music opens up possibilities to engage with and share musical sounds in varied ways, whether through singing along with others in a support group, or disseminating the recording in social networks for listening in private. Varied forms of musical participation influence memory construction, emotional responses, and motivation, as I will discuss further in Chapter 7.

In this chapter, I have focused primarily on participation and embodiment in kanyeleng performance, while recognizing the diversity of ways that people engage with music in The Gambia, including recorded music such as *Teriyaa*. I have suggested that it is through embodied participation in performance that kanyeleng steal power and steal health. From a kanyeleng framework, stealing is a responsibility, not a crime: stealing gives health to kanyeleng and their families, and blessings to the victim. In the arena of public health, kanyeleng steal power by challenging the linear, top-down model of health promotion, stretching it sideways and outward to accommodate different kinds of expertise and different forms of knowledge. Kanyeleng ritual knowledge of fertility and the body underlies their song and dance, and their shamelessness makes room for laughter in the space of health expertise.

The depth of kanyeleng power is not often mentioned in the increasingly conservative Muslim context of contemporary Gambia. But the story of Niuminding Fatty's legendary underwear theft opens a window into kanyeleng practices that have long been concerned with power, and of concern to the powerful. Jawara feared Niuminding for her power, obtained through ritual and theft, and tried to contain it through bribery (Sheikh Omar Jallow, personal communication, November 28, 2012). More recently, Yahya Jammeh cultivated the APGWA kanyeleng among his most outspoken supporters. Kanyeleng involvement in health promotion campaigns combines their longstanding roles in political negotiations of power with their ritual knowledge of the body and reproductive health. This is their transformative labor. Together, these aspects of kanyeleng expertise make them much more than mouthpieces, since kanyeleng voice is but one part of an embodied performance practice that demands interaction and involvement from the group. Kanyeleng frameworks of participation and embodiment are just as important as their verbal messages for promoting health in the local context.

Notes

1 The line between fact and fiction is difficult to pin down, particularly when it comes to kanyeleng practices of thieving. However, Niuminding's account of the underwear theft (NCAC and Fatty 2003) was corroborated by other members of her kanyeleng group, and I take it seriously (regardless of its veracity) as a source of insight into kanyeleng systems of knowledge, ritual, and play.

2 According to Sheikh Omar Jallow, during the referendum campaign, Niuminding and others were hospitalized after being injured in a clash with opposition supporters. Jawara did not visit them or provide compensation. This eventually led to a falling out with Jawara, and Niuminding shifted the allegiance of the Banjul kanyeleng to Sherriff Dibba, helping him to establish the National Convention Party in 1975 (Sheikh Omar Jallow, personal communication, April 25, 2018).

3 Not her real name.

4 Exploiting the rich comedic potential of the topic, Kitabu had audiences in stitches with his portrayal of a male authority figure running into the bushes with diarrhea.

5 In his analysis of Malian jembe drumming, Rainer Polak (2010) suggests that the unequal spacing of subpulses is stable and not dependent on tempo. According to my observations, however, lenjengo performances feature much more marked differences in subpulse durations during the slower-tempo opening section sometimes referred to as the *ngaanyaa* ("showing off") section or *lenjeng ndingo* ("little lenjengo").

7 "Touch the drum and they will come"

Music, tradition, and communication

Introduction

Next to the bustling main road in Brikama, members of the Nyambai College kanyeleng group began to sing. They had arrived early at the Regional Health Directorate to work in the compound, demonstrating to Ministry staff both their health knowledge and commitment to cleanliness. Bent over at the waist, the kanyeleng pulled out weeds as they sang about malaria. Jainaba Saho's beautiful voice rang out across the compound, and the rest of the group answered with the response part. Jarra balanced her yellow bidong on a tree stump and began to play, swaying from side to side. The song called on listeners to get rid of standing water, weeds, and rubbish where mosquitoes proliferate. Then, in rhythmic, heightened speech, Jainaba announced:

Kibaaroo meŋ be kayito to	Information that is on paper
Karaŋnaa le be a karaŋna	Educated ones will read it
Meŋ be taa televisiono to	That which is on the television
Tele tiyo le be a je la	Owners of televisions will see it
Meŋ be taa radio buŋo to	That which is on the radio
Radio tiyo le be wo je la	Owners of radios will see that
Bari meŋ be ntolu daa kono	But that which is in our mouths
Dunia bee le be wo je la	The whole world will see that
(September 22, 2013)	

In typically boastful kanyeleng fashion, Jainaba's saataroo proudly articulated the value of her song for communicating with a broad audience. Written information is accessible to educated people, in a country where almost half the population is illiterate. Mass media broadcasts are heard by those with the means to buy televisions and radios. The information in kanyeleng songs, however, is available for the entire world to hear.

Expressed in a hyperbolic kanyeleng style, Jainaba's song nonetheless reflects the reality that for many people, particularly in rural Gambia, musical performance and other kinds of in-person oral communication are the primary means through which they learn new information. Jainaba's saataroo must be understood in relation to the strong sense of exclusion experienced by illiterate women, in particular, who must constantly ask for assistance from others (often their children) to use their mobile phones, to understand English language news, to interpret their child's report card, or to read a doctor's prescription. In the space of kanyeleng song performances, the hierarchies of language and power are turned on their head, as skill with Mandinka-language wisdom, proverbs, and song structures becomes more important than the ability to read or understand English. Through song, women move the construction and communication of knowledge out of the encrypted realm of written words and colonial language, and into the space of public musical expression and social engagement.

As I have argued in Chapter 6, these ways in which musical performance contributes to inclusion and social engagement are not always adequately recognized in public health discourse that reduces diverse forms of musical participation and interaction to a top-down, linear model of message dissemination. In this model, health communication is a one-directional process of conveying information from experts to a target community, and musicians are simply intermediaries. This approach does not sufficiently capture the important role that performers play in promoting participation, negotiating different understandings of health, and integrating new information into local contexts of communication and sociality. Weaving messages about health into the fabric of musical sound, movement, and social interaction, performers are not only conveying information; they are also embodying ideas about healthy living and healthy relations with others. Lacing together major themes from the book, in this chapter I challenge reductionist notions of top-down message dissemination and unchanging tradition and emphasize instead the broader processes of meaning making and social mobilization that take place through music.

Negotiating tradition

In health development discourse, performers involved in health promotion are referred to as "traditional communicators" or "TCs." The concept of traditional communication is part of a broader discourse in international development that reinforces notions of authenticity and monolithic, unchanging cultural tradition. Development discourse portrays tradition alternatively as harmful and regressive, or as a resource to be exploited to achieve development goals. In either case, as Stacy Leigh Pigg writes, "[I]t is development that is mobile and active; 'tradition' is construed as a passive state of repetition" (1995: 49; see also L. Stone 1992). Public health programs in The Gambia reflect these conflicting views of the traditional, with Gambian health workers situated as intermediaries, negotiating between the requirements of international donors and local communities.

The goal of many health promotion programs is to change people's behavior, whether by encouraging hand washing, exclusive breastfeeding (i.e. giving babies only breast milk for the first six months), or the use of sugar-salt solution to treat diarrhea. Many programs are specifically concerned with changing traditions that are seen to contribute to health problems. Prevention messages for diseases such as Ebola target traditional practices such as funeral rites, or communal eating, that can spread the virus. Contrasting with these ideas about traditional culture as a barrier to be overcome, discourse on traditional communication represents culture as a resource that can be exploited in order to accomplish program goals more effectively (L. Stone 1992). In this framework, health workers are charged with differentiating between "good" tradition and "harmful" tradition.[1] This negotiation of tradition is evident in the work of GAMCOTRAP, an organization that is specifically concerned with addressing "traditional practices" affecting the health of women and children. Using songs to communicate messages and promote community engagement is, for GAMCOTRAP, an important means of asserting the enduring value of certain aspects of traditional culture, even as other practices, such as female genital cutting and early marriage, are targeted for elimination.

Neither the demonization nor the glorification of tradition adequately represents the complex relationships that shape the way people engage with diverse forms of health information and care. Female performers are not passive recipients of tradition but rather active agents in building meaning through music, forging relationships with organizations, and asserting new forms of power through participation in health-related events. Examples from kanyeleng and the Allatentu Support Band reveal that the impact of music programs relies not on unchanging tradition, but rather on performers' adaptability and their capacity to engage local communities, make unfamiliar information accessible, and facilitate memory and engagement.

Female performers emphasize their creativity, innovation, and international connections, challenging the dichotomy between tradition and modernity in public health discourse (see Barz 2006: 88). While terms such as "traditional communication" highlight historical continuity, performers more often use language to accentuate their newness and innovation. For example, health workers referred to the Sankalamba group based in Soma as a kanyeleng group, but Sankalamba members themselves explained that they were actually a political group supporting Yahya Jammeh's APRC party, formed by bringing together all the best singers from Soma and surrounding villages. Members of the Mandinaba performance group (Western Region) similarly rejected being characterized as traditional and referred to themselves as *artistoolu* (artists). Associated with professionalism, creativity, and income generation, the term "artist" is used to describe performers who are not defined by traditional roles. While one must be born into a griot family in order to be a griot, anyone – including griots as well as non-griot individuals – may choose to be an artist.

Fatou and the Allatentu Support Band made use of the variety of sounds available in the recording studio as a way to assert a modern and cosmopolitan musical identity. Rather than restricting themselves to traditional acoustic instruments, they liberally added string sounds, marimba, and flute, among other sounds that were available through the MIDI keyboard in the studio. Fatou used extensive autotune to provide the distinctive robotic, modern-sounding vocal quality preferred by many popular musicians in The Gambia. This feature is particularly evident on the song "HIV Be Keering."[2] The music videos for *Teriyaa* similarly employed the extensive special effects and frequent scene changes that characterize many contemporary Gambian music videos. For example, the song "Let Us Fight" includes what appear to be sunrays moving outward across the screen throughout the entire track, as well as several outfit and hairdo changes for Fatou. The videos show Fatou dancing and singing at tourist resorts and beachside locations in the Greater Banjul Area, suggesting a cosmopolitan life of luxury and wealth. While such images are common in Gambian popular music videos, Fatou intentionally chose backdrops suggesting leisure and prosperity in order to challenge dominant associations of HIV/AIDS with poverty, disgrace, and death. Alluring images of hotel swimming pools, reclining chairs, and beach umbrellas, were outside the realm of everyday experience for most Gambians. Rather than emphasizing tradition, Fatou and the band purposefully drew on these exotic images associated with modernity, cosmopolitanism, and leisure, in order to reconfigure HIV positive identities and challenge stigma.

Kanyeleng likewise make choices to accentuate their creativity and innovation, challenging one-dimensional interpretations of tradition and the stigmatized infertile woman. They delight in defying expectations and incorporating alternative musical styles and behaviors in their performances. One performer with the APGWA kanyeleng is known for her skill as a "rapper," and she has even mastered the style and moves of young male hip hop artists, such as the crotch-grab. Nyali consistently has audiences in stitches with her imitation of a popular radio personality's squeaky voice. Others pretend to speak in a language they do not know, such as English or Chinese, for comic effect. In their performances, kanyeleng also incorporate props such as oversized mobile phones, portable radios, and TVs to portray an absurd and amusing image of an "up-to-date," twenty-first-century kanyeleng.

Similarly, while public health discourse emphasizes the rootedness of traditional communicators in local communities, performers themselves often stress their international connections and travel experiences. For example, members of the APGWA kanyeleng group frequently reminded listeners that they were the only Gambian kanyeleng group to have traveled to Europe. In 2003, the group had spent three months in Germany with Binta Jammeh Sidibeh setting up a museum exhibit on Gambian culture. They performed music and dance along with other activities such as cooking, tie-and-dye, and hair braiding. In one of many examples, in a song at a naming ceremony in Talinding, the lead singer performed the following lyrics in saataroo style:

Gambia muumee bee	The whole of Gambia
Maŋ daŋ Gambia damma	Not stopping at Gambia
Afrika muumee bee	The whole of Africa
Kañeleŋolu, ning i be a fo la	Kanyeleng, if you say it
Moolu be ntolu le jiibe la …	People will look to us …
Kabiriŋ Kartong fo Koina	From Kartong to Koina
Kañeleŋolu meŋ si bula pleno kono, a ye taa	Kanyeleng who can enter inside a plane
tubaabuduu	to go to Europe
Wo keta ntolu doroŋ ne	That happened only to us
(May 15, 2013)	

Using the alliterative phrase "from Kartong to Koina," (referring to towns on opposite ends of The Gambia), the song highlighted the unique position of the APGWA kanyeleng, as the only group in the entire country to have traveled to Europe. The kanyeleng then went on to list all the good qualities of the group, including their commitment to their family and elders, that enabled them to achieve this success.

Other performers likewise highlighted their travel experience and international connections. For example, bidong player Kejawo frequently traveled to neighboring countries to perform. Telling people about her international travel served to highlight her status and prestige as a performer. This was particularly important for Kejawo because the bidong, the instrument that she plays professionally, is also widely played by amateurs and children. Kejawo's international travel mostly involved performances at life cycle celebrations such as weddings and naming ceremonies. Other performers underscored international connections that were mediated by development organizations and tourists. The Sankalamba group based in Soma, for example, had worked with ODAM (The Organization of Development Action and Maintenance), an international development organization based in Asturias, Spain, to produce an album of their songs (ODAM was one of GAMCOTRAP's long-standing donor organizations). Similarly, the Brikama Nyambai College kanyeleng group has connections to multiple organizations, including the Child Protection Alliance, the Child Fund, and the Department of Community Development, as well as the Ministry of Health and Social Welfare. Performers are actively engaged in building relationships with various organizations and negotiating their position in relation to international entities and flows of funding.

The low-tech nature of many kanyeleng performances is consistent with development discourse on "authentic" African tradition (Hough 2006). Unlike the Allatentu Support Band and other popular ensembles that use electric instruments and amplification, kanyeleng performers typically use only a megaphone to amplify their volume. The association of traditional communication with low-tech forms underscores the dichotomy between the "traditional" and the "modern" that permeates development discourse (Pigg 1995: 49; Hough 2006). Furthermore, terminology such as "traditional communication" may actually undermine efforts to include local perspectives by "effac[ing] the differences among localities with a blanket concept of 'the traditional'" (Pigg 1995: 49). Rather than applying "traditional" as a blanket term to signify a globally recognized form of cultural appropriateness, it is necessary to consider the complexity of particular performance practices, performers, and their positions in society.[3] Low-tech forms are not inherently culturally appropriate in African contexts, and different groups within a single society have different preferences and musical tastes.

Incorporating a variety of styles and formats (e.g. radio, live performance, popular music, and kanyeleng groups) can enable health organizations to accommodate differences in preferences shaped by gender, age, ethnicity, or individual predilections. Performers such as kanyeleng as well as Fatou and the Allatentu Support Band have been effective in health promotion programs because of their ability to creatively integrate different forms of knowledge about health and healing, and different ways of engaging their listeners. In other words, it is performers' adaptability, rather than their attachment to tradition, that enables them to effectively disseminate health information and promote community engagement and understanding.

As I have demonstrated in previous chapters, gendered understandings of music and health also shape what is said and how it is heard in music performance contexts. The perception that both musical performance and family health are women's concerns continues to limit the number of men who engage with health-related performances. Staff from the Ministry of Health and Social Welfare and the Allatentu Support Group suggested that radio was often more effective than live performance in targeting men because "to call them together sometimes is ... a very big challenge" (Buba Darboe, personal communication, June 24, 2013). The Ministry uses radio frequently in health promotion programs, and many community radio stations have weekly "health talks" delivered by the Regional Health Education and Promotion Officers. The Allatentu Support Group also does radio programs on occasion, which are focused on HIV/AIDS awareness and incorporate tracks from the *Teriyaa* album as an educational tool to reach out to men specifically. Gendered dynamics of music engagement and participation must be considered by health organizations in order to move away from a narrow focus on women and reductive interpretations of traditional communication.

Gambian health workers and performers are uniquely situated to negotiate between dominant paradigms of communication in global health practice, and local understandings of gender, participation, and living tradition. Many of the most successful initiatives involving musicians, such as the 2015 Ebola prevention campaign (see McConnell and Darboe 2017), were the result of creative thinking on the part of Gambian health workers with knowledge of both public health practices and deeply rooted, adaptable practices of musical communication. By prioritizing performance as a powerful mode of community mobilization and information dissemination, the Directorate of Health Promotion (the "public face" of the Ministry) has developed a strong positive reputation, even when they address issues that are controversial and challenging.

Health performances in The Gambia are the product of multi-layered negotiations between international organizations and funding bodies, national level policy makers, local health workers, and performers of various kinds. Kim Yi Dionne has demonstrated that global health interventions fail when the priorities of the various actors and institutions involved are "misaligned" (2017: 4). Representations of target communities as passive victims, rather than active agents in seeking health, normalizes the disconnect between program planning and prioritization, which takes place externally, and program implementation, which is conducted by local agents. I suggest that a similar dynamic is evident in the way traditional culture is represented in public health discourse as static and passive, as something which may be used by external agents in narrowly defined ways, either instrumentalized in the service of biomedical discourse, or demonized and targeted for eradication. What is evident in the Gambian case is that traditional culture (*coosaanoo*) is understood as active, living, and changing, and musicians are likewise inventive actors engaging meaningfully with health workers to promote well-being in their communities. The creativity of these local health workers and performers must be engaged in program planning as well as implementation in order to avoid the problems outlined by Dionne (2017) and build effective, strengths-based interventions for health. In the following sections, I will unpack some of the components of such a strengths-based approach, including the importance of community involvement, translation, emotional engagement, and memory making.

Community engagement

A combination of different program formats (e.g. live performance and radio) may well be the best strategy to engage meaningfully with diverse populations. At the same time, health workers suggested that performers who are based in rural communities tend to be more influential over the long-term than outsiders who arrive for a short health education program and then leave (see Majalia 2011). A health worker from the Central River Region explained that TCs (usually kanyeleng) were effective because "They stay together with those community members. They know each other! ... Whatever they tell them, they tend to take it [more] seriously ... than a stranger coming trying to teach them" (personal communication, July 1, 2013). Performers such as kanyeleng who are part of the target community may be more accepted than outsiders, and they also have more opportunities to disseminate information. In this sense, kanyeleng can have an advantage over popular music groups that perform for an hour or two and then depart, even though big name performers may attract a larger audience to a specific event. This depends, of course, upon the status and social position of particular performers. Jaliba Kuyateh, for example, is highly respected throughout The Gambia both for his musical abilities and his personal integrity. Programs featuring Jaliba, such as the Allatentu Support Band remix project, typically attract a large audience and listeners do not necessarily see Jaliba as a stranger.[4]

Communicating health information through songs also requires that performers translate biomedical language into language that is more comprehensible to lay people. Buba Darboe from the Directorate of Health Promotion and Education observed that when health workers give talks, they often use technical language and English-language terms that are not widely understood by the general population. He explained, "To translate that language into your local language becomes difficult. People will not get what you are saying. ... They listen more to the TCs [traditional communicators] than us. ... They are the first line of communication" (Buba Darboe, personal communication, June 24, 2013). Using music, performers engage in a process of translation to make biomedical information locally accessible. This translation occurs in the words used to describe health topics (i.e. explaining English language concepts in local languages) as well as in the medium of communication itself. Women attending the Reproductive and Child Health clinics can feel alienated by the lecture format and formal language used by health professionals. Musical performances offer a more engaging and polyvocal medium of communication that makes people feel comfortable and provides the space (or license) necessary to hear and be heard. As ethnomusicologist Jennifer Kyker suggests, "[T]he tensions between music's multivalent, inarticulable qualities and the digestible, fact-based orientation of public health work can be richly productive, inviting audiences to hear different forms of discourse in relation to each other" (2016: 192). When music encourages active participation, it can also break down audience-performer divisions and one-way communication, facilitating the collective construction of health knowledge, hearing and being heard.

This process of translation was evident in the Brikama Nyambai College kanyeleng group's song about malaria performed at the Regional Health Directorate in 2013. In this song, Jainaba Saho translated the "immune system" as *balajata soojaroo meŋ si malaria kele* (the body soldiers that can fight malaria):[5]

Dindiŋo, niŋ malaria ye a muta ...	A child, when malaria infects them ...
Ala balajata soojaroo meŋ si malaria kele, wo buka meŋ	Their body soldiers that can fight malaria, they are not developed
Wo le ye a tinna, a ke kuu dindiŋo la baake, kaari fula ka taa sanji luulo kaŋ.	That is why, be very careful, a child from two months to five years
(September 22, 2013)	

Jainaba discussed the immune system, in terms that are understandable to a Mandinka-speaking listener, in order to underscore the particular risk that malaria holds for children under five. In combination with the engaging and familiar form of Mandinka tulungo performance, this message can be more accessible for people unfamiliar with the language and communication forms typically used by educated health professionals.

Another example that demonstrates the translation of biomedical concepts in performance is a song about breastfeeding that was performed by multiple groups throughout the Western Region. In September 2013, I attended a performance in Kembujeh, the village where I had lived seven years earlier. At the time, I had known Nyima Cham,[6] Kembujeh's village health worker and jalimusoo, for over seven years, and she continually impressed me with the depth of her knowledge and warm-heartedness. In a performance under the mango trees in her compound, Nyima led a song about the importance of colostrum, or first breast milk:

Ali ŋa taa karaŋo la	Let's go learn
Karaŋo le mu londoo ti	Learning is knowledge
Sunjunonoo folo mu boroo le ti	Colostrum is medicine
Niŋ i ye a je n ka fo sunjunono folo mu boroo le ti	If you see we say colostrum is medicine
Sunjunono folo mu dindiŋo la penku folo folo folo	Colostrum is a child's very first vaccination
(September 13, 2013)	

In The Gambia, colostrum is widely viewed as dirty, and many mothers do not feed it to their newborn babies. Nyima Cham used the Mandinka term *sunjunonoo folo* (first breast milk) to describe colostrum. She emphasized the beneficial properties of colostrum by referring to it as *booroo* (medicine). Then she further highlighted the protection that colostrum offers for the immune system by describing it as *dindiŋo la penku folo folo folo* (a child's very first vaccination/injection). Like vaccinations, colostrum protects babies against disease by giving them antibodies from their mothers. Nyima also chose to make the comparison between colostrum and vaccination because vaccinations, and injections more generally, tend to be widely accepted in The Gambia. In fact, many people prefer to receive injections rather than orally administered medications because they believe that they are more efficacious.

Songs such as these reflect a process of translating and localizing health knowledge, embedding new information within existing modes of understanding and relating (Barz 2006: 146; Bingley 2011). This is an example of what Mark Davidheiser describes as "ritualization, using accepted social institutions to make social changes more comprehensible and palatable by incorporating them into shared cognitive frameworks" (2006: 853). Music performance contexts in The Gambia provide an accepted social institution through which participants can communicate, negotiate disparate understandings of health and healing, and enact change.

The process of embedding new information within existing musical forms and practices is evident in GAMCOTRAP's and APGWA's work on the contentious topic of female genital cutting (*nyaka*), which is addressed both as a health issue and a human rights issue (Hernlund 2003; Hernlund and Shell-Duncan 2007). Nyaka was made illegal in The Gambia in 2015, but it is an ongoing topic of debate and controversy. Many Gambians value the nyaka ritual not only as a rite of passage that enables a Mandinka girl to achieve womanhood, but also for the depth of cultural and musical information embedded in the ritual.[7] Movements to eradicate nyaka can be threatening because nyaka is seen as an integral part of what it means to be a Mandinka woman. Undergoing nyaka gives women respect and social capital, enabling them to participate fully in women-centered networks (Shell-Duncan et al. 2011). With the prohibition on female genital cutting, women express concern about the loss of traditional gendered knowledge and women's social capital associated with nyaka. In an attempt to respond to these concerns, GAMCOTRAP and APGWA have embedded their programs in women's networks and women's music making. Both organizations have been involved in programs to maintain aspects of coming-of-age ritual, while eliminating the cutting. Such programs can be valuable in sustaining social networks, cultural knowledge, and musical performance practices, challenging the idea that abandoning nyaka means abandoning one's cultural identity (Shell-Duncan and Hernlund 2000).

The case of GAMCOTRAP also illustrates the politicization of debates about women's rights and women's health in The Gambia under Yahya Jammeh. During his presidency, Jammeh found GAMCOTRAP's work extremely threatening. Jammeh's regime targeted GAMCOTRAP staff, with two staff members detained and subject to a prolonged, politically-motivated lawsuit. GAMCOTRAP staff were threatening to Jammeh primarily because of their strong relationships with rural women groups, built through sustained engagement over time. Jammeh's fear of GAMCOTRAP's political power was not entirely unfounded. In 2016, Dr. Isatou Touray became The Gambia's first female candidate for president, before eventually withdrawing in support of Adama Barrow, the Coalition candidate who went on to defeat Yahya Jammeh in the presidential election. In 2019, she was appointed as Vice President.

Musical performance has formed an essential component of GAMCOTRAP's community engagement strategy that has provided a platform for social and political change. For example, performers working with GAMCOTRAP have used the repertoire of songs associated with nyaka as a form of transformative labor, telling new stories to maintain a sense of continuity even while working for social change. The Sankalamba group based in Soma recorded an album with new versions of nyaka songs, keeping aspects of the gendered knowledge associated with nyaka while rejecting cutting. One of the members of the Sankalamba group explained that even though her daughters have not been cut, they know the specialized song repertoire associated with female initiation. I observed the powerful impact of this approach during one of GAMCOTRAP's training programs in the Central River Region in 2013. GAMCOTRAP staff played new versions of nyaka songs recorded by the Sankalamba group. All the participants in the training program got up to dance and sing along with the recording. The participants then made up their own songs, using familiar melodies to tell their own stories. This experience was the most powerful and engaging part of the event for many of the participants. Singing and dancing together created a supportive environment that enabled people to open up, participate, hear and be heard.

Health workers described the process of message development and translation as one of collaboration between health educators with expertise in health information and performers with expertise in music, dance, and drama. A Regional Health Education and Promotion Officer from western Gambia explained that particular health units and departments came up with the key messages that were conveyed to performers, who then used their own creativity to bring those messages to life in songs and drama. She said, "You can use the same script, but the way they will act it in Fonye will be different from the way it will be acted in Busumbara. ... The cultural aspect of entertainment we leave to their side" (personal communication, January 15, 2013). This illustrates the collaborative nature of the partnership: While health workers contribute bioscientific knowledge about health topics, performers bring their own creativity and expertise in expressive forms that make the communication process work.

The process of bringing the "same message" to diverse populations is, of course, not always straightforward (F. McNeill 2011). Close attention to local understandings of health, healing, and illness is necessary to minimize misunderstanding and conflict in the process of knowledge translation and communication. One example of such misunderstanding results from the translation of the medical terms "hypertension" and "anemia." In Mandinka, these terms are translated as *yeleseloo* (high blood) and *yelejiyoo* (low blood), respectively.[8] The result of the translation and intersection of different medical models is that many Mandinka speakers logically conceive of "high blood" and "low blood" as being mutually exclusive conditions on opposite ends of a continuum (i.e. you cannot suffer from both anemia and hypertension at the same time). It is widely known that individuals suffering from "low blood" (which is widespread among Gambian women) should eat leafy greens (*jamboolu*) because it will help "increase" their blood. Unfortunately, many people suffering from "high blood" intentionally avoid eating leafy greens because they do not want to "increase" their blood further, even though green vegetables are in fact a healthy choice for those with hypertension.

While some health workers with whom I spoke were aware of this issue, I heard others advising patients with hypertension to avoid leafy greens. The process of integrating and translating complex medical knowledges is fraught with difficulty and opportunities for misinformation. Rather than a simple process of translation, health communication work might more accurately be thought of as a multidimensional process of integrating unfamiliar biomedical information into local understandings of health and healing.

Dissemination and memory

Performers and health workers consistently underscored the ability of music, and songs specifically, to reach more people than other communication methods. This is linked to the features of performative license and social contexts of participation as elaborated in previous chapters. Musical sounds serve to call people to an event even if they have not been informed in advance, while also attracting people who would not necessarily attend a lecture-only event (see Barz 2006; Van Buren 2010). When I visited the Taibatou Health Center in the Upper River Region, members of the local kanyeleng group told me:

> First first, if you need people … if you just touch this [drum], they will come. When they come … they will focus their eyes, they will focus their ears. … The way performance and health are related … some mothers can go for two, three months without coming to the nurse here. But if you call kanyeleng here, if you call the drums here, you will see. All the mothers in the village will answer you here. … Kanyeleng can give information, the nurses can give their information, while it was the drums that called them here.

> *Folo folo, niŋ i be sulaariŋ moolu la … niŋ i ye ñiŋ maa doroŋ, i be naa la le. Niŋ i naata … wo be a ñaa le loo la, a be a tuloo le loo la.… Tuluŋo aniŋ jaatakendeya ye ñoo soto daameŋ. … Dimbaa doo si taa fo kaari fula, kaari saba, i maŋ naa noosi jaŋ. Bari niŋ i ye kañeleŋolu kili jaŋ, niŋ i ye tantaŋo kumandi jaŋ, i be a je la, ñiŋ saate dimba bee be i danku la jaŋ. … Kañeleŋolu si kibaaroo dii noo, ila noosoolu si ila kibaaroo dii ila, i si a tara tantaŋo le ye i kili naŋ.*

> (Taibatou/ Kerewan kanyeleng group member, personal
> communication, July 3, 2013)

I witnessed this in action on numerous occasions, including during the 2018 open defecation awareness tour run by the Ministry of Health and Social Welfare (discussed in Chapter 6). During the tour, the sounds of musical performance served to attract and engage large numbers of residents from the surrounding neighborhoods. Even when music does not in itself carry a verbal message about health, it can facilitate health promotion by bringing people together to participate and engage in dialogue (see also Bingley 2011; Barz 2006).

Music can also facilitate information dissemination because when people learn songs at an event, they may continue to sing them in other contexts. In May 2013, I visited the beautiful village of Genieri in the Lower River Region and met with four members of the Genieri Suusundi Timmaring Group dedicated to promoting exclusive breastfeeding. This lively group included both kanyeleng and non-kanyeleng performers who were known for being particularly effective and proactive in their efforts to improve the health of young children in Genieri and surrounding villages. The four group members with whom I spoke asserted that they had seen a reduction in the number of infant deaths as a result of their work.[9] They explained that the influence of their songs was not confined to the original performance contexts because people continued to sing them in other settings. One group member explained that children, in particular, spread the songs beyond their original performance: "When you sing a song ... this child, what we sang, if they are playing with another child, they will be singing it. That makes dissemination easy" (*Ñiŋ tuluŋo, niŋ i be a kaŋ, niŋ i ye denkiloo laa ... dindiŋo ñiŋ, ŋa meŋ laa. ... Niŋ a niŋ dindiŋ doo be feeyaa la, a be tara la a laa kaŋ. Janjandiroo ka soneyaa wo le kono*) (Personal communication, May 4, 2013).

Performers also incorporate information about health in their songs at other community events such as naming ceremonies and weddings. In an interview in his office in Kotu, Momat Jallow, then Program Manager for Health Communication at the Ministry, explained:

> Whenever there are occasions where people gather, they will come and sing those songs, putting the message in. So people will be entertained, at the same time they will receive the health message. And this can be done in various ways, like in naming ceremonies. ... Also, like whenever they have farming sessions ... So during the weeding time also, they will go with the whole village, and when they are weeding the farms, they are also singing and then putting those health messages inside. And definitely, at the end of the day, even small kids in the village will be able to sing those songs, and we think that by singing those songs they can be transformed into actions.
>
> (Momat Jallow, personal communication, January 31, 2013)

The performance of songs about health in all kinds of community meeting places demonstrates the extent to which health workers and performers have worked to incorporate health promotion within established communication contexts and social relations. Performing at regular meeting places such as farms and markets enables performers to reach more listeners than they would otherwise; they also build on social dynamics of baadinyaa and sanawuyaa that can provide the positive relationality necessary for effective communication.

The members of the Genieri Suusundi Timmaring Group worked closely with Saharu Kante, then Regional Health Education and Promotion Officer for the Lower River Region, who similarly emphasized the role that children play in disseminating information through song. Kante felt that musical performance was a particularly effective means of teaching children, who were the future leaders of the community:

> The kids will also pick it up, you know, even going to the market, going to the stream, you know, they will be singing along ... It makes it stick. And as you know, behavioral change has steps, you understand, so if you believe in something for a long time, you find it difficult to change. But when we target the kids, so the kids will take these songs and then be singing, and it sticks! So if we, at least, if we cannot make those people change, the kids, the kids can change, and then they will grow up with that positive behavior.
>
> (Saharu Kante, Regional Health Education and Promotion
> Officer, personal communication, June 5, 2013)

Kante's perspective here is in some ways aligned with global health discourse that represents adult individuals as responsible for the spread of disease, and children as innocent victims in need of care (see Fassin 2013). In this case, Kante asserts the value of traditional communicators for children specifically, because they particularly enjoy singing songs in their everyday play. The role of community-based, multigenerational performances in facilitating information dissemination has broad relevance, however, and it was emphasized by performers and health workers alike. Music has the "ability to trigger memory" and make a message "stick" (Barz 2011: 28; see also de Quadros and Dorstewitz 2011). Even when people do not attend the event where a song is originally performed, they may hear the song and the message it contains, because others learn the song and continue to sing it.

Characteristics such as call-and-response, repetition, and the use of short phrases, can facilitate participation and communication (Alagoa 1968; Bekalu and Eggermont 2014; Bingley 2011; Turino 2000; Van Buren 2006). Particularly when communicating orally to a large group, repetition is necessary because not everyone will hear the words on the first utterance (Ong 1982: 40). In addition, as discussed in Chapter 6, by using musuba and lenjengo melodies that are already familiar, kanyeleng performers facilitate the participation of the people present at health events. Listeners are able to quickly join in and sing the response part to songs about health topics, which helps them to remember the information better (Bekalu and Eggermont 2014; Bingley 2011).

A former staff member of the Gambia Family Planning Association (GFPA) described a communication failure that serves to illustrate the effectiveness of song in rapidly disseminating information. She explained that without thorough training and collaboration between performers and health workers, the information conveyed through musical performance can be superficial or even incorrect. GFPA wanted to promote contraception, but one of the singers they were working with performed a song stating that they conducted abortions, which was (and remains) illegal in The Gambia:

> This woman thought she was doing very good for Family Planning, and she composed a song that says, "There was a girl who got pregnant, she went to family planning. They did an abortion for her and she was the same with all other girls" [*sunkutudoo le konomaata, a baa ye a samba family planning, ye ala harjee tiñaa, i ye a niŋ doolu kañandi*]. ... Then people started singing that song and it went out like wildfire. Family Planning has to go back to correct that message. "No, we don't do abortion." You know, so it can be very dangerous. ... You have to train them.
>
> (Personal communication, August 6, 2013)

Because it was expressed in a catchy song, the incorrect information spread much farther than it might have otherwise, to the consternation of GFPA staff. This cautionary tale shows that in their work as communicators, performers require resources and training. More than just mouthpieces to promote predetermined messages, performers should be thoroughly involved in program development and implementation.

Music, emotion, and integration

Examples throughout this book have demonstrated that performers promote understanding by embedding new and sensitive information in familiar song forms. Maintaining well-known themes also adds important contextual meaning to songs. As discussed in Chapter 5, by preserving an emphasis on love, care, and baadinyaa, performers make new information meaningful in relational terms. In contrast to health education messages that emphasize individual behavior change and health outcomes, women's songs articulate a relational perspective on health as a collective concern and responsibility.

These social and relational meanings in performance events are closely linked to mood, and the way people respond emotionally to music (McConnell 2015). Health workers and performers were very much aware of the way in which participants' mood and energy level shapes the success of a health event. In lengthy training programs, people often become tired, bored, and lose concentration. A communication expert from The Gambia Women's Bureau explained,

> When you continue to talk without having something to give people [an] energizer, you go up to a point, the audience start to drop. The concentration is dropping. But after a session you beat the instrument, entertain them for some time, raise their energy up, and you continue your discussions again.
>
> (Personal communication, November 21, 2012)

Musical performance can energize participants by inspiring positive emotional responses, and encouraging participation and social interaction through singing, dancing, and handclapping.

Particularly for people who have not been to school, the formal context of a health education event can feel foreign and unnatural. Incorporating familiar performance styles into the event can help participants to feel a sense of belonging in an unfamiliar environment. Amie Bojang from GAMCOTRAP explained, "Songs are very powerful and important in the work we are doing. ... Even when the place is tense and the discussion, once a song comes in, everybody goes back to be calm, listen and then engage" (personal communication, January 17, 2013). By using musical performance, health workers and performers facilitate comprehension by decreasing tension in the group and making participants feel comfortable (see also Barz 2006: 61).

Music participation played an important role during the West African Ebola epidemic in 2014–2016. The climate of fear surrounding the disease contributed to social conflicts and emotional distress, while undermining the mechanisms of care and support that people would normally employ in such crises (Leach 2015). As discussed in Chapter 5, because Ebola is spread through contact with bodily fluids, people were not able to express care and support for each other through touch as they normally would. In her research on the Ebola epidemic in Liberia, Ruth Stone found that "songs and sound created together formed safe ways to bridge the physical and emotional space between people" (2017: 89). While Ebola enforced physical distance between people, music created a sense of connection and closeness in the absence of touch. The case of Ebola throws into sharp relief the importance of the way musical participation can enable people to overcome the social distance created by fear and stigma.

In The Gambia, performers often described the connection between music and emotions with reference to the *sondomoo*. The term sondomoo is difficult to translate because it refers not to the physical heart, but rather to the emotional heart, mind, or whole being. Performers explained that music has a powerful effect on the sondomoo and can therefore transform the listener's emotional state. Elsewhere, I have discussed the sondomoo in relation to emotional flexibility, drawing on the work of ethnomusicologist Benjamin Koen (McConnell 2015; Koen 2005, 2006, 2008). The sondomoo is also relevant for understanding performative license, and music's influence on memory and emotion. That is, the emotional content of music can give license to hear, and ultimately to understand and remember. For example, Mariama (a member of the Allatentu Support Group discussed in Chapter 4) told me that she used to listen to people talk about HIV/AIDS, and the information would "enter here [the ear] and exit here [the other ear]" (*a ye duŋ jaŋ, a ye funti jaŋ*). She said that, in contrast, when she listened to the *Teriyaa* songs, the information entered the sondomoo. The involvement of the sondomoo here suggests an emotional engagement with the material as well as longer-term memory.

Metta, the eloquent leader of the Dobong Kunda kanyeleng, discussed the sondomoo in relation to the broader social and emotional impact of performance (tulungo). She said,

> The benefit that tulungo has for health, when you meet here [together], the words that you say to each other that are important, the advice that the singers give, everyone can put that in their sondomoo. When they go, they know how they will proceed.
>
> *A ye nafaa meŋ soto jaatakendeyaa bunda ye, niŋ ali benta jaŋ ali ka kuma le fo ñoo la meŋ i ye a long ko i importanta le. Denkililaalaalu ka yamaroo meŋ dii, moo bee si a bula noo i sondomo kono. Niŋ i taata i ka loŋ ne ko, i be taama la ñaameŋ .*
>
> (Metta, personal communication, July 1, 2013).

As Metta suggests, performances can facilitate interpersonal connections as well as the social construction of knowledge. Rather than being passive recipients of facts, people choose what they want to remember in their sondomoo based on whether they believe that information has benefit for them and those close to them.

I discussed memory and the role of the sondomoo with Nyali from the APGWA kanyeleng. To help me to grasp these concepts, Nyali underscored the difference between hearing and understanding information and eating food. Whereas food is eaten with the mouth and goes directly to the stomach, Nyali specified that words "are not eaten, they are heard." Pointing at her ears and then her heart, she explained that words are heard with the ears, but people must choose "that which is good" to keep in the sondomoo (personal communication, July 17, 2013). Information that has no benefit should be thrown away. It is not worth keeping. Only the information that has value should be saved and shared with family and friends. Nyali presented a view of communication and memory as physical processes involving particular parts of the body, including the ears and the sondomoo. Unlike eating, which involves a straightforward passage from the mouth to the stomach, information does not directly travel from the ears to the sondomoo; it is only remembered in the sondomoo if it appears to be worthwhile and meaningful.

Nyali's explanation raises a question: what makes people see particular kinds of knowledge as beneficial? My view is that people must be able to incorporate new knowledge into their existing worldview and framework for understanding health and illness. Information that does not resonate with an individual's understanding of the world will not settle in the sondomoo. As Nyali suggested, this information will stop at the ears. Musical performance can play an important role here. By integrating physical, emotional, social, and intellectual aspects of experience, musical performance can help information to settle in the sondomoo. Furthermore, beyond the specific contexts of health communication, the ways in which people discuss the sondomoo in relation to emotion and memory points to the deeper significance of music as a site of public healing and collective memory making.

Conclusion

The involvement of local performance groups in health communication activities provides an important counterbalance to the "outside expert" model that continues to be the norm in many health programs (Barz 2006; Bingley 2011; Majalia 2011). According to this model, health problems stem from local ignorance and passivity, and health professionals alone possess the knowledge and expertise to improve health outcomes. The strengths-based approach flips this around, recognizing the importance of indigenous knowledge and capabilities in inspiring positive change. In other words, efforts to achieve social justice and health equity must be grounded in local experience and creativity (Sunderland et al. 2018), rather than "one-size fits-all" approaches that may actually undermine indigenous knowledges and ways of being.

More than just textual messages, musical performances bring to health promotion contexts particular associations and models for social interaction and expression. Songs carry with them emotional and social content that, along with stylistic features of the music, bring people together, promote communication, and encourage memory and engagement. The term "traditional communication" is often used in development discourse to reference low-tech forms of performance associated with notions of authentic, unchanging African tradition. Similarly, performers are portrayed as mouthpieces who disseminate information received from health experts. In this chapter I have argued, however, that innovation and adaptability are defining features of women's performances. More than any particular musical characteristic, female performers' flexibility makes them particularly suited to engaging with contemporary health challenges in The Gambia. A strengths-based approach must recognize performers as partners in the communication process who do much more than convey facts. The influence of musical performance is contingent upon the extent to which performers facilitate local participation, emotional engagement, and the integration of new information into existing worldviews.

Notes

1 In her discussion of female genital cutting in The Gambia, Ylva Hernlund (2003) uses the term "winnowing culture" to describe this process of differentiating between "good" and "bad" forms of traditional culture.
2 This song is Track 4 on the website: www.routledge.com/9780367312725.
3 In research in South Africa, Fraser McNeill (2011) highlights related disconnects between notions of tradition in peer education programs featuring young women performers, and demarcations of traditional knowledge and ritual authority based on age and gender.
4 In his study of popular music and health promotion in Liberia, Michael Frishkopf (2017) argues that celebrity role models are particularly persuasive in inspiring change in health promoting behavior.
5 The recording of this song is Track 7 on the website: www.routledge.com/9780367 312725.
6 Jalimusoo Nyima Cham's participation in the activities of the Kembujeh women's group, comprised primarily of kanyeleng women, demonstrates the limitations of the

idea that tulungo and jaliyaa are completely separate areas of musical expression; in many cases, jalimusoolu participate in performances alongside kanyeleng and other non-jali performers.

7 Some Gambians are also concerned about the move away from coming-of-age ceremonies, and a growth in cutting without ritual. The work of Ylva Hernlund and Bettina Shell-Duncan offers insight into the complex politics of the movement to eliminate female genital cutting in The Gambia and the challenges involved in implementing a ritual without cutting (Hernlund 2003; Hernlund and Shell-Duncan 2007; Shell-Duncan and Hernlund 2000; Shell-Duncan et al. 2011).

8 Mandinka concepts of "low blood" and "high blood" bear some similarities to the concepts used by southerners in the United States, as described by LF Snow (1974).

9 The Regional Health Directorate did not have sufficient data to confirm the group's assertion regarding infant deaths.

8　Beginnings and endings

Introduction

The APGWA kanyeleng took out their clapping sticks and sang louder in an attempt to drown out the sounds of saxophone and Jola *bugarabu* rhythms coming from the other side of the square. The Ministry of Health and Social Welfare had invited them to perform for the August 2013 launching of the new rotavirus vaccine program, which aimed to reduce cases of diarrheal disease, a leading cause of death for children under five. The sky was overcast and the ground was still muddy from the last night's rain. Undeterred, the kanyeleng danced in the mud and sang out in praise of the important guests who had begun to arrive one by one (see Figure 8.1). Their songs inspired well-dressed women (the recipients of praises) to carefully step through the mud in their high heeled shoes in order to reciprocate with monetary donations, dancing with the kanyeleng as they waved their money in the air.

The event had an air of festivity, but the organizers from the Ministry were worried. The invited speakers were late and rain was starting to fall. As it turned into a downpour, the organizers decided to move the event inside, even though the venue was not large enough to comfortably accommodate the large gathering. People crowded in and struggled to find seats in the humid hall as the organizers hastily moved their equipment inside. The official proceedings began with prayers, which were followed by a series of lengthy speeches in English. When the speakers had finished, a brief summary was provided in Mandinka and Wolof. Then the Chairperson announced that the next item on the schedule was supposed to be a performance from the kanyeleng group. She said, "I think we can skip that." Because the event had started late, the group would not get to perform. The kanyeleng were disappointed. They had prepared a song about rotavirus especially for the occasion, and now they would never get to sing it.

I was reminded of the rotavirus event in December of 2018 when I attended an event marking World AIDS Day in Pirang with Ministry staff. As we drove up, I heard the sound of a police whistle and immediately spotted the Pirang kanyeleng group entertaining the waiting crowd under the mango tree next to the mosque. The program began as usual with speeches from Ministry staff and local government officials, followed by a moving testimony from a member of the Allatentu

Figure 8.1 Kejawo Juwara performing at the rotavirus vaccine launching event with other members of the APGWA kanyeleng group, August 2013, photograph by the author.

Support Group for people living with HIV/AIDS. When the kanyeleng were invited to perform, the emcee announced that they would have to be brief because the program was behind schedule and a crowd was already waiting at the next event site in Brikama. The kanyeleng moved into the circle and began their song. After just two minutes, the emcee returned and tried to take the microphone from them. The kanyeleng refused to relinquish the microphone, instead launching into their second song. After another three minutes had passed, the emcee again returned to try to cut them off. The kanyeleng protested that they were not yet finished, but eventually they relinquished the microphone and went to sit down.

The rotavirus vaccine launching and the World AIDS Day event illustrate two important aspects of women's involvement in health performances. Firstly, while this book has shown that female performers play an important role in promoting community engagement with sensitive health topics, their power and influence are often cut short and incomplete. Health events involve tension and negotiation around whose voices should be prioritized, and women's songs are sometimes interrupted or cut out completely. If performative license is about the freedom to hear and be heard, then that freedom is not guaranteed; it is sometimes curtailed or accessed only temporarily. Whereas for kanyeleng, a successful performance involves extended song-dance cycles with high levels of participation, for the organizers of health programs, kanyeleng are expected to break the monotony of the speeches with a short song that enlivens the crowd and communicates information succinctly without causing the event to run late.

At the same time, the rotavirus and World AIDS Day events illustrate the way meaningful musical engagement often takes place outside (and sometimes in conflict with) the official proceedings. That is, women often perform on the sidelines, before, after, or in-between. In some cases, performers refuse to stop singing when they are told their time is up. In other cases, performers interrupt the program to spontaneously express themselves through song.

What I am trying to show here is some of the messiness and friction associated with women's health performances, as well as their potential impact. If community participation is the goal, then it cannot necessarily be achieved in a neat, contained, three-minute performance. As I demonstrated in Chapter 6, participatory performances tend to be longer, messier, and noisier than most event organizers would prefer.

While some health workers joked about unruly kanyeleng songs and sought to contain unplanned interruptions, others emphasized the importance of in-the-moment sung responses in promoting participation and engagement. A staff member from GAMCOTRAP spoke at length about the power of spontaneous singing during GAMCOTRAP training programs. She explained,

> Sometimes, as you are sitting there doing the training, you just hear a woman *shout*. Her vocal comes out like that because of what? The message inspired the woman to come out. And spontaneously they will all be singing. You will not even know how they organized it. … I think one that made me cry was in Jarra Soma. This woman. The hall was filled with people and out of the blue, I didn't even know that she sings. I didn't know she had that ability. She just stood up and she just had this voice echoing all over the room and I was like "my goodness." I couldn't control my tears. … That was a very memorable, I always remember. I felt in love with that woman.
>
> (Personal communication, January 17, 2013)

Spontaneous singing was a common feature in many health events I attended as well as in group interviews and discussions relating to this research. For some interruptions, it was as though the performer could not help but express her reaction to the topic through song, which in turn inspired responses and participation from others. While such spontaneous singing is challenging for program organizers concerned about time constraints, it is often deeply meaningful for participants who emphasize the emotional impact and sense of social connection that performances inspire.

Women's health performances can be transformative on an individual level when they enable the integration of mind and body, emotion and intellect. As Andre de Quadros and Phillip Dorstewitz write, the emotional content of musical performance can provide "the fabric out of which reason is crafted" (2011: 63). This may be particularly important for the performers featured in this book who use their bodies to dance and sing about health, yet those very bodies are labeled abnormal, unhealthy, and dangerous because they harbor HIV, or fail to fulfill societal expectations of female fertility. In this context, women's songs and dances play an integrative role, challenging the social exclusion of HIV positive or infertile bodies and asserting instead the power of the female voice and body in motion. This is their transformative labor. In this manner, songs and dances enact the integration of self and other, imagining a world where an HIV positive body does not signify a woman's moral failure, and where infertility does not destroy her marriage. By integrating emotional, intellectual, and social aspects of experience, participating in music together with others enables people to envision alternative futures and work together to create change.

In addressing sensitive health topics through song, women take advantage of established song repertoires and features of performative license. As discussed in Chapter 4, I interpret performative license not primarily as freedom of expression, but rather as freedom to hear and be heard. This freedom emerges in "moments" (Fabian 1998) and is partial, yet it has the potential to effect change in the world. While the special social position of performers such as kanyeleng enhances their ability to address sensitive topics, for others (such as Fatou) it is the medium of song that facilitates freedom to hear and be heard *despite* their vulnerable social position. Although the extent to which a given performance can inspire sustained transformation may be limited, attending to momentary freedoms in song provides a view of the complexity of women's experiences and reveals cracks in the notion of all-encompassing hierarchy and marginalisation.

On pride and strength

This book has shown that in the challenging context of neoliberal economic restructuring and authoritarian national politics in The Gambia in the era of Yahya Jammeh, women adapted longstanding performance practices to address contemporary global health concerns. I have explored the ways in which, during the last several decades, global health and development organizations have involved female performers in their programs in response to growing international concern for the role of women and gender in development. For organizations, engagement with women's performance groups has provided a demonstration of their commitment to gender equality and local participation. For performers, on the other hand, collaborations with health organizations such as the Ministry of Health and Social Welfare have allowed them to access new opportunities for earning income while bringing women's perspectives and concerns to the public sphere.

An emphasis on African women's marginalization in global health discourse neglects local perspectives on women's power and performance, as discussed in Chapter 2. In The Gambia, women navigate contested ideas about appropriate behavior for Muslim women that simultaneously restrict and expand their performance possibilities. According to Mandinka notions of shame, women are (in theory) more emotionally expressive and more musically inclined. Moreover, religious discourse restricting music associated with men in particular compounds and villages has served to increase performance opportunities for women, amplifying longstanding notions of shame and gendered musical participation. Female performers have translated forms of power in the performance sphere to power in the area of public health, engaging with international donors' concern for gender equality.

Women's performances illustrate a process of negotiating seemingly disparate ideologies of health and value in creative ways. In some ways, the performances of the kanyeleng groups discussed in this book indicate a move toward commoditization of music and an intensification of monetary exchange. Similar processes are evident in the performances of Fatou and the Allatentu Support Band, who engaged with national and international development organizations in order to access funding and other resources. At the same time, through their performances women negotiate social relationships and produce forms of value that are not reducible to commodity exchange. Performers emphasize baadinyaa and related themes in order to embed messages about health into local discourses of responsibility and relationality.

These themes were evident in the Brikama Nyambai College kanyeleng's memorable performance of "Pride in Baadinyaa," a popular lenjengo song that I heard often at community events. Their performance in September 2013 featured Jainaba Saho's improvised saataroo section, as well as her signature expressive melodic variations.[1] Jainaba's agile, bell-like voice cut through the sounds of traffic on the Brikama highway, attracting passersby from the footpath outside the Health Directorate compound. A small boy watched and listened intently, mimicking with his hands the rapid movements of the sticks on the bidong. Jainaba's rendition of "Pride in Baadinyaa" challenged the public health emphasis on deficiencies – what Gambians lack – and described baadinyaa as a cultural strength and a resource for promoting health:

Ɗaañaa, ntolu ka ŋaañaa baadinyaa le la	Pride, we take pride in baadinyaa
Ntolu la Gambia jaŋ	In our Gambia here
N ka ŋaañaa baadinyaa la	We are proud of baadinyaa
Meŋ kamma n ka ñoo le faasaa	That is why we defend each other
N ka ñoo muta	We look after each other
N ka ñoo kanu	We love each other
Ɗaañaa, ntolu ka ŋaañaa baadinyaa le la	Pride, we take pride in baadinyaa
Kanoo meŋ be ntolu teema	The love that is between us
Haani banko kotenkolu, niŋ i taata …	Even other countries, if you go there …
I buka i kanu … ko ŋa n faŋ kanu ñaameŋ	They don't love each other the way we love each other
Ɗaañaa, ntolu ka ŋaañaa baadinyaa le la	Pride, we take pride in baadinyaa
Niŋ luntaŋo naata ñiŋ banku kaŋ jaŋ	If a visitor comes to this country here
Gambia dalita meŋ na, n ka wo le ka i ye … ate maŋ wuluu ñiŋ banku kaŋ	That which Gambia is accustomed to, we do that for them … [even though] they were not born in this country
Ɗaañaa, ntolu ka ŋaañaa baadinyaa le la	Pride, we take pride in baadinyaa
Kanoo niŋ ñoo mutoo meŋ tarata n dammaŋolu teema	The love and social cohesion that exists between just us
Wo kani kiliŋo	That same love
N ka wo le yitandi luntaŋolu la fo n niŋ i ye ka baadinyaa	We show that to visitors until we have baadinyaa with them
Ɗaañaa, ntolu ka ŋaañaa baadinyaa le la	Pride, we take pride in baadinyaa

Programo meŋ be keeriŋ jaŋ, n be Brikama health, Sister's Quarters, Nyambai college kanyeleŋ kafoo le be looriŋ ...	The program that is happening here, we are at Brikama health, Sister's Quarters, Nyambai College Kanyeleng Group is standing ...
Ḍaañaa, ntolu ka ŋaañaa baadinyaa le la Bii n bee be bendiŋ jaŋ Ka ñiŋ kaseto dadaa, pur bankoo bee si nafaa ala ... Nna loodulaa mu ñiŋ ti	Pride, we take pride in baadinyaa Today we all are meeting here To make this recording so that the whole country can benefit from it ... This is our responsibility

The Nyambai College kanyeleng's song illustrates two important themes that have informed this book. The first is baadinyaa. The song is in some ways typical of Mandinka performance practices in which references to baadinyaa are woven into songs to negotiate social relationships and manage conflicts. Baadinyaa provides insight into local conceptualizations of the social basis of health and the role of music in promoting healthy sociality. In this performance, Jainaba Saho also describes baadinyaa as an indication of Gambian exceptionalism. Unlike other countries where people are selfish and individualistic, she asserts, Gambians love each other and take care of each other. This idealistic representation of Gambian sociality was also targeted specifically toward me, the foreign researcher. It can be interpreted in part as an explicit intervention to inform me, and the wider international audience that I represented, about Gambian cultural strengths and expectations regarding social responsibility and care for others.

The second important theme in the Nyambai College kanyeleng's song is *ngaanyaa* (pride), which aligns with the strengths-based approach that informs this book. The Mandinka term ngaanyaa has different meanings depending on the context. In this song, it suggests showing pride or celebrating baadinyaa. In the context of community celebrations such as naming ceremonies or weddings, this song is used to evoke a sense of pride and celebration among family and friends. In Jainaba Saho's saataroo, however, the song's meaning is reframed to suggest a sense of national pride in baadinyaa. By inserting this message alongside her songs about health topics, Jainaba Saho challenges dominant health development narratives that define African culture primarily in negative terms, and articulates instead a narrative of pride, strength, and resilience. The song also expresses pride in kanyeleng capabilities and underscores the importance of the group's musical intervention to profit "the whole country." The song reflects Jainaba's sense of responsibility to use her musical abilities for the benefit of others.

By listening closely to songs such as this one, ethnomusicologists have a unique perspective to offer to interdisciplinary conversations on music and global health. I have suggested that global health scholars and practitioners, as well as ethnomusicologists, must grapple with two major problems of representation in attempting to mobilize resources to address health and social problems in Africa. The first is the tendency to represent Africa and Africans primarily in terms of what they lack (Ferguson 2006; Mbembe 2001), while the second is the inclination to focus on symptoms rather than root causes of health and social problems.

Representing people in terms of negatives (what they are *not*), with inadequate attention to the global political and economic relationships that help to produce conflict and health disparities, undermines efforts to create positive change. Although ethnomusicology is susceptible to these problems of representation, and consequent action and inaction, ethnomusicological attention to cultural strengths and the broader social conditions in which they emerge, can offer important counter narratives and open up avenues for solidarity and sustainable action. Medical ethnomusicological approaches challenge reductive views of culture as a resource for development (see Yúdice 2003; Dirksen 2013) by foregrounding the complexity of music as a social practice that is embedded in particular cultural, political, and historical contexts.

As João Biehl and Adriana Petryna argue, global health discourse must move beyond representing people as "problems or victims" to emphasize their roles as "agents of health" (2013: 11). Pushing beyond one-dimensional deficiency narratives illuminates multiple meanings and diverse forms of transformative labor that women enact through health performances. More than solely information dissemination, women's performances represent enduring social practices grounded in indigenous understandings of illness, health, and the role of musical performance in social life. Performers' transformative labor builds on women-centered networks that link individual, family, and community concerns to sustain continuity and meaning in the face of change (see Mullings 1995). Even as performances communicate information about Ebola, open defecation, or vaccines, they simultaneously enable the strengthening of women's social networks and deeper levels of meaning making to reframe stigma and marginality.

Beginnings and endings

The performers and health workers who are the focus of this book work with minimal compensation in a context of extremely limited access to health education and care. As is true of health programming in The Gambia more generally, unreliable funding and the prevalence of short-term, disease-specific programs make the work of performers particularly challenging. There is a need for ongoing training and support that recognizes performers as skilled collaborators who bring expertise in particular forms of communication and social mobilization. Effective health education requires extended partnerships between health workers, performers, and the communities they serve.

The majority of funding for health services in The Gambia comes from international donor organizations rather than the government budget (see Sundby 2014). Donor programs are, in general, highly focused in terms of both time and target, and as a result, government health workers are frequently bound to address predetermined agendas of donors rather than problems they themselves identify. Donor organizations often prioritize vertical programs that address a specific disease rather than strengthening public sector health care (Biehl and Petryna 2013: 7; see also Pfeiffer 2013). Even in cases where donors and health workers have the same agenda, the short-term nature of much development funding means that health organizations do not always have the resources to invest in long-term training and relationship building. The lack of systematic coordination between the numerous NGOs working on health-related issues in the country and the Ministry of Health and Social Welfare leads to inconsistency and inefficiency, with some duplication of services and some regions better served than others. Although NGOs are doing valuable work in The Gambia, there is a need for more integration with and long-term support for the Ministry in order to ensure that resources are used effectively and equitably.

Effective collaborations require long-term commitment and funding. Moreover, rather than viewing performers as simply voices to disseminate predetermined information, successful collaborations consider performers and health workers as partners in the health promotion effort. In this partnership, health workers bring expertise in biomedical health knowledge, whereas performers such as kanyeleng contribute expertise in musical performance, norms of communication and participation, and indigenous understandings of health and healing.

In January 2013, I spoke at length with Amie Bojang and Dr. Isatou Touray from GAMCOTRAP, who consistently inspired me with their commitment and dedication to their work despite the many challenges that they and their colleagues faced. As Amie Bojang explained, promoting community participation takes time. GAMCOTRAP programs take place over three days. On the first day, women just listen. It is only on the second and third days that they begin to really engage in dialogue and tell their own stories. Positive change requires long-term collaboration and funding that goes beyond what is typical for short-term development programming.

As Dr. Isatou Touray explained,

> Performance has always been my entry point. You could use it as an entry point and also to a closing point and in-between. … Sometimes even some of the kanyeleng will tell me "Heh, I hope we are not disturbing you, but this is the way we communicate our message." … You have to be ready to accept this … and it's quite a powerful tool. A very powerful tool.
> (Personal communication, January 17, 2013)

The performers with whom I work in The Gambia consistently demonstrated the ideas expressed by Dr. Touray. As an "entry point," they use musical performance as a platform to inspire the social engagement and mobilization necessary for action. Performative license, understood as the freedom to hear and be heard, offers a starting point for communication on sensitive health topics related to sex, death, and stigma. Music attracts listeners who might otherwise stay away, and songs have long been a site for public dialogue on issues of concern to women. Female performers have adapted melodies and rhythms commonly performed at community events in The Gambia to articulate messages about health, using playful dynamics of sanawuyaa and baadinyaa to defuse conflict and facilitate multidirectional communication.

In the messy "in-between," performers employ music as an energizer and motivator. I have suggested that musical participation on a small scale (e.g.

through singing, dancing, and handclapping) can potentially translate into larger scale participation and mobilization over the long-term. This is because actively engaging in music together with others can build a sense of collective responsibility and togetherness. Musical interactions entail a push-and-pull between the individual and the group, as separate voices, instruments, and handclaps are audible yet blended together. This modeling of negotiations between individual and group concerns on the micro-level in music events can build momentum for larger collective action to address health and social issues. This is also facilitated through a process of knowledge indigenization, embedding health knowledge in familiar melodies, rhythms, and ways of interacting musically. Local communities are not passive recipients of health knowledge. Rather, they selectively appropriate information and integrate it with their existing worldviews in order to determine the way forward.

Finally, as a "closing point," the resources of musical performance can help people to reflect upon and interpret past experiences in ways that enable them to envision a future. In this work, female performers draw on local understanding of gender, religion, and memory, as well as special social relationships such as sanawuyaa and baadinyaa. More than simply reflecting reality, performers play a role in creating and embodying social, psychological, physical, and emotional health and well-being.

Note

1 The recording of this song is Track 8 on the website: www.routledge.com/ 9780367312725.

Glossary

Afro-Manding   Style of popular music that incorporates the Mandinka language and/or Mandinka musical influences

Baadinyaa   Mother-childness; kinship or positive relationship

Bidong   20-liter plastic jerry can played with two sticks

Bolonkono kafoo   Upcountry group

Griot/griotte   West African hereditary specialist with expertise in praise singing, genealogy, conflict mediation, instrumental performance, and other skills that vary by region, ethnic group, and family

Jali/jalo (pl. jaloolu)   Mandinka griot

Jalimusoo (pl. jalimusoolu)   Female Mandinka griotte

Jaliyaa   The art of the *jali*

Jamundiroo   Praise singing

Jiikijo   Calabash "water drum"

Jinn   Spiritual entity

Jongo   Slave

Kankurang   Mandinka masquerades associated with circumcision events and other recreational events

Kanyeleng   Performers/performance group comprised of women who have experienced infertility or child deaths

Kanyelengyaa   Being a kanyeleng

Kora   21-string bridge harp played by jali

Kuntofengo   Spirit husband who prevents a woman from having healthy children that survive

Kutiro   Mandinka drum played in a three-drum ensemble

Lenjengo   One of the most popular rhythms performed at Mandinka dance events

Luwo   Circle that is formed for performance events

Maloo   Shame

Mbalax   Senegambian popular music that incorporates the rhythms of the *sabar* drums

Musuba   One of the most popular rhythms performed at Mandinka dance events

Nyamaaloo (pl. nyamaaloolu)   Artisan, hereditary specialist

Saataroo   A form of heightened speech (lit. "narration" or "explanation")

Sanawuyaa Joking cousin relationship
Sondomoo Heart, mind
Sooroo Offering, donation
Tantango Drum or drum-like instrument
Tulungo Percussion and dance events (also, "play")

Bibliography

Adams, Tony, and Stacy Holman Jones. 2008. "Autoethnography Is Queer." In *Handbook of Critical and Indigenous Methodologies*, edited by Norman K. Denzin, Yvonna S. Lincoln and Linda Tuhiwai Smith, 373–390. Los Angeles: Sage.

Airhihenbuwa, Collins O. 2007. *Healing Our Differences: The Crisis of Global Health and the Politics of Identity*. Lanham, MD: Rowman & Littlefield Publishers.

Alagoa, Ebiegbere Joe. 1968. "Songs as Historical Data: Examples from the Niger Delta." *Research Review* 5 (1): 1–16.

Albright, Ann Cooper. 2010. *Choreographing Difference: The Body and Identity in Contemporary Dance*. Middletown, CT: Wesleyan University Press.

Allison, Theresa A., Daniel B. Reed, and Judah M. Cohen. 2017. "Toward Common Cause: Music, Team Science, and Global Health." *Journal of Folklore Research* 54 (1/2): 1–13. https://doi.org/10.2979/jfolkrese.54.2.01.

Amon, Joseph J. 2008. "Dangerous Medicines: Unproven AIDS Cures and Counterfeit Antiretroviral Drugs." *Globalization & Health* 4: 1–10.

Ansdell, Gary. 2014. *How Music Helps in Music Therapy and Everyday Life*. Farnham, UK: Ashgate Publishing Limited.

Antonovsky, Aaron. 1996. "The Salutogenic Model as Theory to Guide Health Promotion." *Health Promotion International* 11 (1): 11–18.

Appert, Catherine M. 2012. "Modernity, Remixed Music as Memory in Rap Galsen." PhD Thesis, University of California at Los Angeles, USA.

Appert, Catherine M. 2018. *In Hip Hop Time: Music, Memory, and Social Change in Urban Senegal*. New York: Oxford University Press.

Arnoldi, Mary Jo. 1995. *Playing with Time: Art and Performance in Central Mali*. Bloomington, IN: Indiana University Press.

Barthes, Roland. 1985. *The Grain of the Voice: Interviews* 1962–1980. London, UK: Cape.

Barz, Gregory. 2006. *Singing for Life: HIV/AIDS and Music in Uganda*. New York: Routledge.

Barz, Gregory. 2008. "Confronting the Field(Note) In and Out of the Field." In *Shadows in the Field: New Perspectives for Fieldwork in Ethnomusicology*, edited by Gregory Barz and Timothy Cooley, 2nd ed., 206–224. New York: Oxford University Press.

Barz, Gregory. 2011. "Singing for Life: Song of Hope, Healing, and HIV/AIDS in Uganda." In *The Culture of AIDS in Africa: Hope and Healing Through Music and the Arts*, edited by Judah Cohen and Gregory Barz, 20–34. New York: Oxford University Press.

Barz, Gregory, and Judah Cohen, eds. 2011. *The Culture of AIDS in Africa: Hope and Healing Through Music and the Arts*. New York: Oxford University Press.

Bateson, Gregory. 1972. *Steps to an Ecology of Mind: Collected Essays in Anthropology, Psychiatry, Evolution, and Epistemology.* San Francisco: Chandler PubCo.

Batt-Rawden, Kari. 2010. "The Role of Music in a Salutogenic Approach to Health." *The International Journal of Mental Health Promotion* 12 (May): 11–18. https://doi.org/10.1080/14623730.2010.9721809.

Batt-Rawden, Kari, Susan Trythall, and Tia DeNora. 2007. "Health Musicking as Cultural Inclusion." In *Music: Promoting Health and Creating Community in Healthcare Contexts*, edited by Jane Edwards, 64–82. Newcastle, UK: Cambridge Scholars Pub.

BBC News. 2014. "Ebola Health Team Killed in Guinea." September 19, 2014. http://www.bbc.com/news/world-africa-29256443.

Beaglehole, Robert, and Ruth Bonita. 2010. "What Is Global Health?" *Global Health Action* 3 (1): 5142. https://doi.org/10.3402/gha.v3i0.5142.

Becker, Heike. 2005. "'Let Me Come to Tell You': Loide Shikongo, the King, and Poetic License in Colonial Ovamboland." *History and Anthropology* 16 (2): 235–258. https://doi.org/10.1080/02757200500116162.

Bekalu, Mesfin Awoke, and Steven Eggermont. 2014. "Aligning HIV/AIDS Communication with the Oral Tradition of Africans: A Theory-Based Content Analysis of Songs' Potential in Prevention Efforts." *Health Communication* 30 (5): 441–450. https://doi.org/10.1080/10410236.2013.867004.

Berger, Iris. 2014. "African Women's Movements in the Twentieth Century: A Hidden History." *African Studies Review* 57 (3): 1–19.

Bergh, Arild, and John Sloboda. 2010. "Music and Art in Conflict Transformation: A Review." *Music & Arts in Action* 2 (2): 3–17.

Biehl, João, and Adriana Petryna. 2013. *When People Come First: Critical Studies in Global Health.* Princeton University Press.

Bingley, Kate. 2011. "Bambeh's Song: Music, Women and Health in a Rural Community in Post-Conflict Sierra Leone." *Music and Arts in Action* 3 (2): 59–78.

Bird, Charles. 1976. "Poetry in the Mande: Its Form and Meaning." *Poetics* 5 (2): 89–100. https://doi.org/10.1016/0304-422X(76)90002-4.

Bird, Charles S., and Martha B. Kendall. 1987. "The Mande Hero." In *Explorations in African Systems of Thought*, edited by Ivan Karp, 13–26. Washington, DC: Smithsonian Institution Press.

Blacking, John. 1977. *The Anthropology of the Body.* London, UK; New York: Academic Press.

Boal, Augusto. 1979. *Theater of the Oppressed.* New York: Urizen Books.

Boesten, Jelke, and Nana Poku, eds. 2009. *Gender and HIV/AIDS: Critical Perspectives from the Developing World.* Farnham, UK; Burlington, VT: Ashgate.

Boserup, Ester. 1970. *Woman's Role in Economic Development.* New York: St Martin's Press.

Bourgois, Philippe, and Jeffrey Schonberg. 2009. *Righteous Dopefiend.* Berkeley, CA: University of California Press.

Buggenhagen, Beth A. 2012. *Muslim Families in Global Senegal: Money Takes Care of Shame.* Bloomington, IN: Indiana University Press.

Butler, Judith. 1988. "Performative Acts and Gender Constitution: An Essay in Phenomenology and Feminist Theory." *Theatre Journal* 40 (4): 519. https://doi.org/10.2307/3207893.

Callaway, Barbara, and Lucy E. Creevey. 1994. *The Heritage of Islam: Women, Religion, and Politics in West Africa.* Boulder, CO: Lynne Rienner.

Campbell, Agnes Adama. 2017. "Gambian Women, Violence and Its Intersection with HIV/AIDS: Agency through Feminist Participatory Research." PhD Thesis, University of Sussex, UK.

Carney, Judith, and Michael Watts. 1991. "Disciplining Women? Rice, Mechanization, and the Evolution of Mandinka Gender Relations in Senegambia." *Signs* 16 (4): 651–681.

Carty, John, and Yasmine Musharbash. 2008. "You've Got to Be Joking: Asserting the Analytical Value of Humour and Laughter in Contemporary Anthropology." *Anthropological Forum* 18 (3): 209–217. https://doi.org/10.1080/00664670802429347.

Cassidy, Rebecca Jane. 2011. "Changing Understandings of HIV and AIDS through Treatment Interactions." PhD Thesis, University of Sussex, UK.

Cassidy, Rebecca, and Melissa Leach. 2009a. "AIDS, Citizenship and Global Funding: A Gambian Case Study." *IDS Working Papers* (325): 1–31.

Cassidy, Rebecca, and Melissa Leach. 2009b. "Science, Politics, and the Presidential Aids 'Cure.'" *African Affairs* 108 (433): 559–580.

CDC, Centers for Disease Control and Prevention. 2016. "2014–2016 Ebola Outbreak in West Africa." https://www.cdc.gov/vhf/ebola/outbreaks/2014-west-africa/index.html.

Chapman, Rachel Rebekah. 2010. *Family Secrets: Risking Reproduction in Central Mozambique*. Nashville, TN: Vanderbilt University Press.

Charry, Eric S. 2000. *Mande Music: Traditional and Modern Music of the Maninka and Mandinka of Western Africa*. Chicago, IL: University of Chicago Press.

Cohen, Jon. 2011. "HIV Treatment as Prevention." *Science* 334 (6063): 1628–1628. https://doi.org/10.1126/science.334.6063.1628.

Cohen, Judah. 2011. "Singing as Social Order: The Expressive Economy of HIV/AIDS in Mbarara, Uganda." In *The Culture of AIDS in Africa: Hope and Healing Through Music and the Arts*, edited by Gregory Barz and Judah Cohen, 309–321. New York: Oxford University Press.

Conquergood, Dwight. 1992. "Ethnography, Rhetoric, and Performance." *Quarterly Journal of Speech* 78 (1): 80–97. https://doi.org/10.1080/00335639209383982.

Conrad, David C. 1985. "Islam in the Oral Traditions of Mali: Bilali and Surakata." *The Journal of African History* 26 (1): 33–49. https://doi.org/10.1017/S0021853700023070.

Conrad, David C, and Barbara E Frank. 1995. *Status and Identity in West Africa Nyamakalaw of Mande*. Bloomington, IN: Indiana University Press.

Csikszentmihalyi, Mihaly. 1990. *Flow: The Psychology of Optimal Experience*. New York: Harper & Row.

Daily Observer. 2007. "Lab Test Proves HIV Cure: Dr. Coumba Toure-Kane Guilty of Professional Dishonesty," February 23. http://www.observer.gm/enews/index.php?option=com_content&task=view&id=7399&Itemid=33.

Dave, Nomi. 2014. "The Politics of Silence: Music, Violence and Protest in Guinea." *Ethnomusicology* 58 (1): 1–29.

Davidheiser, Mark. 2006. "Joking for Peace: Social Organization, Tradition, and Change in Gambian Conflict Management." *Cahiers d'Etudes Africaines* 46 (184): 835–859. https://doi.org/10.4000/etudesafricaines.6223.

de Quadros, André. 2017. "Music, the Arts, and Global Health: In Search of Sangam, Its Theory and Paradigms." *Journal of Folklore Research* 54 (1/2): 15–39. https://doi.org/10.2979/jfolkrese.54.2.02.

de Quadros, André, and Philipp Dorstewitz. 2011. "Community, Communication, Social Change: Music in Dispossessed Indian Communities." *International Journal of Community Music* 4 (1): 59–70. https://doi.org/10.1386/ijcm.4.1.59_1.

Deeb, Lara. 2006. *An Enchanted Modern: Gender and Public Piety in Shi'i Lebanon*. Princeton, NJ: Princeton University Press.

Denzin, Norman K. 2003. *Performance Ethnography: Critical Pedagogy and the Politics of Culture*. Thousand Oaks, CA: Sage.

Diawara, Mamadou. 1997. "Mande Oral Popular Culture Revisited by the Electronic Media." In *Readings in African Popular Culture*, edited by Karin Barber, 40–48. Bloomington, IN: International African Institute in association with Indiana University Press.

Diawara, Manthia. 1998. *In Search of Africa*. Cambridge, MA: Harvard University Press.

Dionne, Kim Yi. 2017. *Doomed Interventions: The Failure of Global Responses to AIDS in Africa*. New York: Cambridge University Press.

Dirksen, Rebecca. 2012. "Reconsidering Theory and Practice in Ethnomusicology: Applying, Advocating, and Engaging beyond Academia." *Ethnomusicology Review* 17: 1–35.

Dirksen, Rebecca. 2013. "Surviving Material Poverty by Employing Cultural Wealth: Putting Music in the Service of Community in Haiti." *Yearbook for Traditional Music* 45: 43–57.

Doron, Assa, and Ira Raja. 2015. "The Cultural Politics of Shit: Class, Gender and Public Space in India." *Postcolonial Studies* 18 (2): 189–207. https://doi.org/10.1080/136887 90.2015.1065714.

Dudley, Shannon. 2008. *Music from Behind the Bridge: Steelband Spirit and Politics in Trinidad and Tobago*. New York: Oxford University Press.

Durán, Lucy. 1995. "Birds of Wasulu: Freedom of Expression and Expressions of Freedom in the Popular Music of Southern Mali." *British Journal of Ethnomusicology* 4 (1): 101–134. https://doi.org/10.1080/09681229508567240.

Durán, Lucy. 2003. "Women, Music, and the 'Mystique' of Hunters in Mali." In *The African Diaspora: A Musical Perspective*, edited by Ingrid Tolia Monson, 136–86. New York: Routledge.

Durán, Lucy. 2007. "Ngaraya: Women and Musical Mastery in Mali." *Bulletin of the School of Oriental and African Studies* 70 (3): 569–602. https://doi.org/10.1017/ S0041977X07000845.

Durán, Lucy. 2013. "POYI! Bamana Jeli Music, Mali and the Blues." *Journal of African Cultural Studies* 25 (2): 211–246. https://doi.org/10.1080/13696815.2013.792725.

Dutta, Mohan J. 2008. *Communicating Health: A Culture-Centered Approach*. Cambridge, UK: Polity Press.

Dutta, Mohan J. 2015. "Decolonizing Communication for Social Change: A Culture-Centered Approach." *Communication Theory* 25 (2): 123–143. https://doi.org/10.1111/ comt.12067.

Ebron, Paulla A. 2002. *Performing Africa*. Princeton, NJ: Princeton University Press.

Esteva, Gustavo. 2010. "Development." In *The Development Dictionary: A Guide to Knowledge as Power*, edited by Wolfgang Sachs, 6–25. Johannesburg: Zed Books.

Fabian, Johannes. 1998. *Moments of Freedom: Anthropology and Popular Culture*. Charlottesville, VA: University of Virginia Press.

Farmer, Paul. 2001. *Infections and Inequalities: The Modern Plagues*. Berkeley, CA: University of California Press.

Farmer, Paul. 2004. "An Anthropology of Structural Violence." *Current Anthropology* 45 (3): 305–325. https://doi.org/10.1086/382250.

Fassin, Didier. 1987. "Rituels villageois, rituels urbains: La reproduction sociale chez les femmes joola du Sénégal." *L'Homme* 27 (104): 54–75. https://doi.org/10.3406/ hom.1987.368894.

Fassin, Didier. 2013. "Children as Victims: The Moral Economy of Childhood in the Times of AIDS." In *When People Come First: Critical Studies in Global Health*, edited by João Biehl and Adriana Petryna, 109–132. Princeton, NJ: Princeton University Press.

Fassin, Didier, and Ibrahima Badji. 1986. "Ritual Buffoonery: A Social Preventive Measure against Childhood Mortality in Senegal." *The Lancet* 327 (8473): 142–143.

Fassin, Didier, and Helen Schneider. 2003. "The Politics of AIDS in South Africa: Beyond the Controversies." *British Medical Journal* 326: 495–497.

Feierman, Steven. 1999. "Colonizers, Scholars, and the Creation of Invisible Histories." In *Beyond the Cultural Turn: New Directions in the Study of Society and Culture*, edited by Victoria E. Bonnell and Lynn Avery Hunt, 182–216. Berkeley, CA: University of California Press.

Feierman, Steven, and John M. Janzen. 1992. *The Social Basis of Health and Healing in Africa*. Berkeley, CA: University of California Press.

Ferguson, James. 2006. *Global Shadows: Africa in the Neoliberal World Order*. Durham, NC: Duke University Press.

Flint, Adrian. 2011. *HIV/AIDS in Sub-Saharan Africa: Politics, Aid and Globalization*. London: Palgrave Macmillan.

Foley, Ellen E. 2010. *Your Pocket Is What Cures You: the Politics of Health in Senegal*. New Brunswick, NJ: Rutgers University Press.

Frackowski, Marlena. 1989. "The Laura Boulton Collection." *Resound: A Quarterly of the Archives of Traditional Music* VIII (3): 1–6.

Frank, Barbara. 2004. "Gendered Ritual Dualism in a Patrilineal Society: Opposition and Complementarity in Kulere Fertility Cults." *Africa* 74 (2): 217–240.

Freire, Paulo. 1973. *Education for Critical Consciousness*, 1st American ed. New York: Seabury Press.

Frishkopf, Michael. 2017. "Popular Music as Public Health Technology: Music for Global Human Development and 'Giving Voice to Health' in Liberia." *Journal of Folklore Research* 54 (1/2): 41–86. https://doi.org/10.2979/jfolkrese.54.2.03.

Furniss, Graham, and Liz Gunner. 2008. *Power, Marginality and African Oral Literature*. New York: Cambridge University Press.

Galvan, Dennis. 2006. "Joking Kinship as a Syncretic Institution (Les Relations à Plaisanterie Dans Une Institution Syncrétique)." *Cahiers d'Etudes Africaines* 46 (184): 809–834.

Gaunt, Kyra D. 2002. "Got Rhythm?: Difficult Encounters in Theory and Practice and Other Participatory Discrepancies in Music." *CISO City & Society* 14 (1): 119–140.

Goffman, Erving. 1963. *Stigma: Notes on the Management of Spoiled Identity*. Spectrum Book. Englewood Cliffs, NJ: Prentice-Hall.

Grosz-Ngate, Maria. 1989. "Hidden Meanings: Explorations into a Bamanan Construction of Gender." *Ethnology* 28 (2): 167. https://doi.org/10.2307/3773673.

Guyer, Jane I. 1995. "Wealth in People, Wealth in Things – Introduction." *The Journal of African History* 36 (1): 83–90. https://doi.org/10.1017/S0021853700026980.

Guyer, Jane I. 2004. *Marginal Gains: Monetary Transactions in Atlantic Africa*. Chicago, IL: University of Chicago Press.

Guyer, Jane I., and Samuel M. Eno Belinga. 1995. "Wealth in People as Wealth in Knowledge: Accumulation and Composition in Equatorial Africa." *The Journal of African History* 36 (1): 91–120. https://doi.org/10.1017/S0021853700026992.

Hale, Thomas A. 1998. *Griots and Griottes: Masters of Words and Music*. Bloomington, IN: Indiana University Press.

Hammoudi, Abdellah, and Pascale Ghazaleh. 2006. *A Season in Mecca: Narrative of a Pilgrimage*. New York: Hill and Wang.

Harding, Frances. 1998. "Neither 'Fixed Masterpiece' nor 'Popular Distraction': Voice, Transformation and Encounter in Theatre for Development." In *African Theatre for*

Development: Art for Self-Determination, edited by Kamal Salhi, 5–22. Exeter, UK: Intellect.

Harrison, Klisala. 2014. "The Second Wave of Applied Ethnomusicology." *MUSICultures* 41 (2): 15–33.

Henry, Doug, and Susan Shepler. 2015. "AAA 2014: Ebola in Focus." *Anthropology Today* 31 (1): 20–21. https://doi.org/10.1111/1467-8322.12156.

Hernlund, Ylva. 2003. "Winnowing Culture: Negotiating Female 'Circumcision' in the Gambia." PhD Thesis, University of Washington, USA.

Hernlund, Ylva, and Bettina Shell-Duncan. 2007. "Contingency, Context, and Change: Negotiating Female Genital Cutting in The Gambia and Senegal." *Africa Today* 53 (4): 43–57.

Hill, A. G., W. B. MacLeod, D. Joof, P. Gomez, and G. Walraven. 2000. "Decline of Mortality in Children in Rural Gambia: The Influence of Village-Level Primary Health Care." *Tropical Medicine & International Health* 5 (2): 107–118. https://doi.org/10.1046/j.1365-3156.2000.00528.x.

Hoesing, Peter J. 2013. "Listening to African Wellness in the Twenty-First Century." *Journal of Africana Religions* 1 (3): 390–393.

Hoffman, Barbara G. 2001. *Griots at War: Conflict, Conciliation, and Caste in Mande.* Bloomington, IN: Indiana University Press.

Hoffman, Barbara G. 2002. "Gender Ideology and Practice in Mande Societies and in Mande Studies." *Mande Studies* 4: 1–22.

Hogan, Brian. 2008. "Gendered Modes of Resistance: Power and Women's Songs in West Africa." *Pacific Review of Ethnomusicology* 13. https://www.ethnomusicologyreview.ucla.edu/journal/volume/13/piece/498.

Hough, Carolyn A. 2006. "Disruption and Development: Kanyalengs in the Gambia." PhD Thesis, University of Iowa, USA.

Hough, Carolyn A. 2008. "Re/producing Mothers: Structure and Agency in Gambian Kanyaleng Performances." *Ethnology* 47 (4): 257–269.

Hough, Carolyn A. 2010. "Loss in Childbearing among Gambia's Kanyalengs: Using a Stratified Reproduction Framework to Expand the Scope of Sexual and Reproductive Health." *Social Science & Medicine* 71 (10): 1757–63.

Hughes, Arnold, and David Perfect. 2006. *A Political History of The Gambia, 1816–1994.* Rochester, NY: University of Rochester Press.

Huizinga, Johan. 1950. *Homo Ludens: A Study of the Play Element in Culture.* New York: Roy Publishers.

Hull, Elizabeth, and Deborah James. 2012. "Introduction: Popular Economies in South Africa." *Africa* 82 (1): 1–19. https://doi.org/10.1017/S0001972011000696.

Irvine, Judith T. 1990. "Registering Affect: Heteroglossia in the Linguistic Expression of Emotion." In *Language and the Politics of Emotion*, edited by Catherine Lutz and Lila Abu-Lughod, 126–161. New York: Cambridge University Press.

Jacobson-Widding, Anita, and Walter van Beek. 1990. *The Creative Communion: African Folk Models of Fertility and the Regeneration of Life.* Uppsala: Acta Universitatis Upsaliensis.

Jammeh, Yahya. 2007. "Breaking News: President Jammeh Says Two HIV Patients Died During his AIDS Treatment!" *Blogger New Network*, June 21. http://www.bloggernews.net/17982.

Jansen, Jan. 1996. "The Younger Brother and the Stranger: In Search of a Status Discourse for Mande." *Cahiers d'Etudes Africaines* 36 (4): 659–688.

Jansen, Jan, and Clemens Zobel. 1996. *The Younger Brother in Mande: Kinship and Politics in West Africa*. Leiden: CNWS Publications.

Janson, Marloes. 2002. *The Best Hand Is the Hand That Always Gives: Griottes and Their Profession in Eastern Gambia*. Leiden: CNWS Publications.

Janson, Marloes. 2006. "'We Are All the Same, Because We All Worship God': the Controversial Case of a Female Saint in the Gambia." *Africa* 76 (4): 502–525.

Janson, Marloes. 2013. *Islam, Youth, and Modernity in the Gambia the Tablighi Jama'at*. New York: Cambridge University Press.

Jegede, Ayodele Samuel. 2007. "What Led to the Nigerian Boycott of the Polio Vaccination Campaign?" *PLOS Medicine* 4 (3): e73. https://doi.org/10.1371/journal.pmed.0040073.

Joof, Sulayman. 2007. "Herbal Cure and the HIV/AIDS." *Daily Observer*, February 6.

Kamara, Kewulay. 2016. "Ebola: In Search of a New Metaphor." *Futures* 84 (November): 193–200.

Kea, Pamela. 2013. "'The Complexity of an Enduring Relationship': Gender, Generation, and the Moral Economy of the Gambian Mandinka Household." *JRAI Journal of the Royal Anthropological Institute* 19 (1): 102–119.

Keil, Charles. 1987. "Participatory Discrepancies and the Power of Music." *Cultural Anthropology* 2 (3): 275–283.

Keil, Charles, and Steven Feld. 1994. *Music Grooves: Essays and Dialogues*. Chicago, IL: University of Chicago Press.

Kimambo, I. N., G. Hyden, S. Maghimbi, and K. Sugimura, eds. 2008. *Contemporary Perspectives on African Moral Economy*. Dar es Salaam: Dar es Salaam University Press.

Kjus, Yngvar. 2018. *Live and Recorded: Music Experience in the Digital Millennium*. Cham, Switzerland: Palgrave MacMillan.

Knight, Roderic. 1973. "Mandinka Jaliya: Professional Music of the Gambia." PhD Thesis, University of California at Los Angeles, USA.

Knight, Roderic. 1974. "Mandinka Drumming." *African Arts* 7: 24–35.

Knight, Roderic. 1982. "Manding/Fula Relations: As Reflected in the Manding Song Repertoire." *African Music* 6 (2): 37–47.

Koen, Benjamin D. 2005. "Medical Ethnomusicology in the Pamir Mountains: Music and Prayer in Healing." *Ethnomusicology* 49 (2): 287.

Koen, Benjamin D. 2006. "Musical Healing in Eastern Tajikistan: Transforming Stress and Depression through Falak Performance." *Asian Music* 37 (2): 58–83.

Koen, Benjamin D. 2008. "Music-Prayer-Meditation Dynamics in Healing." In *The Oxford Handbook of Medical Ethnomusicology*, edited by Benjamin Koen, Jacqueline Lloyd, Gregory Barz and Karen Brummel-Smith, 93–120. New York: Oxford University Press.

Koen, Benjamin, Jacqueline Lloyd, Gregory Barz, and Karen Brummel-Smith, eds. 2008. *The Oxford Handbook of Medical Ethnomusicology*. New York: Oxford University Press.

Koinange, Jeff. 2007. "In Gambia, AIDS Cure or False Hope?" CNN International, March 17. http://edition.cnn.com/2007/WORLD/africa/03/15/koinange.africa/index.html?_s= PM:WORLD.

Koné, Kassim. 2002. "When Male Becomes Female and Female Becomes Male in Mande." *Mande Studies* 4: 21–29.

Korsmeyer, Carolyn. 2004. *Gender and Aesthetics: An Introduction*. New York: Routledge.

Kyker, Jennifer W. 2016. *Oliver Mtukudzi: Living Tuku Music in Zimbabwe*. Bloomington, IN: Indiana University Press.

Lachenmann, Gudrun, and Petra Dannecker. 2008. *Negotiating Development in Muslim Societies: Gendered Spaces and Translocal Connections*. Lanham, MD: Lexington Books.

Lallemant, Marc, and Gonzague Jourdain. 2010. "Preventing Mother-to-Child Transmission of HIV—Protecting This Generation and the Next." *The New England Journal of Medicine* 363 (16): 1570–1572. https://doi.org/10.1056/NEJMe1009863.

Langeveld, Kirsten. 2014. "Jola Kanyalen Songs from the Casamance, Senegal: From 'Tradition' to Globalization." In *Women's Songs from West Africa*, edited by Thomas A. Hale and Aïssata G. Sidikou, 34–52. Bloomington, IN: Indiana University Press.

Leach, Melissa. 2015. "The Ebola Crisis and Post-2015 Development." *Journal of International Development* 27 (6): 816–834. https://doi.org/10.1002/jid.3112.

Linford, Scott Valois. 2016. "Interweaving Worlds: Jola Music and Relational Identity in Senegambia and Beyond." PhD Thesis, University of California at Los Angeles, USA.

Lock, Margaret, and Deborah Gordon, eds. 2012. *Biomedicine Examined*. New York: Springer Science & Business Media.

Mack, Beverly B. 2004. *Muslim Women Sing: Hausa Popular Song*. Bloomington, IN: Indiana University Press.

Maher, Stephanie Caroline. 2016. "Barça Ou Barzakh: The Social Elsewhere of Failed Clandestine Migration Out of Senegal." PhD Thesis, University of Washington, USA.

Majalia, Mjomba. 2011. "Ngoma Dialogue Circles (Ngoma-DiCe): Combatting HIV/AIDS Using Local Cultural Performances in Kenya." In *The Culture of AIDS in Africa: Hope and Healing Through Music and the Arts*, edited by Gregory Barz and Judah Cohen, 111–128. New York: Oxford University Press.

Masquelier, Adeline. 2009. *Women and Islamic Revival in a West African Town*. Bloomington, IN: Indiana University Press.

Mbai, Pa. 2007. "Inside The State House With Teeth Bite: Dr. Mbowe Says Jammeh Is Mad!." *Freedom Newspaper*, February 12. http://www.bloggernews.net/14593.

Mbembe, Achille. 2001. *On the Postcolony*. Berkeley, CA: University of California Press. http://hdl.handle.net/2027/heb.02640.

Mbonu, Ngozi C., Bart van den Borne, and Nanne K. De Vries. 2009. "Stigma of People with HIV/AIDS in Sub-Saharan Africa: A Literature Review." *Journal of Tropical Medicine* 2009: 145891. https://doi.org/10.1155/2009/145891.

McConnell, Bonnie B. 2015. "Performing Baadinyaa: Music, Emotion, and Health in The Gambia." *Voices: A World Forum for Music Therapy* 15 (3): 1–22. https://doi.org/10.15845/voices.v15i3.827.

McConnell, Bonnie B. 2016. "Music and Health Communication in The Gambia: A Social Capital Approach." *Social Science & Medicine* 169: 132–140. https://doi.org/10.1016/j.socscimed.2016.09.028.

McConnell, Bonnie B. 2017. "Performing 'Participation': Kanyeleng Musicians and Global Health in the Gambia." *Ethnomusicology* 61 (2): 312–332. https://doi.org/10.5406/ethnomusicology.61.2.0312.

McConnell, Bonnie B, and Buba Darboe. 2017. "Music and the Ecology of Fear: Kanyeleng Women Performers and Ebola Prevention in the Gambia." *Africa Today* 63 (3): 29–42. https://doi.org/10.2979/africatoday.63.3.03.

McNaughton, Patrick R. 1988a. *The Mande Blacksmiths: Knowledge, Power, and Art in West Africa*. Bloomington, IN: Indiana University Press.

McNaughton, Patrick R. 1988b. "The Semantics of Jugu: Blacksmiths, Lore and Who's 'Bad' in Mande." *Anthropological Linguistics* 30 (2): 150–165.

McNaughton, Patrick R. 2008. *A Bird Dance Near Saturday City: Sidi Ballo and the Art of West African Masquerade*. Bloomington, IN: Indiana University Press.

McNeill, Fraser G. 2011. *AIDS, Politics, and Music in South Africa*. New York: Cambridge University Press.

McNeill, William Hardy. 1995. *Keeping Together in Time: Dance and Drill in Human History*. Cambridge, MA: Harvard University Press.

Modic, E. Kate. 1996. "Song, Performance and Power: The Bèn Ka Di Women's Association in Bamako, Mali." PhD Thesis, Indiana University, USA.

MoH, Ministry of Health & Social Welfare. 2012. *National Health Policy, 'Health Is Wealth' 2012–2020: Acceleration of Quality Health Services and Universal Coverage*. Banjul: Republic of The Gambia. http://www.nationalplanningcycles.org/sites/default/files/country_docs/Gambia/gambia_national_health_policy_2012-2020_mohsw.pdf.

Morford, James B., and Aaron David. 2019. "The Swing Spectrum: Fluid Meter and Rhythmic Modes in Mandé Drumming Music." *Manuscript in preparation.*

Morgan, Lynn M. 2001. "Community Participation in Health: Perpetual Allure, Persistent Challenge." *Health Policy and Planning* 16 (3): 221–230. https://doi.org/10.1093/heapol/16.3.221.

Mullings, Leith. 1995. "Households Headed by Women: The Politics of Race, Class, and Gender." In *Conceiving the New World Order: The Global Politics of Reproduction*, edited by Faye D. Ginsburg and Rayna R. Reiter, 122–139. Berkeley, CA: University of California Press.

Nattrass, Nicoli. 2004. *The Moral Economy of AIDS in South Africa*. New York: Cambridge University Press.

NCAC and Niuminding Fatty. 2003. "Kanyeleng Ceremony (Mandinka)." Tape NCAC/RDD/03/5763, National Centre for Arts and Culture, The Gambia.

Ndaliko, Chérie Rivers. 2016. *Necessary Noise: Art, Music, and Charitable Imperialism in the East of Congo*. New York: Oxford University Press.

N'Daou, Mohamed Saidou. 2005. *Sangalan Oral Traditions: History, Memories, and Social Differentiation*. Durham, NC: Carolina Academic Press.

Newton, Robert. 2006. "Of Dangerous Energy and Transformations: Nyamakalaya and the Sunjata Phenomenon." *Research in African Literatures* 37 (2): 15–33.

Niang, Cheikh I. 1994. "The Dimba of Senegal: A Support Group for Women." *Reproductive Health Matters* 2 (4): 39–45.

Nutbeam, Don. 1998. *Health Promotion Glossary*. Geneva: World Health Organization.

Obregon, Rafael, and Collins O. Airhihenbuwa. 2000. "A Critical Assessment of Theories/Models Used in Health Communication for HIV/AIDS." *Journal of Health Communication* 5 (sup1): 5–15. https://doi.org/10.1080/10810730050019528.

Obregon, Rafael, and Silvio Waisbord, eds. 2012. *The Handbook of Global Health Communication*. Hoboken, NJ: Wiley.

Okagbue, Osita. 1998. "Product or Process: Theatre for Development in Africa." In *African Theatre for Development: Art for Self-Determination*, edited by Kamal Salhi, 23–42. Exeter, UK: Intellect.

Ong, Walter. 1982. *Orality and Literacy: The Technologizing of the Word*. New York: Methuen.

Panzacchi, Cornelia. 1994. "The Livelihoods of Traditional Griots in Modern Senegal." *Africa* 64 (2): 190–210.

Parker, Richard, and Peter Aggleton. 2003. "HIV and AIDS-Related Stigma and Discrimination: A Conceptual Framework and Implications for Action." *Social Science & Medicine* 57 (1): 13–24. https://doi.org/10.1016/S0277-9536(02)00304-0.

Parry, Jonathan. 1989. *Money and the Morality of Exchange*. New York: Cambridge University Press.

Peace Corps The Gambia. 1995. *Wollof-English Dictionary*. Banjul, The Gambia: US Peace Corps. http://resourcepage.gambia.dk/ftp/wollof.pdf.

Pellecchia, Umberto, Rosa Crestani, Tom Decroo, Rafael Vanden Bergh, and Yasmine Al-Kourdi. 2015. "Social Consequences of Ebola Containment Measures in Liberia." *PLOS ONE* 10 (12): e0143036. https://doi.org/10.1371/journal.pone.0143036.

Penna-Diaw, Luciana. 2014. "Songs by Wolof Women." In *Women's Songs from West Africa*, edited by Thomas A. Hale and Aïssata G. Sidikou, 124–135. Bloomington, IN: Indiana University Press.

Perrino, Sabina M. 2002. "Intimate Hierarchies and Qur'anic Saliva (Tĕfli): Textuality in a Senegalese Ethnomedical Encounter." *Journal of Linguistic Anthropology* 12 (2): 225–259.

Pettan, Svanibor, and Jeff Todd Titon, eds. 2015. *The Oxford Handbook of Applied Ethnomusicology*. New York: Oxford University Press.

Pfeiffer, James. 2013. "The Struggle for a Public Sector: PEPFAR in Mozambique." In *When People Come First: Critical Studies in Global Health*, edited by João Biehl and Adriana Petryna, 166–181. Princeton, NJ: Princeton University Press.

Pfeiffer, James, Pablo Montoya, Alberto J. Baptista, Marina Karagianis, Marilia De Morais Pugas, Mark Micek, Wendy Johnson, et al. 2010. "Integration of HIV/AIDS Services into African Primary Health Care: Lessons Learned for Health System Strengthening in Mozambique – A Case Study." *Journal of the International AIDS Society* 13: 3. https://doi.org/10.1186/1758-2652-13-3.

Pigg, Stacy Leigh. 1995. "Acronyms and Effacement: Traditional Medical Practitioners (TMP) in International Health Development." *Social Science & Medicine* 41 (1): 47–68.

Plastow, Jane. 1998. "Uses and Abuses of Theatre for Development: Political Struggle and Development Theatre in the Ethiopia-Eritrea War." In *African Theatre for Development : Art for Self-Determination*, edited by Kamal Salhi, 97–113. Exeter, UK: Intellect.

Polak, Rainer. 2010. "Rhythmic Feel as Meter: Non-Isochronous Beat Subdivision in Jembe Music from Mali." *Music Theory Online* 16 (4). http://www.mtosmt.org/issues/mto.10.16.4/mto.10.16.4.polak.html#FN2.

Polzer, Jessica, and Elaine Power. 2016. *Neoliberal Governance and Health: Duties, Risks, and Vulnerabilities*. Montreal: McGill-Queen's University Press.

Rasmussen, Susan. 2014. "Transformations in Tuareg Tende Singing: Women's Voices and Local Feminisms." In *Women's Songs from West Africa*, edited by Thomas Hale and Aïssata Sidikou, 263–290. Bloomington, IN: Indiana University Press.

Reed, Daniel. 2011. "'C'est Le Wake Up! Africa': Two Case Studies of HIV/AIDS Edutainment Campaigns in Francophone Africa." In *The Culture of AIDS in Africa: Hope and Healing Through Music and the Arts*, edited by Gregory Barz and Judah Cohen, 180–192. New York: Oxford University Press.

Rice, Timothy. 2014. "Ethnomusicology in Times of Trouble." *Yearbook for Traditional Music* 46: 191–209. https://doi.org/10.5921/yeartradmusi.46.2014.0191.

Roseman, Marina. 2008. "A Fourfold Framework for Cross-Cultural, Integrative Research on Music and Medicine." In *The Oxford Handbook of Medical Ethnomusicology*, edited by Benjamin Koen, Jacqueline Lloyd, Gregory Barz and Karen Brummel-Smith, 18–45. New York: Oxford University Press.

Roth, Claudia. 2014. "The Strength of Badenya Ties: Siblings and Social Security in Old Age—The Case of Urban Burkina Faso." *American Ethnologist* 41 (3): 547–562. https://doi.org/10.1111/amet.12094.

Roth, Molly. 2008. *Ma Parole S'achète: Money, Identity and Meaning in Malian Jeliya*. New Brunswick, NJ: Lit; Global distributor.

Russell, Ian, and Catherine Ingram. 2013. *Taking Part in Music: Case Studies in Ethnomusicology*. Aberdeen: Aberdeen University Press.

Saho, Bala. 2012. "Ritualizing and Domesticating Space: Kaneleng Women Coping with Childlessness in the Gambia." *Mande Studies* 14: 99–125.

Saine, Abdoulaye. 2009. *The Paradox of Third-Wave Democratization in Africa: The Gambia under AFPRC-APRC Rule*, 1994–2008. Lanham, MD: Lexington Books.

Salhi, Kamal. 1998. *African Theatre for Development: Art for Self-Determination*. Exeter, UK: Intellect.

Sama, Martyn, and Vinh-Kim Nguyen. 2008. *Governing Health Systems in Africa*. Dakar: Council for the Development of Social Science Research in Africa.

Sayer, Andrew. 2000. "Moral Economy and Political Economy." *Studies in Political Economy* 61 (1): 79–103.

Schocken, Celina. 2004. *Overview of the Global Fund to Fight AIDS, Tuberculosis and Malaria*. Washington, DC: Center for Global Development.

Schroeder, Richard A. 1999. *Shady Practices: Agroforestry and Gender Politics in the Gambia*. Berkeley, CA: University of California Press.

Schulz, Dorothea Elisabeth. 1997. "Praise without Enchantment: Griots, Broadcast Media, and the Politics of Tradition in Mali." *Africa Today* 44 (4): 443–464.

Schulz, Dorothea Elisabeth. 2000. *Obscure Powers, Obscuring Ethnographies: "Status" and Social Identities in Mande Society*. Berlin: Das Arabische Buch.

Schumann, Anne. 2008. "The Beat That Beat Apartheid: The Role of Music in the Resistance against Apartheid in South Africa." *Wiener Zeitschrift für kritische Afrikastudien* 14: 17–39.

Scott, James C. 1976. *The Moral Economy of the Peasant: Rebellion and Subsistence in Southeast Asia*. New Haven, CT: Yale University Press.

Scott, James C. 1985. *Weapons of the Weak: Everyday Forms of Peasant Resistance*. New Haven, CT: Yale University Press.

Shell-Duncan, Bettina, and Ylva Hernlund. 2000. *Female "Circumcision" in Africa: Culture, Controversy, and Change*. Boulder, CO: Lynne Rienner Publishers.

Shell-Duncan, Bettina, Katherine Wander, Ylva Hernlund, and Amadou Moreau. 2011. "Dynamics of Change in the Practice of Female Genital Cutting in Senegambia: Testing Predictions of Social Convention Theory." *Social Science & Medicine* 73 (8): 1275–1283. https://doi.org/10.1016/j.socscimed.2011.07.022.

Sidikou, Aïssata G. 2001. *Recreating Words, Reshaping Worlds: The Verbal Art of Women from Niger, Mali, and Senegal*. Trenton, NJ: Africa World Press.

Sidikou, Aïssata G., and Thomas A. Hale. 2012. *Women's Voices from West Africa: An Anthology of Songs from the Sahel*. Bloomington, IN: Indiana University Press.

Sieveking, Nadine. 2007. "'We Don't Want Equality; We Want to Be Given Our Rights': Muslim Women Negotiating Global Development Concepts in Senegal." *Africa Spectrum* 42 (1): 29–48.

Simmons, Andrew. 2007. "Meet the President – Yahya Jammeh: Gambian President Claims to Heal Aids Patients with Fruit and Nuts, but Only on a Saturday." *Al Jazeera English*, May 14.

Skinner, Ryan Thomas. 2010. "Civil Taxis and Wild Trucks: The Dialectics of Social Space and Subjectivity in Dimanche à Bamako." *Popular Music; Cambridge* 29 (1): 17–39. https://doi.org/10.1017/S0261143009990365.

Skinner, Ryan Thomas. 2012. "Cultural Politics in the Post-Colony: Music, Nationalism and Statism in Mali, 1964–75." *Africa* 82 (4): 511–534. https://doi.org/10.1017/S0001972012000484.

Skramstad, Heidi. 2008. "Making and Managing Femaleness, Fertility and Motherhood within an Urban Gambian Area." PhD Thesis, University of Bergen, Norway.

Small, Christopher. 2011. *Musicking: The Meanings of Performing and Listening.* Middletown, CT: Wesleyan University Press.

Snow, L. F. 1974. "Folk Medical Beliefs and Their Implications for Care of Patients. A Review Bases on Studies among Black Americans." *Annals of Internal Medicine* 81 (1): 82–96.

Soares, Benjamin F. 2004. "Muslim Saints in the Age of Neoliberalism." In *Producing African Futures: Ritual and Reproduction in a Neoliberal Age*, edited by Brad Weiss, 79–105. Leiden: Brill.

Soares, Benjamin F. 2005. *Islam and the Prayer Economy: History and Authority in a Malian Town.* Ann Arbor, MI: University of Michigan Press.

Stokes, Martin. 2002. "Marx, Money, and Musicians." In *Music and Marx: Ideas, Practice, Politics*, edited by Regula Qureshi, 139–163. New York: Routledge.

Stokes, Martin. 2004. "Music and the Global Order." *Annual Review of Anthropology* 33: 47–72.

Stone, Linda. 1992. "Cultural Influences in Community Participation in Health." *Social Science & Medicine* 35 (4): 409–417. https://doi.org/10.1016/0277-9536(92)90333-L.

Stone, Ruth M. 1988. *Dried Millet Breaking: Time, Words, and Song in the Woi Epic of the Kpelle.* Bloomington, IN: Indiana University Press.

Stone, Ruth M. 2008. *The Garland Handbook of African Music.* New York: Routledge.

Stone, Ruth M. 2017. "'Ebola in Town': Creating Musical Connections in Liberian Communities during the 2014 Crisis in West Africa." *Africa Today Magazine* 63 (3): 79–97.

Strong, Catherine, and Barbara Lebrun, eds. 2015. *Death and the Rock Star.* Burlington, VT: Ashgate.

Sugimura, Kazuhiko. 2008. "Contemporary Perspectives on African Moral Economy." In *Contemporary Perspectives on African Moral Economy*, edited by I. N. Kimambo, G. Hyden, S. Maghimbi and K. Sugimura, 3–15. Dar es Salaam: Dar es Salaam University Press.

Sundby, Johanne. 2014. "A Rollercoaster of Policy Shifts: Global Trends and Reproductive Health Policy in The Gambia." *Global Public Health* 9 (8): 894–909. https://doi.org/10.1080/17441692.2014.940991.

Sunderland, Naomi, Natalie Lewandowski, Dan Bendrups, and Brydie-Leigh Bartleet, eds. 2018. *Music, Health and Wellbeing.* London: Palgrave Macmillan.

Swiss, Liam. 2012. "The Adoption of Women and Gender as Development Assistance Priorities: An Event History Analysis of World Polity Effects." *International Sociology* 27 (1): 96–119. https://doi.org/10.1177/0268580911423047.

Tang, Patricia. 2008. *Masters of the Sabar Wolof Griot Percussionists of Senegal.* Philadelphia, PA: Temple University Press.

Thompson, E. P. 1971. "The Moral Economy of the English Crowd in the Eighteenth Century." *Past & Present* 50: 76–136.

Thorsén, Stig-Magnus. 2004. *Sounds of Change: Social and Political Features of Music in Africa.* Stockholm: Sida (Swedish International Development Cooperation Agency).

Tsuruta, Tadasu. 2006. "African Imaginations of Moral Economy: Notes on Indigenous Economic Concepts and Practices in Tanzania." *African Studies Quarterly* 9 (1&2): 103–121.

Turan, Janet, and Laura Nyblade. 2013. "HIV-Related Stigma as a Barrier to Achievement of Global PMTCT and Maternal Health Goals: A Review of the Evidence." *AIDS Behav* 17 (7): 2528–2539.

Turino, Thomas. 2000. *Nationalists, Cosmopolitans, and Popular Music in Zimbabwe.* Chicago, IL: University of Chicago Press.

Turino, Thomas. 2008. *Music as Social Life: The Politics of Participation.* Chicago, IL: University of Chicago Press.

Turner, Victor. 1982. *From Ritual to Theatre: The Human Seriousness of Play.* New York City: Performing Arts Journal Publications.

UNAIDS, The Joint United Nations Program on HIV/AIDS. 2018. "Gambia: HIV/AIDS data." http://www.unaids.org/en/regionscountries/countries/gambia.

UNdata. 2000. "Per Capita Government Expenditure on Health at Average Exchange Rate (US$)." http://data.un.org/Data.aspx?q=per+capita+government+expenditure+on+health+&d=WHO&f=MEASURE_CODE%3aWHS7_104.

Vail, Leroy, and Landeg White. 1991. *Power and the Praise Poem: Southern African Voices in History.* Charlottesville, VA: University Press of Virginia.

Van Buren, Kathleen. 2010. "Applied Ethnomusicology and HIV and AIDS: Responsibility, Ability, and Action." *Ethnomusicology* 54 (2): 202–223.

Van Buren, Kathleen. 2011. "Music, HIV/AIDS and Social Change in Nairobi, Kenya." In *The Culture of AIDS in Africa : Hope and Healing Through Music and the Arts*, edited by Gregory Barz and Judah Cohen, 70–84. New York: Oxford University Press.

Van Buren, Kathleen Jenabu. 2006. "Stealing Elephants, Creature Futures: Exploring Uses of Music and Other Arts for Community Education in Nairobi, Kenya." PhD Thesis, University of California at Los Angeles, USA.

Waterman, Ellen. 2019. "Performance Studies and Critical Improvisation Studies in Ethnomusicology: Understanding Music and Culture through Situated Practice." In *Theory for Ethnomusicology: Histories, Conversations, Insights*, edited by Harris M. Berger and Ruth M. Stone. New York: Routledge.

WEC International. 1988. *A Practical Orthography of Gambian Mandinka.* Banjul: WEC International.

WEC International. 1995. Mandinka-*English Dictionary. Revised edition.* Banjul: WEC International.

Weil, Peter M. 1976. "The Staff of Life: Food and Female Fertility in a West African Society." *Africa* 46 (2): 182–195.

WHO, World Health Organization. 2006. *Constitution of the World Health Organization.* Geneva: World Health Organization.

WHO, World Health Organization. 2014. "The Gambia: Immunization Country Profile." Geneva: World Health Organization. http://apps.who.int/immunization_monitoring/globalsummary/incidences?c=GMB.

WHO, World Health Organization. 2016. "Global Health Expenditure Database." Geneva: World Health Organization. https://apps.who.int/nha/database/ViewData/Indicators/en.

WHO, World Health Organization. 2018. "The Gambia: Country Cooperation Strategy at a Glance." Geneva: World Health Organization. https://apps.who.int/iris/handle/10665/136857.

Wilkinson, Annie, and Melissa Leach. 2015. "Briefing: Ebola–myths, Realities, and Structural Violence." *African Affairs* 114 (454): 136–148. https://doi.org/10.1093/afraf/adu080.

Wise, Christopher. 2006. "Nyama and Heka: African Concepts of the Word." *Comparative Literature Studies* 43 (1): 19–38.

Wong, Deborah Anne. 2004. *Speak It Louder: Asian Americans Making Music.* New York: Routledge.

Wooten, Stephen R. 2009. *The Art of Livelihood: Creating Expressive Agri-Culture in Rural Mali*. Durham, NC: Carolina Academic Press.

World Bank. 1998. "Implementation Completion Report, Republic of The Gambia Women in Development Project." The World Bank.

Wright, Donald R. 2010. *The World and a Very Small Place in Africa: A History of Globalization in Niumi, the Gambia*, 3rd ed. Armonk, NY: M.E. Sharpe.

Yahya, Maryam. 2007. "Polio Vaccines—'No Thank You!' Barriers to Polio Eradication in Northern Nigeria." *African Affairs* 106 (423): 185–204. https://doi.org/10.1093/afraf/adm016.

Yúdice, George. 2003. *The Expediency of Culture: Uses of Culture in the Global Era*. Durham, NC: Duke University Press.

Index